Irish Homes and Irish Hearts (1867)

CLASSICS OF IRISH HISTORY
General Editor: Tom Garvin

Original publication dates of reprinted titles are given in brackets

Irish Homes and Irish Hearts

✳

FANNY TAYLOR

With a foreword by Eithne Leonard SMG
and an introduction by Mary McAuliffe

UNIVERSITY COLLEGE DUBLIN PRESS
Preas Choláiste Ollscoile Bhaile Átha Cliath

First published in 2013 by University College Dublin Press

© Mary McAuliffe

ISBN 978-1-904558-73-7
ISSN 1393-6883

University College Dublin Press
Newman House, 86 St Stephen's Green
Dublin 2, Ireland
www.ucdpress.ie

Cataloguing in Publication data available
from the British Library

Typeset in Ehrhardt by Ryan Shiels, Scotland
Text design by Lyn Davies,
Frome, Somerset, England
Printed on acid-free paper by
Antony Rowe, Chippenham, Wilts.

CONTENTS

FOREWORD
Eithne Leonard SMG

Poor Servants of the Mother of God:
Spirit and Spirituality

The youngest volunteer nurse in the Crimean War finished her 3rd edition of *Eastern Hospitals and English Nurses* (1857) with the words:

> Oh! that someone would rise up to plead the cause of the Poor and awake in us all a spirit of Union and Charity that we may join in the great work of succouring the poor, not only by doling out to them alms of this world's goods but by those words and actions which can make them feel we have alike one hope, one end and one Master.[1]

This may be the language of Victorian England but the spirit is that of a great woman: Frances Taylor, daughter of the Anglican Pastor of Stoke-Rochford, Lincolnshire. Her exasperation at the red-tape of the army-authorities was not annoyance with petty legalism, it was fury against the waste of life. Soldiers were dying while food and medicine rotted away because no one had the courage to override a civil-service mentality. The enormous loss of life in the Crimean hospitals is well documented. Frances found too often all there was left for her to do, as soldiers died in their thousands, was to write their farewell letters home. She wrote, kneeling on the floor, as the dying men whispered their brief messages. The letters often had to be re-written at night, the page was so blotted by her tears. *Eastern Hospitals and English Nurses* became a best-seller and Frances herself, touched to the depths of her soul by the faith and courage of the Irish soldiers, became a Catholic. Her life-long spirituality was deeply rooted in the preciousness of every human being. The decade following the Crimean War was a time of searching for Frances and from 1856 until 1864–6 she struggled to find her calling in life. The 'someone' she prayed might rise up to help the poor turned out to be herself. She tried setting up a ragged school in London. She travelled to the Daughters of Charity in Paris only to be told her vocation was for the English speaking poor.

In 1864 Frances set out for Ireland to seek advice from Irish friends, the Sisters of Mercy whom she had worked with in the Crimea. Mother Bridgeman and other Mercy Sisters engaged directly with nursing or caring for the destitute in workhouses or orphanages. Frances admired the works and praised their excellence. But Frances, strongly practical, was interested mainly in the business details of the foundations, especially in their sources of income and financial viability. She was generous in her praise but reflected 'the more I see of other Congregations the more convinced I am we must found our own'.[2] She was often nonplussed at the way many religious congregations mirrored privileged society. Those with dowries became professional nurses and teachers and Mother Superiors; those without dowries or education became lay sisters. Frances was determined there would be no social division in her congregation. In 1855 Fr Sidney Woollett SJ, war-chaplain, had received Frances into the Church. She remained faithful to Jesuit spirituality adopting it for her Congregation and Ignatian Spiritual Exercises were the basis of her discernment and direction. Frances was attracted to the role of Mary in the public life of Jesus. In contemplation her heart warmed to find St Ignatius had a servant maid helping Mary. This was an inspiration to Frances and gave her new Congregation the title: *Poor Servants of the Mother of God (SMG)* officially recognised by the Church on 12 February 1872.

From the memoirs written by the first Sisters we can see that Mother Magdalen Taylor was deeply loved. When peals of laughter followed the opening of the convent door, the reaction was: 'Ah! Mother is home!' To the early Sisters Mother Magdalen was their inspiration as well as the Founder of their Congregation. As novices they looked forward to their daily session with her when she shared her own love and enthusiasm for Jesus, Son of God. When it came to stories of Jesus the young religious were moved to deep love and very often to tears. Frances Taylor had a beautiful speaking voice, so as their love for Jesus grew so did their veneration and gratitude to Mother Magdalen. So recreation too was a function none of them would miss. She was a great-story teller and she had an infectious sense of humour. There are still boxes of riddles and jokes written in the founder's handwriting. She prepared for recreation, perhaps when worries about income or the health of her young nuns made the world look grim, she made sure laughter would be generated.

Frances, Mother Mary Magdalen of the Sacred Heart, made her first foundation in Ireland in Carrigtwohill, Co Cork in 1875. In 1888 the Poor Servants of the Mother of God took over St Joseph's, Portland Row, Dublin. The last foundation before her death in June 1900 was the Workhouse in Rathdown Union. Residents there had straw pallets to sleep on. It is now St Colmcille's Hospital, Loughlinstown. It was only following the Special General Chapter in 1969 that our *Charism*, the founding grace that motivated Frances Taylor, became the object of our search. Her writings were republished and early biographies were also made available. It was an invigorating and inspiring time for us. It was heartening to see old and young SMGs sharing the newly discovered human person who had been smothered under a sanctimonious wish for uniformity. The Poor Servants of the Mother of God are celebrating 140 years of their foundation. There are now services for the elderly with special facilities for Alzheimer's sufferers in North Carolina, USA, in England's Liverpool and London and in Dublin and Cork. The mission in Venezuela is still very much alive, through the associate movement, a web of spirituality and catechesis attached to all our communities. Sisters visit annually and honour Frances Taylor/Mother Magdalen with gratitude. Kenya, Kitui and Nairobi have our most youthful membership with parish services, schools, health-service stations, and clubs for street-boys. The cause of her beatification continues: Francs Taylor, Mother Magdalen is now titled, 'The Servant of God'.

Notes to Foreword

1   Fanny Taylor, *Eastern Hospitals and English Nurses* 3rd edn (London, 1857), p. 356.
2   F. C. Devas, *Mother Magdalen Taylor* (London, 1927), p. 123.

INTRODUCTION
Mary McAuliffe

BIOGRAPHICAL NOTE[1]

Frances (Fanny) Taylor was born in January, 1832 in Stoke Rochford Parish in Lincolnshire, where her father Henry Taylor (1777–1842), an Anglican clergyman, was Rector. She was the youngest of ten children (seven girls and three boys) born to the Revd Taylor and his wife Louisa Maria (nee Jones, 1793–1869). Louisa Taylor's surviving diaries paint a happy early childhood for Fanny and her siblings, with the girls being educated privately at home, while the boys were sent off to school. An image emerges of Fanny Taylor as a serious yet fun loving child, well versed from an early age in devotion to the Church and in doing good works. Even at a young age the Taylor children were exposed to religious discussion and debate, in later life Fanny wrote of hearing her father, who had some Tractarian sympathies, speak of the Tractarian controversy[2] and of those involved as 'good men . . . [who] will do a great deal of good'; indeed Tractarian philosophy was to prove very influential in his daughters' spiritual development.[3] Tragedy stuck in 1842 when Revd Taylor died of tuberculosis. The family were not wealthy and the loss of income and the only home they had known hit hard. Influential friends came to the rescue, and a wealthy friend and neighbour Lady Caroline Turnor paid an annuity of £50 per annum for four years to Louisa Taylor which allowed her to keep her family together and move to London.

In London the Taylor family settled in Michaels Grove, Brompton close to the parish Church of the Holy Trinity. Here the family, especially Fanny and her sisters, came under the influence of the Rector of Holy Trinity, Dr W. J. Irons[4], who was 'High-Church' like her father. Irons was also influenced by Tractarianism, so much so, that in 1855 there appeared a pamphlet, signed A. E., which asked 'Is the vicar of Brompton [Irons] a Tractarian?'[5] Attracted to Tractarian doctrine and its emphasis on the sacraments Taylor was particularly attached to the sacrament of baptism. She would have been aware of the controversies in the Church, in particular, the Gorham Controversy which occurred when George Gorham was appointed as vicar of Brampford Speke Parish, Exeter by the crown in 1847. Gorham did not accept fully the theology of baptism, indeed his views that spiritual regeneration was not conferred by baptism were regarded by his High Church colleagues as heretical. This controversy led to 14 prominent Anglicans, including Henry Edward Manning[6] (later Cardinal Manning), who was to play a prominent role in the life and spiritual development of Taylor, leaving the Anglican Church and becoming Roman Catholics. Nearer home, two of her own preachers at Christ Church, Albany Street, Revd Dodsworth and Revd Gordon also converted to Catholicism.

The influence of Tractarianism on Taylor's life continued through the 1840s. Sometime after 1845 the family moved to St Mark's Crescent, Regents Park where they lived near the leading 'Tractarian' church, Christ Church, Albany Street. Even as a young teenager she felt the need to work among the poorest in London and there is evidence that she considered becoming a member of St. John's House in Fitzroy Square, which was a nursing school and Anglican religious community run along Tractarian lines.[7] By 1849 her elder sisters Emma and Charlotte had joined an

Anglican Sisterhood, the Sisters of Mercy of the Holy Trinity (Devonport), known as the 'Sellonites' after their founder Priscilla Lydia Sellon. Sellon set up the 'Sellonites' in Plymouth in 1849, where her spiritual advisor was the leading Tractarian, Edward Pusey. Sellon had ambitions for her foundation and within a few years had set up an industrial school, homes for delinquent boys, refuges for girls, five 'ragged' schools, lodging houses for the poor as well as setting her sisters to work among emigrants. Like the Catholic Sisters among whom Fanny Taylor would later work, Priscilla Sellon believed that work was the way to protect girls who might otherwise get involved in prostitution, she had a printing press set up to provide work for these women. Many Tractarian adherents were interested in the material, moral and spiritual welfare of the bourgeoning populations in working-class urban areas. They were concerned that these populations were not being ministered to adequately by any churches; this concern about the welfare of the working poor and the urban destitute was to play a large part in the life of Fanny Taylor. Between 1848 and 1852, searching for her way in life, Taylor worked among the poor in London, setting up a 'ragged' school' for destitute children.[8] In 1852, again following the example of her sisters, she went to live as a 'visitor' with the Sellonites. Here she was involved in nurse training and hospital work in Bristol and gained some valuable nursing experience during an outbreak of cholera in Plymouth in 1853.

In 1854 the Crimean War broke out. Within months there was a public outcry when the deplorable conditions in which the British wounded were being treated were graphically reported in the British press; in particular there was embarrassment when it became clear that wounded French soldiers were well treated and had a better chance of survival than their wounded British allies.[9] There was a demand, by a public horrified at the high British death rate that hospitals be set up, well supplied with medicine and equipment;

women were also encouraged to go to the Crimea to provide nursing services for the men.

Florence Nightingale offered her services and as her previous work in organising nursing care was known to the then Secretary of War, Sidney Herbert, he asked her to take sole charge of the administration of the nursing care of the British wounded in the Crimea. By 4 November 1854 Nightingale and her party of 38 nurses, including six Catholic Sisters of Mercy from Bermondsey in England, had arrived at Scutari in Turkey. A second group of nurses left London in December 1854, including 15 Irish Sisters of Mercy led by Mother Francis Bridgeman, as well as paid nurses and lady volunteers led by Mary Stanley, and among these, the 22- year-old Fanny Taylor.[10] Although Taylor did have nursing experience, the conditions which awaited the group in the Crimea were beyond what any of them had previously encountered.

We have a detailed account of Taylor's time in the Crimea as, in 1857, she published her first major work entitled, *Eastern Hospitals and English Nurses: The Narrative of Twelve Months Experience in the Hospitals of Koulali and Scutari by a Lady Volunteer.*[11] Taylor's sojourn in the Crimea was important in her on-going spiritual development and in making contacts and friendships with Irish people, in particular, the Irish Sisters of Mercy. From the beginning there was tension between the Sisters of Mercy, Mary Stanley, leader of the second group of lady volunteers and Florence Nightingale. When the Sisters of Mercy arrived at anchor in Golden Horn Bay, near Scutari, in December 1854, Nightingale told them to return home as they were not needed; she felt that she was already overburdened with the administration of the nurses she had and that 'the fifteen new nuns (in conjunction with Mary Stanley) [were] leading me a devil of a life'.[12] For Nightingale the problems with both the Irish Sisters and Mary Stanley's lady volunteers were to do with control, leadership and sectarianism. Both Bridgman and

Stanley had concerns with Nightingale's sole control, with Bridgeman particularly reluctant to place her Sisters under any leadership except her own. Nightingale was also aware of the powerful anti-papist lobby back in England which had already complained about the inclusion of Catholics in the original party of nurses; with the new arrivals the number of Catholic nurses would increase 'from 25 to 84'.[13] Taylor had been among those who were told there was no room for them to work in Scutari. In *Eastern Hospitals and English Nurses* she states that 'it was most unaccountable that 47 women should be kept idle at Therapia while there was so much work to be done in Scutari'. She also details the ever-increasing number of deaths at the hospital in Scutari 'in September, 165; in October, 256, in November, 388 and in December 667 and now they have reached the frightful number of 90 per diem . . . the deaths in January having been 1473 [while] there were at the time, only 10 nurses at the General Hospital and 30 at the Barrack Hospital'.[14]

Eventually Taylor and the other arrivals were set to work among the wounded and by January 1855 she was working in the General Hospital in Scutari. Soon after she made ward rounds with Nightingale and mentions that 'she (Nightingale) carried her lantern, which she would set down before she bent over any of the patients. I much admired her manner with the men – it was so tender and kind'.[15] However Taylor was not uncritical of the manner in which the hospital was run by both Nightingale and the military authorities. She was appalled that the strict military discipline meant that men who were calling piteously for a drink could not be helped unless a direct order was given to the nurses. She complained of the strict enforcement of this discipline which meant that 'an infringement of one of its smallest observances was worse than letting twenty men die from neglect'.[16] One of the Sisters of Mercy wrote in her diary 'Miss Fanny Taylor repeatedly remonstrated with Miss Nightingale on the misery of hearing those sufferers imploring . . . a drink . . .

and have no possibility of supplying it . . . Miss Nightingale would not allow even those who had private funds . . . use them'.[17] However, in her book Taylor was careful not to be overly critical of Nightingale personally, rather she criticised the system in which Nightingale and the English nurses had to operate.

After two weeks Taylor left Scutari and went with the Mary Stanley group to work at the Koulali English Hospital. Here she found a similarly crowded hospital but a less authoritarian regime, which was much more to her liking. As well as nursing Taylor was continuing her spiritual search. She had become close with the Sisters of Mercy and was not trusted by some of the English lady volunteers who suspected her of having 'catholic tendencies' as it seemed that she 'had too much sympathy with the nuns'.[18] Indeed later in life Taylor mentioned that, at the time, she was 'very High-Church' and she 'lived in terror of being reported to the Government as [a] proselytizer'.[19]

It is during this time nursing in the Crimea that Taylor encountered both Irish religious sisters and Irish soldiers in the British army. As well as her friendship with and admiration of the Irish Sisters of Mercy, Taylor wrote in *Eastern Hospitals and English Nurses* of her admiration of the stoicism and simple faith of the wounded Irish soldiers, in later life she would say that the expression of faith among these Irishmen is what led to her conversion. At the time she was a young woman searching for spiritual meaning in her life, and the simple faith of a dying Irish soldier, attended by a Sister of Mercy, who on 'perceiving the crucifix hanging from her [the Sisters] girdle, [would] eagerly seize it with his dying grasp, and press it fervently to his lips'[20] impressed her. These encounters with the Irish in the Crimea also led to a lifelong interest in and association with Ireland, the Irish people, Irish Catholicism, and particularly the Irish poor in England.

In April 1855, while in the Crimea, Taylor was received into the Roman Catholic faith, as one of her biographers states: 'Father Woollett did not convert Miss Taylor...the work of conversion was already done by the sick and dying Irish soldiers, by the nuns'.[21] This momentous event in her life she had to keep secret until after she returned to England in November of that year. For the next 15 years she would spend her life searching for a meaningful way to express her Catholicism and her desire to find an active ministry among the poor and vulnerable in society. Her mentors for much of this period were the convert Dr Henry Edward Manning, later Catholic Archbishop of Westminster, and Lady Georgiana Fullerton (also a convert).[22] Manning encouraged Taylor to find her vocation among the poor of London, especially the Irish emigrant poor who were arriving in overwhelming numbers. Fullerton encouraged her literary output and as well as *Eastern Hospitals and English Nurses* (which sold very well and was reprinted several times) she published her first novel *Tyborne* in 1859. At this time she was also proprietor and editor of *The Lamp*, a Catholic periodical.

Taylor was one of many Victorian ladies who was drawn to serious highbrow journalism and commentary. In common with other converts of the time she recognised the importance to the Catholic cause of publishing books and periodicals which would combat the often virulent anti-popery and prevailing sectarianism in English society. Her books were well received and in *The Lamp* (which she edited from 1863–71) and the Catholic periodicals she founded – *Fireside Readings* and *The Month* – she undertook 'to supply Catholics with papers of general interest which they read without fear of meeting objectionable passages'.[23] These Catholic periodicals were vital to the dissemination of the ideas of English Catholicism and many well-known converts appear among the contributors, including Lady Georgiana Fullerton and Cardinal

John Henry Newman who submitted his famous poem 'The Dream of Gerontius' to *The Month*, where it first appeared in the May and June 1865 editions. Uplifting moral tales were an important literary genre of the day and with a pressing need to earn money for her family at this time due to unwise financial investments by a brother, Taylor began writing novels; her first *Tyborne* (1857), set in Elizabethan England with the persecution of Catholics as its subject, was a best seller.

As well as her literary work Taylor was also searching for a place within Catholicism for the expression of her spiritual aspirations, it is clear she was considering becoming a nun as 'between 1859 and 1866 . . . she . . . tried her vocation with the Daughters of Charity in Paris and the "Filles de Maries" (Daughters of the Heart of Mary) in England'.[24] However, none of the congregations she visited while doing research for her book, *Religious Orders* (published in 1862), were precisely what she was looking for.[25] Remembering her friends, the Irish Sisters of Mercy, she decided to visit Ireland and study the work of the female religious orders there. As well as observing the work of the Irish Orders she wanted to see how they defended the faith of the poor Catholics against proselytisers in their own land, as she saw 'her main mission as welfare and parish work among the Irish immigrants in urban England'.[26] These visits to Ireland culminated in the publication of *Irish Homes and Irish Hearts* in 1867.

Back in London after her Irish journeys Taylor heard of a Polish Congregation of Sisters who seemed to offer the model 'of the kind of life and work' that she was drawn too.[27] These were the Little Servant Sisters of the Immaculate Conception, their Rule appealed to Taylor as the sisters lived in community, worked directly with the poor, the convent required no dowries from those entering and the congregation tried to be self-supporting. She asked the Founder of the Order, M. Edmund Bojanowski, to send some of his Sisters to England which he was unable to do. However, he did give her permission to establish a congregation in London herself. By September 1869, with the encouragement of Archbishop Manning, Taylor and two other women were received as postulants. Taylor took Mary Magdalen as her name in religion, and the women began to live in community and minis- ter among the poor in London. Until 1872 the women trained and lived by the Rule of the Little Servant Sisters of the Immaculate Conception, however the Superior General of that Congregation, Elizabeth Szkudlapska and the Archbishop of Poznan, Cardinal Ledóchowski refused to allow changes to their Rule as proposed by Mother Magdalen; this decision left Mother Magdalen with little choice but to found her own congregation.

On 12 February 1872 Mother Magdalen took her final vows and this date is kept by her Order, the 'Poor Servants of the Mother of God (SMG)', as their foundation date. Their principal work was visiting the sick, as well as spiritual ministering to the poor and rescue work among women at risk of, or involved in, prostitution, 'with the early foundations of the congregation including refuges, night shelters, schools, a workhouse, a home for the elderly and a free hospital'.[28] By 1879 the constitutions of the congregation were written and Mother Magdalen took them to Rome; by August 1879 she received the *Decretum Laudis* signed by Pope Leo XIII; and in 1892 the Brief of Approbation of the Institute and Constitutions was granted, with the definitive approval granted in July 1900.

From its foundation in 1872 the congregation of the Poor Servants of the Mother of God had a strong and on-going connection with Ireland and many of its Sisters were Irish. One of the earliest foun- dations outside London was a short-lived school in Limerick in 1874, but more long-lasting Irish connections were made when the Order established schools at Carrigtwhohill, Cork in 1875, in Monkstown in Cork in 1881, and two schools in Dublin in 1888 and 1889. While further Poor Servants of the Mother of God foundations were set up in Ireland in the twentieth century, the Rathdown Union Workhouse in Dublin was one of the last in the lifetime of Mother Magdalen.

She had suffered from oedema for many years and was diagnosed with diabetes in 1894. Her health deteriorated in 1899 and she died on 9 June 1900 in the Soho Square Convent, London. The life of Frances (Fanny) Taylor, Mother Magdalen, was one of spiritual searching, devotion to God and dedication to working among the poor in her society. Her legacy continues in the work of her successors in the SMG congregations worldwide.[29] Many of her literary endeavours (she continued writing and publishing well into the 1890s) were published to critical acclaim, and her editorship of influential English Catholic periodicals established her as an important historical figure in both English and Irish religious historiography.[30] In particular, her conversion to Catholicism and her oft declared love of the expression of faith among Irish Catholics allows the reader a unique, albeit not completely uncritical insight into mid-nineteenth-century Ireland, from the point of view of a supportive and informed outsider. Research in the SMG central congregational archive shows that Mother Magdalen read many histories of Ireland in preparation for her journeys between 1864 and 1867; she was particularly well informed on the social and political concerns of the country. Most especially she was interested in the female religious congregations based in Ireland and their activities in rescue work among the poor, children and women, in education, in health care and it is these interests which inform the narrative of *Irish Homes and Irish Hearts*.

IRISH HOMES AND IRISH HEARTS, 1867

Until recently it was believed that Fanny Taylor paid only one visit to Ireland in 1867, and based on this visit she wrote a series of articles for her magazine, *The Lamp*, these excerpts were then gathered into book form and published as *Irish Homes and Irish Hearts* later that year. However work in the SMG central archive has uncovered a more detailed chronology of four extended visits by Taylor to Ireland between 1864 and 1867. It is also clear that few articles on her Irish visits appeared originally in *The Lamp*, and that most of the material was published first in book form in *Irish Homes and Irish Hearts*. The dedication on the first edition of the book gives a very broad hint of Taylor's reasons for visiting Ireland: she dedicated the book to 'those who under strange skies [the Crimea] . . . first taught me the worth of Irish character, the warmth of Irish hearts and the depth of Irish faith'.[31] By the 1860s the numbers of poor Irish in London and the plight particularly of poor Irish women and children had come to Taylor's attention. A letter from her friend Father William Ronan, SJ, suggests a further reason for her attention to the Irish poor. Ronan wrote that Archbishop Manning wanted her to create a new foundation in London specifically to rescue 'the poor Irish in London from the proselytisers'.[32] Manning and Fullerton agreed that in order to understand the needs of the Irish in England and how to meet those needs, Taylor should visit Ireland.

Irish Homes and Irish Hearts is organised so that the religious institutions visited by Taylor in Dublin are covered in the first chapters of the book, while subsequent chapters cover her visits north (Drogheda and Newry), south (Limerick, Cork and south Kerry), west (Athlone, Galway, Gort, Loughrea, Clare) and finally back to Dublin. The final chapter is a broad discussion on politics, history and religion in Ireland. However despite this organisation Taylor's first visit to Ireland was actually to the south in 1864, when she indicated that she was present 'immediately after the erection of the statue to Father Mathew, at the top of Patrick St. [Cork] which occurred in October 1864'.[33] It is perhaps not unusual that Taylor's first trip to Ireland was to Cork as she still had contact with the

Sisters of Mercy whom she had known in the Crimea and who were now based in the convents in the area.

In *Irish Homes* Taylor illuminates both the foundation histories of many of the native Irish orders and her admiration for their founders. Among the orders discussed were her old friends, the Sisters of Mercy, founded in Dublin in 1831 by Catherine McAuley; the Presentation Sisters, founded in Cork in 1775 by Nano Nagle; the Irish Sisters of Charity founded in 1815 in Dublin by Mary Aikenhead; the Sisters of Holy Faith founded in Dublin in 1864 by Margaret Aylward; and the Irish Sisters of Loreto established in Ireland in 1823 by Frances Mary Ball. She also visited the foreign orders which were established in Ireland in the nineteenth century; the Poor Clares, the Sisters of St Vincent de Paul, the Sisters of the Good Shepherd and the Carmelite Sisters. While she did not deal with the male orders at length she did visit some institutions run by the Irish Christian Brothers, founded by Edmund Rice in 1802. She visited the orphanages, refuges for fallen women, industrial schools, schools for the blind, hospitals and infirmaries run by the various congregations. She also visited some state run institutions (workhouses and training schools) of which she was unfailingly critical. She entered no Protestant-run institutions, although she did include some criticism of them, which indicates her very specific interest and bias in terms of religion and ministry. She travelled the country by almost every mode of transport available, steamboat, train, canal-boat, carriage, outside car and open cart. The development of the railways in Ireland in the 1840s and 1850s allowed Taylor to access the towns and cities outside of Dublin and in her travels out of the capital she gained a more nuanced, broader view of the social and political landscape of the country. Indeed her travels were so extensive that her friends worried about her health; Fr Ronan, writing in 1900, stated that he saw her several times in Ireland 'after the Crimean war . . . and always in a state of wretched health from overwork'.[34] Despite this heavy workload Taylor completed her series of visits and had the full manuscript ready for publication in 1867.

Taylor's perspective in *Irish Homes* is that of a reflective and informed traveller. She displayed a certain sense of Irish history and Irish political issues gained from reading Irish histories and following the political debates of the day. Unlike many of her English contemporaries Taylor did not regard the Irish as an uncivilised race, mainly because of their 'persevering, unconquerable faith'. Taylor believed that it was because of this faith the Irish had achieved much that was not acknowledged, in fact, the Irish had

> out of their poverty, and their suffering, and their difficulties . . . raised one after another of these noble institutions [*the religious establishments of Ireland*], which in all material things may vie with the grand establishments in England, on which English wealth has been so lavishly expended, while from the spirit in which they are carried on, they far excel the results of our splendid efforts[35]

She was concerned about the English attitudes to the Irish; she was perturbed, for example, that during the 'recent Fenian outbreak' an English writer could call for 'revival in Ireland of the stern measures of Cromwell'.[36] She believed such suggestions were only possible because the English knew little of the dire and fatal consequences Cromwellian policies had had on the country and, in particular, on the religion that she now held so dearly to her heart. Despite the beauty of the country, the picturesque ruins, the ancient history and the hospitality of the people Taylor wrote that Ireland remained a land of injustice and oppression. Unlike many of her English contemporaries she was unafraid to point the finger of blame for this at English governance of Ireland.

At the time Taylor was in Ireland the Fenian movement was seen as a major threat to the stability of English rule and it is a subject to which Taylor obviously gave some thought. From her reading of history she felt that the wrongs done by English mis-government in Ireland should be made known to all English people; that the English tried not only to 'suppress a religion' but also attempted to 'extinguish a nation'.[37] She wrote of the passion the Irish had for their nation: 'for even the heart of the nun in the quiet convent beats quick when Ireland is spoken of'.[38] Taylor also wrote that, while the Irish brood, perhaps too much, on the injustices of the past, no Irishman of education and standing truly wants to break the connection with England. Fenianism, she wrote, was 'disliked, feared, and disapproved of; looked on as politically unwise and morally wrong'.[39] However until the English could prove themselves loved and trusted by the Irish people, until these continuing political and religious injustices were stopped there would remain among Irish people 'a keen sense of injustice in the present'.[40]

Irish Homes also reflects Taylor's understanding of the language of respectability in use by those working among and with the poor. Most middle-class philanthropists accepted that the virtues of sobriety, moral restraint, hard work, education and thrift were vital in terms of social improvement. Proper education and the practice of faith would lead to a moral, upstanding, respectable workforce. Like many of those drawn to work with the poor Taylor demonstrates a belief that the education given to the children of the poor should also reflect their class and status in society. Most in society were, she felt, 'particular about caste' and that it was 'a terrible risk of serious evil' to educate a child above his or her class and expectation.[41] Children of the working class were to be educated for their station in life. In Kenmare she approved of the fact that the Poor Clare Sisters 'try to classify the children, giving to each the education most suited to their position, and . . . their capabilities';

middle-class girls were given a more literary education: 'there are girls of a superior grade, who are being trained for school mistresses . . . they receive a solid and excellent education'.[42] The Sisters of Mercy impressed her with the work among 'the, respectable laboring poor, servants . . . the lower middle classes . . . who could be helped resume their former station' and among those most reduced in circumstances

> the pauper class, the lowest, most wretched, most ignorant, most neglected of the population, and therefore most needing instruction and elevating influences. Among this class of sufferers the Sisters of Mercy in Limerick go about consoling, teaching, and helping.[43]

These Sisters of Mercy were, Taylor wrote, the first to solve the problem of reforming 'female criminals' which was 'a harder task' than reforming male criminals as the woman had gone more 'against the instincts of her better nature' so 'the consequences of her crime have a more hardening effect on her'.[44] Female criminals who had been in a 'state of chronic rebellion and passion' in jail were, when moved to finish their sentences with the Sisters of Mercy at the Goldenbridge Refuge (opened in 1856), 'redeemed. . .to virtue, society and God'.[45] It was the 'absence of hope' which made these women 'wild' and it was repentance, work, and a renewed sense of virtue and respectability that gave the women hope. The Sisters continued to work with the women after they left the Refuge, helping them find 'proper, respectable' work placements and trying to keep them away from 'malign influences' and 'former friends'.

Taylor's visit to St Brigid's, the orphanage run by Margaret Aylward's Sisters of the Holy Faith, allowed her debate the merits of 'boarding-out' poor children to foster families, which was a method used by Aylward and her Sisters, or, alternatively, the merits of raising children in the more institutional setting of the orphanage or the workhouse, a method which was more common among the other orders and the State. She found much to praise in the system adopted by St Brigid's. The children were provided with homes, friends and education in their native religion, they were trained by their foster parents in trades and work; this, she wrote, fitted the orphan for 'the rough path in life they have to pursue'.[46] Life in the orphanage was, she felt, too gentle and easy, especially on the female orphan who when she left the genteel life of the convent orphanage 'hears rough words, and meets the petty injustice ... she is dismayed, frets to get back again, and finding that impossible, often gives up the struggle in despair'.[47] What Taylor and many others were most concerned with was that these girls be trained for their station in life, to be domestic servants and 'the tendency of girls of the lower classes to reject this mode of livelihood, is certainly injurious to them'.[48] Taylor believed that without the ability to be gainfully employed in the outside world the chance that these girls would fall into sin was increased.

Taylor would later use much of what she observed in the institutions of care run by the various female religious orders in Ireland in her own foundation. Her order, the Poor Servants of the Mother of God, also ran schools, asylums, hospitals and orphanages for the poor. She visited Magdalene asylums run by Mercy and Good Shepherd sisters as well as those run by the Sisters of Charity and other orders. For the Sisters of Charity of Refuge and the Good Shepherd nuns, running these asylums was their main missionary work. Most of their asylums were self-supporting, as hard work was seen as a route to salvation and redemption. Taylor was particularly taken with the laundries attached to many of the convents where the women, referred to as 'penitents', whom she claimed 'willingly entered these sheltering walls, and are trying to regain their good name, and to make their peace with God', and worked for their keep and as penance in the laundry.[49] She noted that in the Good

Shepherd convents 'the "penitents" . . . are not expected or urged to remain for life, and the greater part do not'.[50] She noted, nonetheless, that the Sisters of Charity in Donnybrook, Dublin encouraged the 'penitent' women to stay for life as the Sisters believe that

> very few of those who have lost their good name, and, generally speaking, have contracted habits of intemperance, idleness, and other vices, will be able to resist temptation if exposed to the rough contact of the world again.[51]

Taylor, however, was not certain that encouraging the women to remain in the Magdalene asylum for life was a viable option. She understood that the women themselves do much better in the asylum when they 'knew a certain time of probation only was required' and that they would, in time, leave the asylum.[52] In the Cork Magdalene she was struck by the magnificent laundries and the 'quiet manner and modest demeanor of many of the women, giving evidence of the improvement which had been wrought in their characters'.[53] She also described the method by which different groups of the poor were kept separate in these convent systems. The children in the industrial schools, reformatories and orphanages attached to these convents were separated from the 'fallen' women in the Magdalene asylums. This allowed the sisters, she observed approvingly, to cater for each population according to the perceived needs of that group and prevent moral contagion from one group to the other. She was, especially, highly critical of the workhouse system and wrote that workhouse training engendered particularly in girls 'bad habits . . . inveterate idleness, and a tendency to cunning and deceit'.[54] The workhouse system she declared was 'calculated to demoralise a large portion of the population', where '*unmarried* [her italics] mothers and their babies' were lodged together, an 'evil' fact, which she wrote, 'needs no comment' in a Christian country.[55] She believed that only when the religious sisters took over the running of these institutions were the poor saved from themselves and the 'wild, savage' children turned into 'useful members of the population'.[56] The 'fallen women' was regarded as a site of moral contagion in nineteenth-century Ireland, their propensity to spread disease or immorality had to be contained within a system that kept the 'fallen' women away from those who were 'respectable'. Taylor, like many of her contemporaries, approved of these methods of confinement, regulation, penance and reform by which the Irish orders worked to 'rescue' these 'fallen' women.

Taylor made the most of her journeys in Ireland and as well as her detailed observations on the work of religious orders, she proved to be a good travel writer, commenting on the landscape, architecture, ancient ruins and the general character of the ordinary people. She described Limerick as a fine old city and the beauty of Cork 'surpassed expectations . . . [as the sun shone] the river, the churches, the steeple of 'Shandon' and the quaint picturesque houses [lying] glittering in its rays'.[57] While she was complimentary of much convent architecture, she was generally unimpressed by church architecture, finding only in Killarney, a cathedral, designed by Pugin 'worthy of the name . . . [with its] great height of the roof, the noble pillars, the sense of space and grandeur, made one think of some of the beautiful cathedrals of old'.[58] On her way from Killarney to Kenmare she was taken with the dramatic beauty of the countryside, wondering whether a 'more beautiful drive . . . can be had anywhere . . . the memory of it will . . . be a joy forever'.[59] She visited the Poor Clare Convent in Kenmare and mentioned that several works of 'considerable' importance had been composed by a member of the community, although she did not mention the author by name. She also noted that this unnamed writer was under-taking 'a long awaited work', a popular and illustrated history of

Ireland. This, of course, was Mary Francis Cusack, known as the 'Nun of Kenmare', a convert who had, like Taylor's sisters, once been a Sellonite and who would also go on to found her own order of Catholic nuns, the Sisters of St Joseph of Peace. In Clare and Galway Taylor was impressed by the simple faith of the ordinary people. She also had a keen eye for the people and described many of the characters she met from the hard-working nuns, to the women 'in their red petticoats and blue clocks, when standing together in groups formed a subject for an artist' at Sunday mass in Gort, Co. Galway.[60] She also noted the heartbreak of emigration, describing scenes of weeping at Gort as young emigrants boarded the coach for Ennis which was 'a strange and sorrowful sight', where the emigrating people were exhorted to 'send money over and bring the others out'.[61]

Taylor believed that the Irish female religious orders were carriers of the Catholic religion and that their philanthropic missions to the poor in Ireland were necessary to combat proselytism. The Holy Faith Sisters were, as noted in *The Month*, the 'chief bulwark in Dublin against the machinations' of the 'soupers'.[62] Proselytism was considered by Taylor, Manning and other English Catholics as a major problem among the Irish poor in London and Taylor wished to recreate a similar order of women in England to serve, protect and educate the Catholic poor in the virtues of work, morality, respectability and in their tenets of their own Catholic faith. Several times she wrote about 'souperism', especially the prevalence of this practice during the Irish Famine (1845–50) and its growing popularity, as she understood it, in the 1860s. Many Protestant organisations, she noted, gave help and charity willingly to the starving Irish during the Famine, but, there were some 'who took advantage of the misery of the poor to tamper with their consciences'.[63] Taylor wrote vehemently against the 'evils of souperism', which she argued was closely connected with the philanthropic practices of the Established Church. This was the practice by which meals and religious instructions were provided by some non-Catholic organisations.[64]

On her visit to St Brigid's Orphanage, set up by Margaret Aylward in 1857, she was impressed by the work of the Sisters of the Holy Faith in protecting the Catholic faith of poor children. She wrote that the Sisters

> besides undertaking the large amount of work which the management of such a widely-scattered family as the children of St Brigid must entail, have opened in various parts of Dublin six poor schools, for besides the orphanages the "soupers" have started poor schools, where clothing, food, and other bribes are freely given, and the Sisters of the Faith found that additional schools to the existing ones were needed to combat this evil.[65]

It is possibly while visiting the Sisters of Holy Faith that Taylor received her most immediate education on 'souperism' in Ireland. Aylward had been involved in combating the 'evils' of 'souperism' for many years at this stage and as her many writings indicate she seemed convinced that there 'was a great scheme to rob Ireland of her Catholics'.[66] There can be little doubt that 'souperism' was a main topic of discussion on Taylor's visit to St Brigid's – she mentioned that Aylward had already spent 'six months in prison on most unjust grounds' because of her 'exertions on behalf of the poor'.[67] She also used research published by Dr John Forbes in 'Memorandums made in Ireland in the autumn of 1852', detailing his inquiries among proselytisers in Connemara, which, she wrote, demonstrated the failure of this practice despite the money thrown into the effort. Much to Taylor's approval, Forbes concluded that it was 'unjustifiable to seek to attain Protestantism in Ireland at the risk . . . of the peace of a nation which is profoundly devoted to Catholicism'.[68]

It must be noted that Taylor's dislike of 'soupers' was well developed before her Irish visits. In her magazine *The Month* articles on Protestant proselyting in Ireland had already appeared in which it was stated that the main features of these missions were 'fraud and hypocrisy'.[69] Margaret Aylward was, in the 1850s, asked by Paul Cullen, Archbishop of Dublin, to 'keep a watchful eye on the movements of the proselytisers' especially among the poor, orphaned children of the city.[70] Like Taylor, Aylward was of the opinion that the education the children received should 'make them strong in faith' and fit them 'for their position in society'.[71] Taylor approved of the continuing efforts by Aylward's Holy Faith Sisters and the other female religious congregations to educate Catholic children in their own faith and to train them in suitable trades and occupations.

Her descriptions of the number and the work of the female religious congregations demonstrate the extraordinary growth in influence of the conventual movement among women in nineteenth-century Ireland, and also among English converts like herself, in England. Through the nineteenth century many areas of work were closed off to middle-class, educated women, for whom the domestic life of wife and mother was still expected. For women searching for a life outside of the domestic, philanthropy was one acceptable avenue. Charitable good works, suitable to the nurturing and caring nature of women, was a respectable path for the educated women seeking an outlet for their intelligence, ability and vocation. Among middle-class Catholic women there was a proliferation of vocations to religious life, and many new congregations sprung up to cater for this need. Joining convents gave women status, respect, influence and employment they could not get elsewhere, especially for those who felt called to a life of service among the poor. The growth of religious vocations among women in nineteenth-century Ireland was extraordinary, rising from 120 nuns in Ireland in 1800, to 8,000 by 1901, making up more than a 'quarter of the professional adult women workers' in the 1901 Census.[72] Most of the female congregations established in this century were active orders, working in education, nursing, asylum care, prison care and visiting, and more.

As well as extensive detail on the work of the female religious, *Irish Homes* also allows readers an intimate view of the convents. In the Convent of the Irish Sisters of Charity, Harold's Cross, Dublin, Taylor attended a profession of a nun and notes that

> the chapel is a perfect gem. It is built in the form of a cross and the lightness and beauty of its colouring, its stained glass windows, and its decorations are admirable. The spectators of the ceremony were hospitably entertained by the Sisters at breakfast, after which we were allowed a thorough inspection of the Chapel and also to visit the schools, which are built half-way down the avenue leading from the high road. These schools are well attended and seemed to be in excellent order.[73]

While Taylor was obviously a dedicated admirer of the work of the Irish nuns it is perhaps overly harsh to say that her work 'reads more like a lengthy propaganda pamphlet for the religious institutions than a critical and factual account of these'.[74] *Irish Homes* is not, in fact, completely uncritical of the female religious orders, as Taylor did question some of the work and care practices in the institutions she visited. She was unsure of the beneficial effects of the upbringing and training girls received in orphanages; the fact that so many employers complained of the inability of these girls to do well in domestic service cannot, she wrote, be ignored. She was also not convinced that 'fallen' women should be persuaded to remain in Magdalen asylums for life. Many of the women in these Refuges were, she felt, 'more sinned against than sinning', and with the help of the nuns could be reformed and made fit for a life of faith and work in the outside world. Taylor did, nonetheless, like her Irish and English contemporaries believe in the efficacy of rescue, repentance and reform, particularly of 'fallen' women, orphans and the poor. As part of this rescue and to prevent moral contagion, it was accepted that penance, hard work, silence and prayer were necessary to bring a 'sinner' back to acceptance in 'respectable' society. These orders of nuns provided the 'rescue' and 'reform' for those whom nineteenth-century Irish society deemed in need, they strove to inculcate ideals of chastity and virtue as well as 'respectable' morality, particularly in women, as well as the self-discipline, sobriety and devotion to faith considered necessary to be a proper member of Irish Catholic society. Taylor drew inspiration from the pastoral work of the Irish nuns among those considered most in need in society – this is the type of work her own Order would later undertake in England.

Irish Homes was published to very good reviews, although some of these did come with a warning. The *Pall Mall Gazette* noted that 'Miss Taylor (of Crimean fame) in "Irish Homes and Irish Hearts" gives a history of Irish conventual establishments . . . in which she recognises one of the greatest works, means and circumstances considered, of recent days'.[75] The *Church Times* of 25 May 1867 gave the book a detailed review but warned readers that Miss Taylor was 'thick and thin Roman' however the review conceded that if the reader took onboard this 'tainted' atmosphere in the book there was much to satisfy.[76] The *Dublin Review* described her style as 'lucid and eloquent' in detailing the great works of the religious congregations and her exposure of the 'detestable evil' of souperism. Her final chapter on the political situation in Ireland might, the reviewer suggested, serve as a small text on the 'Irish question'.[77]

Irish Homes provides a snapshot of the workings of the various institutions run by the orders and the reasoning behind their operations, at a time when institutions run by these religious sisters were becoming an integral part of a systemic attempt to educate, train and provide for a 'respectable' poorer class and also provide an education for a growing, wealthier and more politically influential Catholic middle class. Taylor's descriptions of the work of the nuns demonstrate clearly the process of 'gathering in' the poor, to 'separate them into groups according to need and to control and manage them in formalised settings' which 'took root' in nine-teenth-century Ireland.[78] On her return to England Taylor continued looking for an order whose rule she might adopt for her own work among the poor, particularly the Irish Catholic poor, in England; finally she founded her own Order in 1872. The stated aim of her foundation was to require no dowries from novices, to be self-financing, to help the urban poor, especially women and children, to protect their Catholic faith and to educate and train them for suitable, 'respectable' employment (namely domestic service or laundry work). While Taylor did not join any of the Irish orders, the nuns she encountered on her visits to Ireland had clearly given her ideas and inspired her future work. Her depictions of the institu-tions, towns and areas that she visited and her opinions of the work carried out by the Irish orders of nuns, their aims and concerns, in *Irish Homes* allows the reader today, a unique, if sometimes uncritical and biased, first-hand account of religious, institutional and social histories of mid-nineteenth-century Ireland.

Notes to Introduction

1   This note is based on several biographies of Frances Taylor/Mother Magdalen, including Francis C. Devas, *Mother Mary Magdalen* (London, 1927); Mother M. Geraldine SMG, *Born to Love; Fanny Margaret Taylor* (Roehampton, 1970); Sister Mary Campion Troughton SMG, *Life of Mother Foundress* (Roehampton, 1972); Ruth Gilpin Wells, *A Woman of her Time and Ours: Mother Magdalen Taylor SMG* (NC, 1994); Eithne Leonard SMG, *Frances Taylor, Mother Magdalen SMG: A Portrait 1832–1900* (Roehampton, 2005), and archival sources from the Central Archive of the Poor Servants of the Mother of God, St Mary's Convent, Brentford, Middlesex (hereafter SMG Archives). Special thanks are due to the archivist at Brentford, Paul Shaw, for all his advice and help and to Alison Quinlan who has written on Mother Magdalen and her literary output,

in particular her excellent work on *Irish Homes and Irish Hearts*, including her contribution to *Irish Homes and Irish Hearts – Extracts and Personal Reflections* by Joseph Richard Dunne (Roehampton, 2011), and her article 'Fanny's Forays in Ireland 1864–6' in the congregational publication *Pray and Promote*, vol. 3 no. 5 (June 2011).

2 More popularly known as the 'Oxford Movement', among whose proponents were Cardinal John Henry Newman and Revd Edward Pusey.

3 Devas, *Mother Mary Magdalen*, p. 7.

4 Revd W. J. Irons (1812–83), Church of England clergyman and writer. His best known work was *An Analysis of Human Responsibility* (1869).

5 *Oxford Dictionary of National Biography*. http://www.oxforddnb.com/view/article/14459 Revd W. J. Irons. Those who were involved in the 'Oxford Movement' (1833–45) came to be known, popularly, as Tractarians and their beliefs as Tractarianism after a series of pamphlets, *Tracts for the Times*, published between 1833 and 1841. As Peter Nockles explains Tractarianism was 'a religious and intellectual revival in defence of the Church of England as a divine institution . . . a repository of apostolic succession', affirming the liturgical use of vestments, ritual and high ceremony within the church. Tractarians evinced a desire to assert the independence of the church in the face of state interference and, in looking back to the Elizabethan and Stuart churches, wanted to restore the 'faith and practice of the Early Church and the High Church ideals of seventeenth-century Anglicanism'. The influence of the Oxford Movement was seen mostly in High-Church Anglicanism, with a return, as leading Tractarian Edward Pusey (1800–82) wrote, to the 'beauty of holiness' – particularly the use of vestments and more traditional rituals.

6 Henry Edward Manning (1808–92), youngest son of William Manning, a West Indies merchant and Tory MP. He was ordained in the Church of England in 1832 and was a proponent of High Church Anglicanism. He resigned from the Church of England in the wake of the Gorham controversy and was received into the Catholic Church in 1851. In 1865 he became Catholic Archbishop of Westminster and in 1875 he was elevated to the office of Cardinal. He died in 1892.

7 Sr Ida Kennedy SMG, *A Brief Life of Mother Magdalen Taylor* (Roehampton, 2008), p. 4.

8 Ragged schools were charitable institutions set up to provide a free, basic education as well as food, clothing and sometimes lodging to these needy children.

9 Mark Bostridge, *Florence Nightingale: The Woman and her Legend* (London, 2008), ch. 9, also see Maria Luddy (ed.), *The Crimean Journals of the Sisters of Mercy 1854–56* (Dublin, 2004). The *London Times* was notable in its exposure of the squalor in which wounded British soldiers were treated and the horrific rate at which they were dying at Balaklava and Scutari. These reports ignited public outrage and nearly toppled the government of Lord Aberdeen.

10 Mary Stanley (1813–79), an ardent Puseyite and daughter of Edward Stanley, later Bishop of Norwich. She was initially a supporter of Florence Nightingale, but is now known chiefly for the dispute she had with Nightingale in the Crimea. She converted to Catholicism and on her return from the Crimea devoted her life to philanthropic causes.

11 Fanny Taylor, *Eastern Hospitals and English Nurses: The Narrative of Twelve Months Experience in the Hospitals of Koulali and Scutari by a Lady Volunteer* (London, 1856). *Eastern Hospitals* came out again in a two-volume edn, in March 1856, and it appears to have been only the second published first-hand account of Crimean nursing to be produced, according to Bostridge. Florence Nightingale did not approve of it. The so-called 'third', cheap, revised edn appeared in February 1857.

12 Luddy, *The Crimean Journals*, p. xiii.

13 Bostridge, *Florence Nightingale*, pp 238–40.

14 Taylor, *Eastern Hospitals*, p. 31.

15 Ibid., p. 39.

16 Ibid., p. 47.

17 Luddy, *The Crimean Journals*, p. 215.

18 Ibid., p. 152.

19 Campion SMG, *Life of Mother Foundress*, p. 26; SMG Archives, ref 1/A/10 pt.

20 Taylor, *Eastern Hospitals*, p. 203.

21 Devas, *Mother Mary Magdalen*, p. 42.

22 Lady Georgiana Fullerton (1812–85) daughter of the 1st Earl of Granville, married Irishman and convert to Catholicism, Alexander George Fullerton. She herself converted in 1846. She was the author of several novels including *Grantley Manor* (1847), *Lady Bird* (1852), *Too Strange to be not True* (1862) and *Ellen Middleton* (1884). She devoted much of her life to works of charity and in 1856 joined the Third Order of St. Francis. She was a loyal supporter of Mother Magdalen and the Poor Servants of the Mother of God. She died in Bournemouth in 1885.

23 Joyce Sugg, *Ever Yours Affly: John Henry Newman and his Female Circle* (Leominster, 1996), p. 154.

24 Kennedy, *A Brief Life of Mother Magdalen Taylor*, p. 6.

25 Fanny Taylor, *Religious Orders: Or, Sketches of Some of the Orders and Congregations of Women, by the author of 'Eastern Hospitals'* (London, 1862). This was published by Emily Faithfull's 'Victoria Press'. Faithfull was associated with the 'Langham Place Group', a group of politically minded women who were engaged with issues such as the education of women, changes to marriage laws and the need for women's employment, particularly in the sphere of writing and journalism.

26 Susan O'Brien, 'Terra Incognita: The Nun in Nineteenth-Century England', in *Past & Present*, no. 121 (Nov., 1988), p. 131.

27 Wells, *A Woman of Her Time and Ours;* p. 91.

28 Kennedy, *A Brief Life of Mother Magdalen Taylor*, p. 11.

29 There are now SMG foundations in the USA and Kenya as well as in Ireland, the UK and Rome.

30 As well as the journals she founded, amongst her many publications were *Holy Confidence or Simplicity with God* (London, 1869); *The Catholic Pilgrim's Guide to Rome*, 1st edn (London, 1887); *Life of Father John Curtis of the Society of Jesus*, revised by Father Edward Purbrick SJ (Dublin, 1889); *Forgotten Heroines or History of a Convent in the Days of Luther and the Nun's Centenary* (London, n.d.); *Memoir of Father Augustus Dignam SJ, with Some of his Letters*, 1st edn (London, 1895); *The Inner Life of Lady Georgiana Fullerton, with Notes of Retreat and Diary* (London, *c.*1899), as well as many works of fiction.

31 Dedication in *Irish Homes and Irish Hearts* (1867).

32 SMG Archives, 'Letters of W. J. Ronan SJ', dated July 1900, ref. C. G5, p. 4, A–C; SMG Archives, 'Letters of W. J. Ronan SJ', dated July 1900, ref. C. G5, p. 4, A–C.

33 Fanny Taylor, *Irish Homes and Irish Hearts* (London, 1867), p. 142.

34 SMG Archives, 'Letters of W. J. Ronan SJ', dated July 1900, ref E2/12 and E2/35.

35 Taylor, *Irish Homes*, p. 234.

36 Ibid., p. 218.

37 Ibid., p. 219.

38 Ibid., p. 232.

39 Ibid., p. 217.

40 Ibid., p. 218.

41 Ibid., p. 132.

42 Ibid., p. 169.

43 Ibid., pp 136–7.

44 Ibid., p. 53.

45 Ibid., pp 53–9.

46 Ibid., p. 102.

47 Ibid.

48 Ibid., pp 102–3.

49 Ibid., p. 89.

50 Ibid., p. 140.

51 Ibid., p. 28.

52 Ibid.

53 Ibid., p. 153.

54 Ibid., p. 155.

55 Ibid., p. 191.

56 Ibid., pp 191–2. Taylor mentions that Daniel O'Connell was also convinced of the 'evil workhouses do', and had 'raised his voice up against them', p. 191.

57 Ibid., p. 141.

58 Ibid., p. 163.

59 Ibid., p. 165.

60 Ibid., p. 202.

61 Ibid., p. 206.

62 'Irish birds' nests', in *The Month* (Dec. 1866), pp 568–9.

63 Taylor, *Irish Homes*, p. 97.

64 See Miriam Moffitt's *Soupers and Jumpers: The Protestant Missions in Connemara* (Dublin, 2008).

65 Taylor, *Irish Homes*, p. 100.

66 Margaret H. Preston, *Charitable Words: Women, Philanthropy and the Language of Charity in 19th-Century Dublin* (Connecticut, 2004), p. 85.

67 Taylor, *Irish Homes*, p. 100. This was in November 1860 when Aylward was accused of kidnapping a child a Protestant mother tried to reclaim from St Brigid's. While she was cleared of these charges she was sentenced to six months in prison for contempt.

68 Ibid., pp 228–9.

69 'Irish birds' nests', in *The Month* (Dec. 1866), pp 568–9.

70 Jacinta Prunty, *Margaret Aylward, 1810–1889: Lady of Charity, Sister of Faith* (Dublin, 2011), p. 50.

71 Ibid., pp 102–5.

72 Maria Luddy, *Women and Philanthropy in 19th-Century Ireland* (Cambridge, 1995), p. 23. See also Caitriona Clear, *Nuns in Nineteenth-Century Ireland* (Dublin, 1988).

73 Taylor, *Irish Homes*, p. 31.

74 Rebecca Lea McCarthy, *Origins of the Magdalene Laundries: An Analytical History* (London, 2010), p. 23.

75 *The Pall Mall Gazette*, 31 May 1867 – at this time *The Pall Mall Gazette* was a conservative paper.

76 *The Church Times*, 25 May 1867, p. 182. *The Church Times*, an Anglican newspaper, was founded in 1863 by George Josiah Palmer to campaign for Anglo-Catholic principles.

77 *The Dublin Review of Books*, vol. 61 (1867), p. 240.

78 Clear, *Nuns in Nineteenth-Century Ireland*, pp 106–7.

IRISH HOMES AND IRISH HEARTS.

CHAPTER I.

THERE is certainly no lack of books about Ireland. ' Tours' and ' Visits' to, and ' Sketches' and ' Scenes' in, the Emerald Isle abound on all sides; and at the present time the subject of Ireland is in everybody's mouth, and her wants and their remedies, her shortcomings and her difficulties, are discussed on all sides. I do not desire to follow in this beaten track, or to enter into a disquisition on these vexed questions; my object is only to show an aspect of Irish life as it happened to come under my notice—an aspect which I believe is little known in England, but which gives a stranger a very fair idea of Irish hearts and Irish homes. I would speak of that marvellous net of religious institutions spread over the land, and of those deeds of charity, which in reality form a powerful element in Irish life.

It would greatly tend, I believe, to a right understanding of the state of the country, the character of the people, and her prospects for the future, if we would take due account of the religious and charitable institutions which have risen on Irish soil, and which have been for

the most part originated and brought to maturity by the
Irish nation themselves. Of late years the attention
of English people has often been drawn to the admirable religious and charitable institutions of France and
Belgium, and they have interested us, not only on
account of their excellence and their number, but also
because of the wonderful celerity with which they
sprung up after a long convulsion of anarchy and
irreligion. Still more worthy, then, are the religious
institutions of Ireland of notice, for they have risen
up and flourished in spite of greater difficulties than
have ever been contended against in any country in
Europe.

To understand them thoroughly it is absolutely necessary to take a glance into the past history of Ireland.
It is often made a matter of reproach to the Irish, that
they dwell so exclusively in the history of the past as to
unfit themselves for the duties of the present. I believe
this evil would be greatly obviated if English people
would remember what Irish people would perhaps do
well to forget. For if it be unwise for the descendants
of the injured to brood over the injuries which cannot
now be effaced, it surely is well and fitting for the
descendants of those who were the aggressors to regret
the folly and injustice of their ancestors, and thus if
possible, by a generous sympathy, to heal the rankling
sore handed down from father to son.

Few things strike the English visitor to Ireland more
than the different effect which religious persecution and
penal laws, existing for two centuries, have wrought in
that country, as compared with their influence in England. In the latter, slowly but surely they accomplished

their end, gradually destroying the priesthood, and so blotting out the faith from the hearts of the people. The middle classes and the poor were rent from the ancient faith, and catholicity lingered only among a remnant of the nobility and gentry, and found its refuge within the walls of a few mansions whose owners bore an ancient and a stately name. Religious houses were swept from the land, and men and women who wished to consecrate themselves to God were compelled to seek a refuge on foreign shores. But in Ireland the case was different. In vain were bishops and priests hunted like wild beasts, their heads being sought for in common with those of wolves;[*] in vain was it enacted that to harbour them should be punished with death,[†] their faithful people would not betray them; they were hidden ' in deserts, in mountains, in dens, and in caves of the earth,' loved and honoured by their scattered and suffering flocks as the priesthood of no other country had ever been. As in England, the devastator's hand threw down the monasteries and the abbeys which had overspread the land, but the hearts of the people clung to them still. The ' ancient places ' of Ireland have never been deserted; still to this day the people carry their dead to rest beneath the shade of some old priory, or by the ruins of the churches which were once

Set like stars around some saintly hermitage.[‡]

---

[*] 'The second beast is a priest, on whose head we lay ten pounds—if he be eminent more.'—BURTON'S *Parliamentary Diary*, 1657.

[†] 'And for the Jesuits, priests, fryers, munks, and nunnes, 20ᵘ will be given to any that can bring certain intelligence where any of them are. And whosoever doth harbour or conceal any one of them is to forfeit life and estate.'—*Several Proceedings in Parliament, from 21st to 28th of November*, 1650, p. 912. 　　　　[‡] Keble.

Though long ages have passed since the Church's
offices have ceased, and the wind whistles through
the broken arches, and the birds build their nests on
the ivy-covered walls, the voice of prayer is rarely
silent: pilgrim after pilgrim has told the ' round of the
beads ' by each ruined altar; and when sorrow and
anguish are more than usually heavy on the soul, the
mourner will take long journeys bare-foot along the
roughest roads to offer up petitions where the bones
of the saints are resting.   As in England, the parish
churches of the land were confiscated to the state
religion, but their ministers had to content themselves
with bare walls and empty benches; the people fled
from them to mud cabins or mountain caves, or, if these
failed, the blue sky was their canopy, and a heap of
stones their altar.   In one point only did these cruel
enactments succeed : they *almost* entirely destroyed
the religious orders, especially those for women ; nuns
in their habit were dragged before magistrates, and
driven as criminals from the cities.   Here and there
they lingered still, putting on secular attire, and often
begging their bread; but the great mass of religious
women, and a large proportion of men, were either
banished from their native shores or died unable to
leave others to fill their places.   But by those who
were left the battle was bravely and resolutely fought
through the lapse of two long centuries, and in 1745,
when England had become thoroughly Protestant,
Ireland remained Catholic to its core.   In the reign of
James the First, Lord-Deputy Chichester had been
forced to exclaim, ' I know not how the attachment to
the Catholic Church is so deeply rooted in the hearts of

the Irish, unless it be that the very soil is infected with
popery.' His successor in the reign of George the
Second could have endorsed his remark, and yet it is a
fact that up to St. Patrick's Day, 1745, not one single
place of Catholic worship, of that faith professed by a
whole nation, was allowed by the law to be open. On
that morning a crowd of people assembled in an old
warehouse in Dublin to hear mass; the pressure was
too great, the floor gave way, and nine persons, including the officiating priest, were crushed to death. The
calamity attracted the notice of government and permission to open Catholic churches, carefully called
' chapels,' was accorded. And now that light was beginning to dawn, and the worst heat of the battle was
over, the generals of the army had time to count up
the ravages that the war had wrought, and to prepare
for the future. For the conflict was not yet over.
Very slowly and very grudgingly justice was meted
out. ' The government discountenanced, and the laws
absolutely prohibited, any education by Catholics. The
people were sunk in the lowest state of political degradation. They were silent—and history makes no mention of their sufferings—but it was the silence of despair.'
Nor was the danger only a negative one. Finding that
all efforts had failed to bring over the adult Irish to the
new religion, and having totally deprived them of the
means of educating their children in their own way,
the advocates of Protestantism endeavoured to sap the
faith of Ireland by drawing its children into their own
schools. In 1743 there were forty-seven charter schools,
into which every effort was made to draw Catholic children. ' On entering them,' writes an Irish priest,

' their names are changed so that they may have no
communication with their parents, and after a little
time they are transferred to another parish that the
isolation may be more complete. Premiums are
given to those who show most proficiency in the
catechism, which is composed purposely for these
schools and is nothing but a continuous invective
against the Catholic church. ... They get portions
on condition that they marry Protestants with the
consent of the directors of the schools.' To these
schools no less than one million was voted by Parliament. There were various others of the same kind,
and it was then law that all children of Catholics who
asked for relief should be brought up as Protestants.

At such an unpropitious time as this, and in the face
of these tremendous difficulties, the first new order in
Ireland sprung into being. Its foundress was a Miss
Hanoria Nagle, who was born at Cork in 1728, and
whose family was closely connected with that of the
celebrated Father Mathew. Miss Nagle was not one
of those children who give very early indications of
being marked out to do an extraordinary work. It is
recorded of her that she was particularly wayward,
and gave her mother much uneasiness; but that her
father would sometimes take her part and declare she
' would be a saint yet.' Perhaps there was a strength
of character and an intensity of will in the giddy child
which made him foresee that if she once turned with
earnestness to serve God, it would not be done by halves.
Unable, as all families of the upper classes in Ireland
then were, to procure the necessary education for their
children at home, Miss Nagle was sent to Paris. Her

education finished, she was plunged into a round of
gaiety and dissipation very easily to be found in the
brilliant court of Louis XV. But the gay, frivolous
girl had a noble destiny before her; and in the midst
of her enjoyment a Divine voice made itself heard in
her heart. There had been a grand ball in Paris, and
the morning dawned ere the most eager of the pleasure-
seekers—and among them Miss Nagle—were willing to
quit the scene. At last her carriage rolled through
the empty silent streets, and she, wearied and jaded at
last, felt that sad void in the heart which so often suc-
ceeds worldly pleasures. Suddenly her attention was
arrested by a group of people standing at a church door.

They were poor—those whom hard labour scarcely
permits to snatch the necessary hours for sleep; yet
they were willing to forego some of this brief repose,
that they might spend a short time with God. In
order to be in time for the *first mass*, they were at the
church doors before they were open. The silent lesson
went with powerful force to Miss Nagle's heart. When
she and they, she mused, should stand before the
judgment-seat to give an account of their time, how
different would their answer be! Tears flowed from
her eyes; and she resolved from that moment God should
be to her all in all—a resolution she faithfully kept.
She determined to leave the gay world of Paris and
return to Ireland.

She at once began to occupy herself in such works
of charity as were within her reach; and the lamentable
state of her poor country people thus forced itself
on her notice, and the very magnitude of the evil
appalled her. What could she, single-handed, do

amidst such a wilderness?   She had no private fortune ;
and none of her friends were likely to second her efforts
and enter into her views.   Catholics of all classes had
hardly done more than begin to breathe in safety ; and
the richer and educated naturally desired to lead a
quiet life, and not to stir up fresh animosity.

One course only, therefore, seemed open to Miss
Nagle ; it was to return to France and there enter a
religious order, devoting herself in prayer and penance
as a victim for the sorrows and woes of her beloved
country.   So she bade farewell to all she loved, and
sailed for France.   But she was not at rest.   A voice
was whispering in her heart that the path she had
chosen was not the one destined for her.   She reasoned
and debated with herself: one day thinking herself
under a delusion ; the next, unable by that solution to
stifle her doubt.   Morning and night the thought of
Ireland haunted her ; and little children seemed to
stretch out their hands to her for aid.   Again and
again she argued with herself, what *could she do*?
Had she not proved it to be useless and hopeless?   But
no argument could quiet her mind.   At last she
resolved on seeking counsel from the Fathers of the
Society of Jesus in Paris, in whose discernment and
wisdom she had great confidence.   To them she laid
open 'the agitation of her mind, her settled disgust for
the world, her ardent desire for the religious state, her
feeling for the poor of her own country, her strong
propensity to contribute to their relief ; that, from the
first moment she discovered their ignorance, she could
never divest herself of the thought ; but that she
attributed all to her heated imagination.   As matters

stood, it was morally impossible for her to be of service
to them. The penal laws were an insuperable bar, and
she had no pecuniary resources. Her constitution was
delicate; yet though the prospect before her if she
returned was wretched and hazardous, and almost
hopelesss, she felt inwardly impelled to follow it, she
knew not why.'

She poured out her heart, and then she hoped her
delusions would vanish, and her path to the convent
be smooth and easy. A very different decision was
given. 'She was called,' said her guides, 'not to religious life at that moment, but to instruct ignorant
children in Ireland.' The want of money and freedom
to act, and the existence of penal laws, were no matter;
she must ' do what she could.'

So astonished was Miss Nagle at such counsel, that
she ventured to argue the point and to remonstrate;
but all in vain; the decision remained the same. Then
she entirely submitted herself to the Divine will, thus
made known to her, and prepared herself for a life of
toil, anxiety, and hardship.

Miss Nagle's parents were then dead, and the only
home she had to return to was that of a married brother,
who resided at Cork. Thither she went, and soon
learned that a rich uncle had determined to make her
his heiress, provided her conduct was such as should
please him. Nothing could be more likely to displease
both him and her brother than to carry out her intention
of founding a school for poor children. But her purpose was fixed, and she commenced her work. Deter-
mining to act with all possible prudence, she began in
secret.

The first Catholic school in Cork was opened, and thirty children were gathered into it; and the young lady, not long before a Parisian belle, found her greatest pleasure in its care and management. Of course, as she expected, in time the secret came to her family's ears, and a storm burst on her devoted head. But, angry as her relations were, they could not help admiring her patience and self-denial, and their opposition changed into warm support.

Her uncle died, and left her his whole fortune entirely at her own disposal. In nine months the thirty children had grown into two hundred, and she was compelled by eager demands to open schools for boys as well as for girls; so that she soon had five schools for girls and two for boys under her care.

It is true their education was not up to the mark of the 'Revised Code.' In secular knowledge they were confined to the three R.'s; but they learned the catechism, were taught to say their beads, were brought to mass and to monthly confession.

' Twice a year,' said Miss Nagle, ' I prepare a set for first communion; and I may truly say it is the only thing that gives me any trouble. In the first place, I think myself very incapable; and in the beginning, being obliged to speak for upwards of four hours, and my chest not being as strong as it had been, I spat blood, which I took care to conceal, for fear of being prevented from instructing the poor. . . . If everyone thought as little as I do of labour, they would have very little merit. I often think my schools will never bring me to heaven, as I only take delight and pleasure in them. . . . I can assure you my schools are beginning to be of service to a great many parts of the world. This is a place of great trade. They are heard of, and my views are not for one object alone. If I could be of any service in saving souls in any part of the globe, I would do all in my power.'

And doubtless her work did not end there. The children poured out from her schools, and were lost to sight; they bore with them the seeds she had sown; and who can tell what fruit they brought forth—what treasure was lying stored up for her in eternity when, her long life ended, she went to her reward?

One sorrow only troubled her; she felt that her work was temporary, and that at her death the fabric she had raised might probably fall to the ground. Neither had the desire for religious life ever left her heart. She therefore formed the idea of inviting a religious community to come over from France and undertake the work; and her project was approved of by Father Doran, S.J., and his nephew the Abbé Moylan, afterwards Bishop of Cork.

In 1769 an application was made to the Ursuline house in Paris, which had been founded sixty years before by the saintly Madame Acarie. But the thought of an Irish foundation terrified the French nuns. No one could conceal from them that it entailed certainly severe hardships, and not improbably risk and danger. The penal laws were still unrepealed, and any outburst of popular fury might put them again in force. The Ursulines would not come; but they consented to receive and train Irish ladies, who should hereafter form a community of their own. Accordingly four young ladies entered the novitiate in 1769.

In 1771 they set out on their return to Ireland, and
halted for the night at the Carmelite Convent of St.
Denis, the prioress of which was then the saintly
Louise of France.   When she learnt their errand, the
princess was filled with a holy envy, and told them
that, had she been permitted, she would willingly have
gone with them; for she thought so highly of their
labours that she would 'be glad to be at the feet of
an Ursuline in heaven.'

The Irish nuns stayed two days at St. Denis, storing
up in their minds the holy counsels of the prioress.
Sister Angela Fitzsimons was remarkable for the
beauty of her voice, so the nuns asked her to sing to
them; and full and sweet, in the quiet chapel of St.
Denis, rose that Eastertide the strains of 'Regina
cœli,' while the nuns listened in delight.

Strange vicissitudes of human life ! Some of those
Carmelite nuns, who then lived in such calm security
with a princess at their head, were to see the day when
they would be driven to death or exile, and their
convent razed to the ground; while they who were
going forth in faith on a perilous and uncertain exile
were to see their work prosper and enlarge, their pro-
scribed religion once more come forth in strength and
vigour, and were to raise on Irish soil a magnificent
building, forming a striking object to the traveller who
enters Ireland by her great southern port, and tra-
verses

   The pleasant waters of the river Lee.

And now it might have seemed as if Miss Nagle's
task were almost done; and as if with little further
trouble her ardent desire for religious life might be

satisfied, and her work placed on a permanent footing. But it was not to be. As is very often the case in these negotiations, matters had been misunderstood. The Ursuline rule forbade its members to devote themselves exclusively to the poor; and indeed, though poor schools are attached to each of their convents, the education of the upper classes is their primary object. On the other hand, Miss Nagle had become assured by experience that the wants of the Irish poor could only be adequately met by an order devoted exclusively to their service. The long hoped-for and expected arrival, therefore, was only to be a heavy disappointment; and, moreover, the very friends who had gathered round Miss Nagle to be her helpers and companions were now Ursuline nuns, and unable to assist in her cherished undertaking. But God blessed even the disappointments of His faithful servant; and before she died she must have learned to see how much better it had been for her to have her first designs crossed.

The wants of the poor were perhaps the greatest in Ireland; but the wants of the upper classes for the education of their children were also very pressing. A vast number of young ladies were trained to become good Christians by the Ursuline nuns; and by their means the faith was preserved and revived in many and many a home, while many another pupil owed her vocation to the religious life to the holy lessons she learned in her convent-school; and up and down among the various convents which now overspread the face of Ireland are to be found numbers of pupils from Ursuline convents.

There were others who had intended to enter the

Ursuline community when it should arrive in Cork, and who shared Miss Nagle's disappointment. Instead of entering the convent they gathered round her, and gradually a new religious institute grew into being. Its history reminds us of that of the Visitation Order. Like the first nuns of St. Francis de Sales, the Sisters of the 'Presentation' sought out children from their own homes, brought them to school, and educated them. They visited the sick, and relieved the poor.

It was said of Miss Nagle that she did not leave a garret in Cork unvisited.

Of course, like all new institutes in the Church, the progress of the 'Presentation' was slow. It consisted at first of a simple congregation of pious women, bound by annual vows. Indeed it would seem as if Miss Nagle's designs for her community did not extend beyond this; and during her lifetime she did not contemplate enclosure. The institute may have been said to have been founded on Christmas-day 1777; and on that day fifty-four poor persons were entertained by the foundress, and she served them with her own hands. This custom she kept up all her life, and it is still observed in the convents of the order. Her compassion extended to all classes of her fellow-creatures. She founded an almshouse for the aged poor, and took a warm interest in all that concerned the reformation of penitents. Some idea of her good works may be gathered from fragments of her letters, which her biographer* has given to the world. 'I am sending boys to the West Indies. Some charitable gentlemen

---

* *Memoirs of Miss Nagle.* By the Rev. Dominick Murphy.

put themselves to great expense for no other motive. These boys being well instructed, and the true religion decaying very much there, by reason of those who leave this country knowing nothing of their religion, made them lay this scheme, which I hope may have the desired effect. All my children are brought up to be fond of instructing, as I think it lies in the power of the poor to be of more service that way than the rich. These children promise me they will take great pains with the little blacks, to instruct them. Next year I will have pictures for them to give the negroes that learn the catechism.'

Sentences here and there, scattered about her letters on business, serve to give an insight into her character, and show us plainly, even if her works did not already bear witness to the same, how noble and generous was her soul. Speaking of another person: ' She is one of those modern religious persons who think every inconveniency such a cross that there is no bearing it.'

' Whoever we live with, we must expect to have something to suffer, as the world is not to be our paradise.'

' I should imagine you were laughing at me, to think I fatigue myself in the least. I can assure you I never thought there was the least trouble in acting in regard of the schools.'

Miss Nagle possessed many eminent virtues, but they were all fostered and sustained in her by her spirit of prayer. Never did she make her active, laborious life an excuse for lessening spiritual duties; on the contrary, she gave to them a larger share than is sometimes allotted by those who lead a far more retired life than she did. Four hours every morning were consecrated to this holy exercise. She never failed to make an annual retreat of eight days; and it was her custom to spend the whole night of Maundy Thursday watching before the sepulchre. When at prayer, she was always accustomed to kneel, and would rarely choose any other attitude. Yet after death it was discovered that her knees were excoriated, and partly ulcerated, and must have been in that state for years; so that every moment of the long hours spent on her knees must have been one of acute agony. Yet no one had ever known or guessed the secret. No word of complaint had passed her lips, nor had her sufferings disturbed the serenity of her aspect. It had been her custom, as we have already said, to traverse Cork from one end to the other (no slight distance), to visit the poor. For the last three years of her life she added the still more painful and laborious task of begging for alms from the houses of the rich. And after her death only it was discovered that she had large tumours on the soles of her feet, which would have made most people give up walking altogether. She did not have much of her reward in this world. In the very streets of the city for which she did so much, she was frequently insulted, and accused of frightful crimes.

So her life passed away; and at last, at fifty-six years of age, she was called to her rest and reward. She endured her last illness with perfect resignation; received all the consolations of the Church; and then called her community round her to receive her last advice; it was to be the motto of their future lives. 'Love one another as you have hitherto done,' she said; and soon after her spirit passed into eternity. She was interred within the convent enclosure, in the centre of the cemetery set apart for the religious. There she rests to this day, while the seeds she sowed have grown up, and blossomed, and bórne fruit around her grave. No less than nine hundred poor children attend those schools, openly and without fear of molestation, which she opened with a handful in secret and in terror. The convent forms a fine pile of buildings. A new church and choir of great beauty have recently been added to it. The almshouse for poor aged women which Miss Nagle began still exists; and the building in which forty-two of them reside is attached to the convent.

We have said that the history of the Presentation order resembled that of the Visitation. Like it, in course of time, its first design has somewhat changed. It was desired that it should be raised from a congregation into an order; that its members should take perpetual vows, and keep enclosure; also that they should devote themselves exclusively to one branch of charitable labour, i.e. the education of poor children within the convent walls. Thus as the wise providence of God had overruled the designs of a saint on earth, so did He think fit to deal with the intentions and projects of another faithful servant after her death. Doubtless the rapid multiplication of religious orders was greatly needed in Ireland; and it was perhaps chiefly owing to this alteration in the original work of the Presentation nuns that the orders of Charity and Mercy sprang into being. The rules and constitutions were remodelled, and were approved of by Pius VII. in 1805.

The *first* Apostolic brief was granted to the Presentation order by Pius VI., September 3, 1791. Thus at the very time when the religious houses in France were swept from the country, and those of all Europe were endangered, Ireland, after her long sufferings, and in the midst of her poverty and privation, put forth the first evidence of her new life and strength.

One of the first convents I visited in Dublin was that of the Presentation, for it possesses the enviable distinction of being the oldest. It was built on George's Hill, far away from the fashionable and well-known parts of Dublin, in the midst of a poor population, and its first stone was laid in 1788. There is nothing remarkable in its appearance. It is a large plain building, with schools attached. The first superioress of this convent was a Miss Mullally, who, like Miss Nagle, had been teaching poor children, and inducing others to join her; they formed themselves into a community, and adopted the Presentation rule. I was kindly received by the nuns, who showed me over their large poor schools and orphanage. Many hundred children are taught in their schools, and since its establishment many thousands must have passed through them. Their orphanage is designed for the children of respectable parents, fallen in circumstances and unable to provide fittingly for their children. These girls receive a solid and excellent education, and there is no difficulty in finding them suitable situations. Many of them become religious chiefly in foreign convents, where Irish and English subjects are much in request.

The Presentation order made rapid progress in Ireland, where it has about fifty houses. It has also thirteen houses in Newfoundland, and is established in England, Madras, and Australia.

CHAPTER II.

THE Irish Sisters of Charity are but little known out
of their own country, and are an entirely distinct order
from the well-known ' Sœurs de Charité' of foreign
lands.   When it was settled that the Presentation
order should be exclusively devoted to the care of poor
schools and should keep enclosure, the necessity for
an active order able to undertake all works of charity
that might present themselves pressed heavily on the
mind of Dr. Murray, then Archbishop of Dublin.
Providence soon threw in his way a person well adapted
to be the foundation stone of the new institute.   Mary
Aitkenhead was born at Cork in 1787, and she was but
twenty-five years of age when Dr. Murray fixed on her
as the foundress of a new order in Ireland.   In 1812
such a task must have seemed a formidable and dreary
one ; and the world was smiling before her, for she was
a richly-endowed being.   She possessed rare personal
loveliness, great and varied talents, and a peculiar gift
of winning the affection and confidence of others.   But
she responded to the call, and was ready to devote all
she had to God.   With the prudence which always
characterised her, Miss Aitkenhead determined to prepare herself well for the future before her.   If she were
to rule others she would first learn to obey, and with

one companion she entered the novitiate of the Convent
of Our Lady at York—an order which was one of the
first established in England after the persecutions, and
whose members devoted themselves to the education
of both rich and poor. This novitiate lasted, at Miss
Aitkenhead's own request, for three years instead of
two, as in ordinary cases; and she and her companion
returned to Dublin in 1815, when they made their
profession, and the institute of the ' Religious Sisters of
Charity' was founded. Members soon came to join
them, and in 1833 the order was approved by the Holy
See.

This order differs greatly from the French Sisters of
Charity. The Irish Sisters adopted the rule of St.
Ignatius; they have a novitiate of two years and a
half, after which they take perpetual vows, and unite
the exercises of religious life to their active duties; but,
like the French sisters, they are free to undertake any
work of charity, and the institutions under their care in
Ireland evidence that almost every form of human
misery has found a helping hand from them. It is not
easy to describe adequately the admirable way in which
these institutions are managed, and no one can visit
the convents of this order without being struck by the
number of superior, refined, and intelligent ladies who
fill its ranks.

One of their principal houses is St. Vincent's Hospital, standing in the large open square known as
Stephen's Green. It was the first Catholic hospital in
Dublin, and was opened in 1834. The house chosen
had formerly belonged to the Earl of Meath, and was
given for the purpose of being used as an hospital by a

generous benefactress. The Sisters took possession of it, and ten patients were at first received. The number of beds is now one hundred and twenty, and various additions and improvements have been made in the hospital from time to time. From the very first St. Vincent's was fortunately under the medical charge of Dr. O'Farrel, by whose energy and skill it has long since attained a high medical rank. Wherever it is practicable it would, we suppose, be better to build an hospital than to adapt any large house for the purpose ; nevertheless there is a home-like air about St. Vincent's Hospital which is very delightful. The wards are lofty and well ventilated, the most spotless cleanliness and perfect order prevail, and, watching the patients in their comfortable beds, with their snowy curtains, and the gentle faces of the Sisters bending over them and doing everything they could to alleviate their sufferings, we felt this was indeed a home for the sick poor. St. Vincent's Hospital receives both men and women, and when we visited it one poor fellow was rapidly passing to another world. Very tenderly were the Sisters watching beside him to soothe and strengthen the parting soul, and his deathbed was neither lonely nor forsaken. There is an exquisite little chapel in the hospital. No pains have been spared on its decorations, and there such of the patients as are able to get about may constantly be seen kneeling in silent prayer, and there also daily mass is said.

But, passing through an hospital like St. Vincent's, one sad thought strikes upon the mind : What becomes of those who are discharged from hospital cured or with their sufferings much alleviated ? What a question !

Is not everybody glad to get out of hospital? who would stay an hour longer in a sick room than he can help? Alas! there are many who would gladly stay in an hospital like St. Vincent's. They are so far well that it would not be fair to let them fill the beds and enjoy the care required by greater sufferers, but they are generally very far from being fit to return to their wretched home or to their employment.

The artisan, the mother of a family, how can they, with their aching heads, their trembling limbs, return to the crowded rooms, the hard work of their ordinary life, and how 'get up their strength' on the scanty and hard fare that awaits them? And what of those who have no home to go to, servants who fell ill at place, young men without friends, and who must now at once seek fresh employment? They surely need an intermediate refuge between hospital and work, in short, a 'convalescent home.' It has long been the wish of the Sisters of Charity to establish one. 'We have often shed tears,' said one of them, 'when we parted with some of our patients, knowing how unfit they were to return to their wretched homes, and seeing them come creeping slowly down stairs, and so unwilling to go.' They accomplished their wish in the summer of 1866, and were able to open a sanatorium or convalescent home near Blackrock and Stillorgan, and thither I proceeded for a visit in the autumn of the same year. I alighted at the Blackrock station on the Kingstown line, and after a pleasant twenty minutes' walk through country lanes, and beneath avenues of trees golden with the autumn tint, I found myself at the gate of St. Vincent's Convalescent Home.

The house, which rejoices in the name of castle, was formerly a gentleman's country residence, and is fitted up with every comfort. There is a pretty garden both before and behind the house, which when I saw it was gay with autumn flowers. In the little parlour to which I was shown a tall white lily of rare species was perfuming the room, and presently came a bright looking Sister of Charity to show me round the house. It would turn the brain of a workhouse guardian to see this establishment, and to find out that the Sisters think nothing too good for their beloved poor. The men's ward was on the ground floor, the two wards for women above. The comfortable beds, spotlessly clean and neat, filled the room, without overcrowding. There were easy chairs, tables on which stood lamps ready for lighting ; books, games, dominoes to while away the tedious hours ; the whole range of the garden and several fields beyond were free for the patients to walk in. On one side of the house rises a tower of several stories. The small rooms on these floors are occupied by the Sisters, but at the top of the tower are flat leads, on which the patients can walk or sit. Here before their gaze lies outspread that lovely view which those who have seen can never forget, Dublin Bay, Howth, and Kingstown, and the fresh sea breezes blow on them, bringing health and vigour in their train. Is it any wonder that the patients look on this home as a sort of paradise, and count the hours of their stay as they fly ? ' We shall never have such a time again,' they say, and they enjoy it to the utmost, and go away strong and able for a fresh battle with the ills and cares of this weary world.

One of the first houses founded by Miss, or rather
Mrs., Aitkenhead (for so it is customary to call her)
was in Stanhope Street, Dublin.   It was opened in
1819 as a home for training girls for domestic service.
It exists in a flourishing condition to this day, and when
I visited it, contained a hundred girls.   They are
taught to be servants, and will, when trained, be provided with situations.   They are instructed in house,
kitchen, laundry, and needle work, besides the habits
of order, cleanliness, and diligence.   The greatest
praise that can be given to this institution is to say
that the servants sent out from it are much sought
after, and ladies who have had one will come again
for another.   The utility of the institution is great.
There is a singular inaptness in Irish girls for domestic
service, and they will choose many a rough and hard
employment in preference to it.   Yet when an Irish
girl is really trained, no servant can be compared to
her; she may not indeed ever acquire the studied
neatness, the gift of order that is natural to her
English sister; but her fidelity and affection, her diligence and carefulness more than counterbalance these
imperfections.   We in England have little experience
of good Irish servants, the simple reason being that
the good ones can always get employment at home, or
else yield to the glittering prospects of enormous wages
held out to them by the ' cousins in America ' with
which every Irishwoman is provided.

The Sisters of the Stanhope Street Convent teach
the poor schools of the parish, containing 600 children.
They also visit the sick and poor, and a number of
prisoners.

In Upper Gardiner Street is another large convent
and schools belonging to the Sisters of Charity. They
are *the* schools, *par excellence*, of the order. I visited
them repeatedly, being never weary of observing the
admirable management and the excellent mode of instruction pursued in them. They are not under
government inspection, but are most fully up to the
mark which could possibly be required by any ' Committee of Council.' I have visited many schools of
all kinds in England, Ireland, and foreign countries ;
but I never saw any one which excelled, and but few
that equalled, the perfect order, and the simple but
thorough teaching of the Gardiner Street schools. More
than once Protestant clergymen have visited these
schools, and tested the children in biblical knowledge.
They found, however, the scholars fully equal to the
occasion, not baffled by the query, ' How many chapters
are there in each of the epistles ?' and the gentlemen
went away, we hope, convinced that the Holy Scrip-
tures are fully familiar to the intelligent Irish poor.
In Gardiner Street, as in all other Irish schools, I was
struck by the beauty of some of the children, and the
variety of its types. Here the brunette complexion
and full dark eyes, there the golden curls and large
blue orbs ; and here, now and then, one of those
witching Irish faces, with eyes neither black, nor brown,
nor blue, but each in turn, with a smile breaking like
sunbeams over the face, and with a head and bust such
as would send an artist wild with delight. And there
the owner stood in her place, gentle and modest, and
perfectly unconscious of her own loveliness. On the
opposite side of the street on which the convent stands

the Sisters have taken a house, and call it St. Catherine's Industrial School. It is a home for young
seamstresses, and is managed by a matron, under the
superintendence of the Sisters. They found many stray
cases among those whom they had to visit and help, of
girls wanting protection, and yet ineligible for the
existing institutions. They were too old for orphanages, and not suited for servants. Sometimes they
could get work, but had no home, sometimes they were
without both. The Sisters accordingly opened this
house, took in as many as it would hold, devoted the
ground floor to work rooms, and employ as many girls
as they can find work for; and that finding work is
the difficult matter. It is very hard that when people
are ready and willing to work, the employment is often
not within their reach. St. Catherine's Home is as
yet in its infancy, and will, we hope, rapidly increase in
size, and therefore in its means of usefulness. No
charity seems to us a greater one than an industrial
school, if some means could be found of supplying it
with regular occupation. It is hard to see the poor
willing to help themselves, and be unable to assist them
in doing so, and thus see them driven into beggary,
often into sin; and surely any effort, however small,
made to stem the tide of this formidable evil is worthy
of deep sympathy and co-operation.

A little way out of Dublin, on the Stillorgan road,
is Donnybrook Green, so celebrated for its annual fair,
where Irish fun ran riot, when

> An Irishman in all his glory was there,
> With his sprig of shillelagh and shamrock so green;

and the riot had so disastrous an ending, that, happily,

after a long struggle with custom, the fair was abolished. On the green now stands a new and handsome church, dedicated to the Sacred Heart, and at a little distance is a convent and Magdalene asylum of the Sisters of Charity. This house can receive seventy inmates, and its mode of management differs somewhat from that of the penitentiaries generally known in England. The wish and intention of the Sisters is that their inmates should remain with them for life. Of course no coercion is used; every one is free to go when she likes, and a certain number always do leave, but the Sisters believe that very few of those who have lost their good name, and, generally speaking, have contracted habits of intemperance, idleness, and other vices, will be able to resist temptation if exposed to the rough contact of the world again. There is much to be said on both sides of the question. If such a plan be adopted, the difficulty of rescuing these poor creatures would be increased, for the number of refuges for them must be multiplied. On the other hand, no means to attain a perfect reformation should be thought too costly. It is certain, however, that both systems should be in operation; for many characters among this class of unhappy women could neither brook a lifelong restraint, nor even the idea of it, and would do far better in an asylum where they knew a certain time of probation only was required. At all events, the progress of the Donnybrook Refuge has been eminently satisfactory. As we passed through the rooms, I was much struck by the superior appearance of many of the women, as compared with those of other asylums, and when I remarked on it to the Sisters,

they told me such and such an one had been so many
years in the asylum. There had been time for the
fierce passions to be subdued, and the wild history of
the past to fade out of the mind.

Terrible are the inward conflicts these poor creatures
have to endure at times, especially soon after their
entrance. 'I want to leave, ma'am,' said a poor woman
one day respectfully to the superioress. ' Why so ?
are you unhappy ? Do we not do all we can for you ? '
' Yes, ma'am, and I am most grateful, but I *must go.
I will tell you the truth. I *must* have gin; I cannot
live any longer without it.' This poor creature had
struggled on for four months. The Sisters did their
utmost to help and encourage her, persuading her to
stay on day after day, till at last the temptation was
conquered, and the poor woman found she could live
without her bane and her enemy. The penitents are
employed in laundry and needlework, and thus do all
they can to earn their own support. Those who have
been a long time in the house are of great assistance
to the Sisters in watching over and encouraging the
new comers. Many of the former are really true
penitents, and they take infinite pains with their
weaker companions, showing them how they in their
turn may overcome temptation, and regain peace and
content. The chapel at Donnybrook is rich in carving and decoration; it is one of the most beautiful
and devotional of convent chapels. A portion is set
apart for the penitents, and here they with the Sisters
have daily mass, and all the other services of the
church. The convent is surrounded by large grounds,
and there is an excellent fruit and kitchen garden.

Passing through these we were led to a spot full of interest to me, and very dear to the Sisters of Charity.

It is the cemetery not only for the inmates of this asylum but for the whole community of Sisters of Charity. It is a quiet sheltered spot shut in by trees, and meet for recollection of those ' gone before ' and prayers for their repose in Christ. A simple wooden cross marks the grave of each Sister; but in the centre of the ground rises a beautiful cross of grey limestone, beneath which repose the mortal remains of Mary Aitkenhead, foundress of the order. From 1815 to 1858, a space of forty-three years, she laboured unceasingly for the good of others; she forgot one thing only—herself. A large picture in the parlour of St. Vincent's Hospital, gives us now some idea of the grace and loveliness of her personal appearance. Even to her old age traces of her great beauty lingered, and when she was no longer able to leave her room her children found her still the same, the sunshine of their lives, their comforter in trouble, their support in perplexity. Before her death she had founded ten houses of her order and gathered round her many hundreds of Sisters likeminded with herself. The Magdalene Asylum was one of her dearest works; her compassionate heart yearned over the most unfortunate of God's creatures, those who had defiled His image in their souls, and cut themselves off from a bright eternity. She laboured long and bravely to bring back such souls to her Lord, and singularly enough it was on the feast of St. Mary Magdalene, the patroness of the asylum, and the pattern she had so often striven to put before the poor inmates, that she was called to her rest or reward.

> Well may we hope their peaceful rest,
> Whose labours thus their life attest.

Another pleasant little village in the neighbourhood of Dublin is that called Harold's Cross. There stands the mother house and novitiate of the Sisters of Charity, and thither on St. Augustine's Day, I bent my steps at an early hour in the morning to witness the profession of a nun. The chapel of this convent is a perfect gem; but of an entirely different style from that of Donnybrook and much larger; it is built in the form of a cross and the lightness and beauty of its colouring, its stained windows, and its decorations, are most admirable. The nave is lined with stalls for the Sisters, and at the end is a small portion reserved for seculars. The ceremony of profession was very simple, but also very impressive. The Sisters came in procession carrying lighted tapers; the postulants first, then the novices, the professed sisters, and lastly, the novice to be professed with the superioress. Certain prayers were said, and then the Sister, kneeling at the foot of the altar, answered the solemn questions put to her whether she had well considered the step she was about to take; whether she were ready of her own free choice to adopt for her future days a life of devotion to God and the poor? To all she assented clearly and firmly, and in the course of the mass which followed she made her vows and pledged herself for ever to be the spouse of Christ. The ceremony concluded with the exchange of the white veil for the black and the reception of the crucifix to be worn on the breast and

the ring for the left hand.   The dress of the Sisters of
Charity is black with a white coif underneath their
veil, and it is very simple in its whole arrangement.
The spectators of the ceremony were hospitably entertained by the Sisters at breakfast, after which we were
allowed a thorough inspection of the chapel and also to
visit the schools, which are built half-way down the
avenue leading to the convent from the high road.
These schools are well attended and seemed to be in
excellent order.   The sick and poor surrounding the
convent are also visited by the Sisters, and the novices
are thus trained for the work of their future lives.

Beside the Portobello Bridge of the Grand Canal
is a large white stone building, on which is inscribed ' St. Mary's Home for the Blind.'   This institution again is under the charge of the Sisters of
Charity, and is another proof of the admirable way in
which they discharge the duties allotted to them.   Of
all the charitable institutions I ever visited this is,
without exception, the *happiest*.   A spirit of joy and
cheerfulness pervades the whole house ; the sound of
merry laughter meets your ear continually ; peace and
joy is written almost on every face, and yet this is the
home of a class of deeply-afflicted beings—those who
have never seen or who must never see again the light
of day, the fair world around them, or the kind faces
of those they love.   The cheerfulness of the blind is
indeed often remarked by strangers ; but a peculiar joy-
fulness seemed to characterise the girls of St. Mary's.
When we came to know more of the management of
the institution we ceased to wonder at their happiness.
They are surrounded by those whose one thought it is

how to make their life a happy and a holy one. The
most watchful care is exercised for their comfort ; the
most careful training given to their capabilities. The
superioress of the house is one of those beings who has
the gift of drawing the hearts of others to her and of
influencing them for good. She has a singular aptitude
for understanding the characteristics of the blind, and
is untiring in her exertions to promote their welfare.
And surely a special blessing is theirs who smooth the
difficulties and lighten the burdens of those whom God
has stamped with the seal of suffering, whom He has
shut up in a cloister of His own making ; for in whatever class of life blindness falls, it is always a heavy
misfortune. There are indeed exceptional cases, where
the mind is so richly gifted, where the other faculties
of the body are so marvellously quickened, that a blind
person becomes the centre of a home, the support of
all around him; but these cases are rare; and, generally
speaking, the blind member of a family is a burden and
an anxiety, even among the wealthier classes. But
how is this misfortune doubled when it regards the
poor ! The poor families to whom it is a struggle to
get the children through their early childhood, and who
look forward to each member becoming independent at
as early an age as posible—what a burden must not a
blind child be to them! It requires double watching through its infancy ; and when school-time comes,
brothers and sisters may go, but not the blind child.
Shut out from the pleasures and employments of childhood, how sad and desolate is a blind child's life !
Look, again, at the blind children in workhouses : what
a miserable life is theirs ! what aggravations of the

unhappy lot of all workhouse children ! how completely
are they at the mercy of rough officials, and when
they grow up to man and womanhood, how manifold
the hardships and dangers to which they are exposed !
Hardships mostly as regards boys, but fearful dangers
as regards girls. Then in the matter of faith also—
in this respect how unprotected are the blind ! The
outward symbols of the faith have no power to retain
their affections ; they cannot see the altar gloriously
arrayed, the priest in the vestments—which each convey
a lesson ; they may not look upon even the veiled presence of their Lord ; they cannot gaze on the beautiful
pictures, the ' storied window,' the imposing worship of
the sanctuary ; above all others they are dependent on
teaching, upon the efforts of fellow-creatures to en-
lighten their minds, and instruct them in the truth.

It would be difficult to describe the effect produced
on the mind by a visit to this asylum. We found two
large rooms filled with the pupils : one the older, the
other the younger portion of the school. Looking
round on those faces, we were struck by the *listening
look* common to the blind when the intelligence has
been cultivated. Sometimes the faces of the blind
display a touching beauty ; and even when the blindness has proceeded from some çause which has dis-
figured the face, it is almost always accompanied by
that expression of mute resignation which goes straight
to the spectator's heart. The intelligence of these
children was truly remarkable ; they were far beyond
seeing children of the same age. The love and desire
of learning had been better than eyes to them. Specimens of beautiful needlework done by them were for

sale. To listen to their music and singing was really a treat. The love of and aptitude for music is proverbial among the blind; but in this case it had been brought to perfection. An excellent music-master had come constantly to give lessons; and under his care the girls had acquired a refinement of taste in singing which took us fairly by surprise. The attitude of the group who stood round the organ was worthy of a sketch; the rapt faces, the *listening look* more marked than ever, as if they caught some echoes of a music that we are too deaf to hear, were most striking.

Notwithstanding all this intelligence, the blind are exceedingly helpless in many things; and not all the training in the world will ever make them otherwise. They require to be under the watchful and tender care of religious. There are other classes of the poor who are, perhaps, rather unfitted for their contact with the rough world by the gentleness and kindness of a nun; not so the blind. Kindness, encouragement, sympathy, are to them as the air they breathe. We could not help noticing the extreme difference between the Dublin asylum and one in a provincial Irish town, which was under secular management. Not that there was anything in the managers to find fault with; they were kind, just, and active, but fulfilled their work as an irksome duty, for which they were paid. The Sister of Charity watches over the blind as a labour of love. She is never weary of devising plans for their comfort and improvement; she is sorry to be called away from them, glad to return; she counts them over as the jewels that are one day to sparkle in her crown.

This helplessness prevents the blind from entirely earning their own support, save in rare instances, and this especially applies to blind girls. Blindness generally arises from illness, sudden accident, or disease in the parents; it is ordinarily accompanied by a delicate constitution, so that a blind woman is incapable of long and persistent labour at mat and basket making, the branches of business generally open to them. In this matter the deaf and dumb are much better off than the blind; there are a dozen occupations to which they can be trained; in many large houses an intelligent deaf-and-dumb servant would be rather an acquisition than otherwise; but who would engage a blind servant? The blind inmates of the Portobello Asylum are not, therefore, a changing community; vacancies seldom occur. When we visited it one child was dying. She lay in the pretty little infirmary, gasping for breath, the death-dew on her brow; but she was ready to die, ready to open her eyes at last and gaze upon the vision of Eternal Beauty: she had only one earthly wish, that her little blind sister might be taken into the asylum and there 'taught how to die.' The superioress told us she had four pressing applications for the bed when death should have made it vacant.

The union among the blind children is remarkable. The Sisters of Charity—accustomed as they are to every kind of labour among the poor—consider the charge of the blind the easiest and pleasantest of their works; there is seldom a dispute, or a reproof needed; the children are gentle, obedient, and loving, and most fervent in faith. As they pass up the broad staircase, you see them bow their heads. 'What do you do that for?'—'Because the images of our Lady and St. Joseph are there,' they answer; '*you told me so.*' Their prayers rise up like incense before God, for they are the prayers of sinless hearts : happy are those who, by becoming their benefactors, have a right to be remembered by them at the throne of God !

Though the hope of teaching blind women to support themselves entirely is a fallacious one, there are many families who would find it an immense benefit to have a child *educated* at this school, and then sent home when she is grown up. Instead of the helpless, useless, unhappy being she would have been, if allowed to pass all her life without education, and under a system of *petting,* she returns home an intelligent, happy creature, dependent on others for many things, it is true, but able to render them services in return. For though the Sisters of Charity show their blind charges every possible kindness, they are never weakly indulgent. They are careful to train their characters; to treat them, in short, as far as possible, *as if they saw* ; providing with quick foresight for the occasions when they cannot help themselves; but exacting from them what is within their capacity, and therefore preventing them from feeling a constant sense of helplessness.

One of the temptations peculiar to blindness is suspiciousness ; it is also, as we know, the temptation of old or infirm persons who are dependent on others. Who can wonder ? How easy is it to deceive the blind ! How often advantages might be taken of their

weakness by evil, designing people ! and, not to go so
far, people who are deficient in *judgment* may make
many mistakes and cause much suffering to the blind.
It is easy, therefore, to see the immense benefit it is to
have a blind asylum watched over by religious.   As
soon as the blind girls knew the nuns, all suspicion
vanished, and has never returned.   Instinct was as
strong as sight, and revealed to them the character
written on those faces which we looked upon—they
felt the refined sense of honour, the patient self-denial,
the heartfelt affection which we *saw* in the gentle Sisters
of Charity.

After our first visit to the asylum we were invited
by the kind superioress to witness a *play* acted by the
blind ; and truly it was worth seeing.   The scene was
laid in the time of the French Revolution ; and Marie
Antoinette, Madame Elizabeth, and other personages
of the period, did their parts with admirable self-pos-
session ; the Abbé Edgeworth, in berretta and cloak,
gave his blessing with sacerdotal dignity.   Several
choral pieces were introduced into the play to enliven
the scene ; while the remarks of a comic character,
who, somehow or other, had something to say to every
one, effectually dissipated the mournful character of
the play.   The burden of her tale was the superior
merits of ' old Ireland' over any other country in the
world ; and some stanzas of her parting song, composed
by herself, were as follows :—

> Come to old Ireland and seek information—
>   'Tis there you'll see sights that will soon make you stare ;
> Sure half what you hear of is all botheration—
>   Come judge for yourself, and you'll find I speak fair.

Come to old Ireland and see those fine places
  They have raised in this land for the use of mankind;
'Tis the first in God's Heart, if the last in His creatures',
  That beautiful spot called the 'Home of the Blind.'

Come to that place where they're all so united,
  Though born in counties divided afar—
They're from Dublin and Cork, Tipperary and Kerry,
  Kilkenny and Waterford, Limerick and Clare.

These simple pleasures are highly prized by the blind
children; and surely it is of no little moment to give
pleasure to those who are cut off from the many enjoyments which strew our paths.

Once a year the blind girls undergo an examination,
and assist at a concert in aid of their asylum given in
the Rotunda, Dublin.

The present asylum of the Sisters of Charity has
two great disadvantages: it is too small, and has no
outlet; there is no garden or ground of any kind; the
portion of the house for the Sisters is very inconvenient
and unwholesome, but they would bear it uncomplain-
ingly if they were not pained by having to refuse
so many pressing cases. They are now only able to
receive one hundred inmates.

Air and space for exercise also are necessary for
the comfort of the blind; for to take them out of
doors is always a difficult and sometimes a dangerous
undertaking. The Sisters therefore had long been
wishing to move, and they had intended to build at
Harold's Cross, when a house and grounds at Merrion,
the second station from Dublin on the Kingstown line,
fell vacant and were for sale. Many difficulties stood
in the way of the purchase, but the blind girls prayed
heartily, and in simple faith believed their prayers were

granted, when the obstacles one by one were removed and the place was theirs.

The house at Merrion is small, and buildings must therefore be added before all the blind girls can be moved from Portobello. At present they come in detachments for change of air, and their enjoyment of their new home is indeed a pleasant sight to witness. The grounds are very spacious; well planted with trees. On one side is a very pretty garden, and beyond it are fields belonging to the Sisters. The house fronts the sea, and is divided from it only by the high road and railway; but a passage beneath the line enables anyone to pass safely to the beach and enjoy sea bathing. A more perfect spot for the purpose could not have been found, and with thankful hearts the Sisters have taken possession of it.

The first stone of the new buildings was laid by the Cardinal Archbishop of Dublin, on September 18, 1866. When they are completed, the house at Portobello will be given up, and all the blind girls transferred to Merrion, while fresh cases will then be admitted. When the new arrangements are finished ' St. Mary's Home for the Blind ' promises to be one of the finest blind asylums in the three kingdoms.

CHAPTER III.

THE Irish Sisters of Charity were founded in 1815
and before they had been twenty years in existence, a
new order sprang into being, similar to them in many
respects, but differing in others. The foundress of this
new order was a Miss, or (as it is now usual to call her)
Mrs. Katherine McAuley, an Irish lady, who finding
herself left in middle life without pressing domestic
duties, and the owner of a large fortune, resolved to
devote both time and money to the service of the poor.
She had no thought of being a nun, but intended to
pass a retired life with a few ladies who had gathered
round her. She purchased ground in Lower Baggott
Street, on the south side of Dublin, and desired an
architect to build a house for her. Some large rooms
fit for teaching poor children, and a chapel, was the
order she gave him; but without intending it he built a
convent, and without intending it Katherine McAuley
and her friends were training themselves as religious
by their life of self-denial and devotion. When she
saw what the designs of Providence were, she meekly
submitted; and at fifty-two years of age went to
serve a year's novitiate in the Presentation convent
in George's Hill. There her cell can still be seen,
the tiny room in which no doubt many secret victories were won, and many fervent prayers breathed

for the anxious future before her, by the humble,
patient novice.

In 1831 the Institute of the Sisters of Mercy was
founded; in 1841 it was approved by the Holy See,
and in that same year Mrs. McAuley died, leaving
fourteen houses of her institute in existence. The
most remarkable features of this order have been its
extreme popularity and its marvellous spread. New
orders generally grow slowly at first, and have hard
frosts and keen winds to contend against. Not so the
Sisters of Mercy : like the Sisters of St. Vincent in
France they caught the *genius* of their native country,
and have been and are likely to remain the favourite
among Irish orders. Before their foundress died they
spread into England; now they possess in England
and Scotland together forty houses ; they have gone
to Australia, New Zealand, California, and America,
while in Ireland their convents are like a network
over the land; almost every town of importance possesses one of their communities, and a large portion of
the education of Irish children is in their hands. Dr.
Forbes, in his ' Memorandums in Ireland,' speaks of
the ' noble Sisters of Mercy so widely spread over
Ireland, and so constantly to be found where good
is to be done.' He adds that, ' As in all Catholic
countries so in Ireland, Sisters of Charity or Mercy
are found, educating the young, nursing the sick,
feeding the hungry, clothing the naked, harbouring
the homeless, imparting religion to improve the good
and to restore the bad, and all with that utter self-
abnegation and self-devotion, and with that earnestness, tenderness, and patience which can only spring

from the profoundest conviction that in so labouring
they are fulfilling God's will as revealed to man.' *

The difference between the Irish Sisters of Charity
and the Sisters of Mercy consists chiefly in their form of
government. The Sisters of Charity are governed by a
superioress-general, subject to an ecclesiastical superior,
the bishop of the diocese in which the mother house is
situated. They have but one general novitiate in which
all novices must be trained, and any Sister may be sent
to or from any house of the order as the superioress-
general may wish. With the Sisters of Mercy each
house is independent of the others, is governed by its
own superioress, subject to the bishop of the diocese,
and receives and trains its own novices. No Sister can
be sent from one convent to another without her own
consent and that of her bishop. When it is desired to
make a new foundation of Sisters of Mercy, one of the
existing convents is prayed to send out a filiation, i.e.
to give up two or more of its Sisters to found the new
community; and it is hoped and believed that they
in their turn will receive novices and grow into a
large community; like a swarm of bees they go forth
from the parent house and find honey for themselves.
Sisters of Mercy can also found branch houses which are
dependent on and supplied from one community, and
this is frequently done in large towns or in different
parts of one diocese. There is much to be said in
favour of both these forms of government, both are
equally sanctioned by the church, and both have their
advantages and drawbacks. But it is curious to ob-

* *Memorandums in Ireland*, vol. ii. p. 27.

serve that in France the tendency to the centralised form of government is strong, and by far the most popular; all their modern orders have, without exception, adopted it; while in Ireland, the form of government of the Sisters of Mercy is undoubtedly the favourite and most popular, and best suits the wants of the country.

The convent in Baggot Street is an extensive building, but with a very plain exterior. Within, much pains have been spent on decorations of a strictly conventual character. The cloisters and convent chapel are beautiful; there are immense poor schools in the rear of the building, a large House of Mercy, and a home for pupil teachers. The three main objects for which Mrs. McAuley designed her order were the care of poor schools, the visitation of the poor, and the charge of a House of Mercy, and to these three works whenever practicable the Sisters are bound by rule to attend.

The House of Mercy is meant as a temporary refuge for respectable girls and women out of employment. It is chiefly filled by servants out of place, and has often proved a most valuable place of refuge for those in danger. The inmates are taught to labour for their own support, either at needle or laundry work, and the Sisters try to get situations for them. It is not intended that they should remain any length of time in the house, but only till they can find employment. In addition to these three works of charity the Sisters may undertake any other, either under their own roof or in branch houses. The Sisters of Mercy in Dublin being the largest and most important house of the order, have five branch houses, the three principal among which I visited, and will now speak of.

The Charitable Infirmary, Jervis Street, is one of the oldest hospitals in Dublin. It was founded in the year 1728 by a small band of medical men; it began on a very small scale in Cook Street, but was soon moved to Inns Quay where it became considerably enlarged, and occupied the site of an old Dominican priory. After sixty years it was driven from its place to give room to the 'Four Courts,' the most beautiful public building that Dublin possesses. The Infirmary took refuge in Jervis Street, and was accommodated in a large house, the property of Lord Charlemont.

In 1792 a charter for this hospital was granted by government, and the managers were incorporated as the 'Guardians and Governors of the Charitable Infirmary, Jervis Street.' Upon the present board there are no medical men. The building has a plain brick exterior. It contains a reception room, board room, lecture room, and six wards, capable of containing seventy patients. This hospital was, until about thirteen years ago, served by the usual class of hospital nurses, under charge of a matron. The medical men were by no means satisfied with their mode of service. The patients were neglected, the hospital was extremely dirty, and it was resolved that the Sisters of Mercy should be asked to undertake the nursing; and the request was made and granted. A certain number of Sisters were sent from the convent in Baggot Street, and a few small and inconvenient rooms, but well separated from the rest of the hospital, were allotted to them, and the Sisters began their work. In a very

short time cleanliness and order reigned throughout the
place—the patients were made comfortable, and the
doctors found that their orders were carried out.   Stimu-
lants now went down the patients' throats instead of
those of their nurses, and all that careful nursing could
do to alleviate suffering was performed.   Jervis Street
Hospital is chiefly used for ' accidents,' and other sur-
gical cases, and there are few under medical treatment.
The house is not well suited for an hospital—the top
wards being far too low and not very capable of sufficient
ventilation.   I understand it is the intention of the
governors to build a new hospital shortly.   The Sisters
are able to do much for the souls of their patients,
taking care to instruct the ignorant—to teach them to
suffer patiently and to turn their thoughts to the God
they have forgotten in their time of health.   More than
once a *wedding* has taken place, in the little chapel,
between those whom sickness had led to repent of the
past and desire to lead a Christian life for the future.

The second branch of the Sisters of Mercy is at the
Mater Misericordiæ Hospital, the chief Catholic hospital of Dublin, and one which bids fair to become
equal in importance to any in Europe.   The idea of
its creation originated with the Sisters of Mercy, who,
not contented with being ready to devote their labour
to its care contributed 10,000*l.* towards its expenses.
They then undertook the arduous task of begging, and
obtained from the public 17,000*l.*   With this sum a
portion of the hospital was built and furnished.   The
Sisters of Mercy took possession of it in 1861, and
receive about a hundred patients.   In Dr. Bristowe's
report to government on the hospitals of the United
Kingdom, the following mention is made :—

' The Mater Misericordiæ Hospital, founded in the year 1861 by the Sisters of Mercy, and as yet incomplete, lies to the north of Dublin, on the confines of the town; it occupies an elevated site, and is surrounded by large open spaces. On the score of salubrity, the site seems wholly unobjectionable.

' The hospital, when complete, will form a quadrangular building, and will hold, we believe, about 500 beds. At present the anterior portion only is in existence. This is a handsome symmetrical three-floored building, presenting on each floor a corridor at the back, extending from end to end, with wards and other rooms opening out of it in front, and with staircase, operating rooms, and offices (forming a compact block), extending from its central part backwards.

*   *   *   *   *

' The hospital is kept scrupulously clean, and its ventilation, and indeed all its internal arrangements, seem admirable. Patients are admitted without any recommendation other than the fitness of the case for admission, and all classes of disease are eligible, except infectious fevers.

' This hospital promises, in our opinion, to be, when complete, one of the finest hospitals in Europe. It is built on the corridor plan; but the distribution of corridors, and wards, and beds, is such as entirely to neutralise any ill effects that could possibly flow from the adoption of this plan, while all the advantages that spacious, cheerful, well-ventilated corridors afford, are thoroughly secured.' *

---

* *Report to Government on the Hospitals of the United Kingdom.* By J. S. Bristowe, M.D.

During the year 1866, 1,100 patients passed through
the wards of this hospital, and 3,491 were treated as
out patients. In the autumn of that same year Dublin
was visited by the terrible scourge of cholera. The hospital instantly opened its doors to the victims, a certain number of wards were set apart for them, and 206
patients were received and well cared for. At all
hours of the day and night the Sisters and medical men
were ready to take them in, and the tenderest and most
vigilant care was bestowed on them. It fell to the task
of one Sister to compose the limbs and shroud the
bodies of more than one hundred victims of this terrible disease. In common with the other hospitals of
which I have been writing, immense spiritual good
is wrought within these walls. Kind and gentle words
make a great impression on the careless; the example
of self-devotion they see before their eyes tends to
strengthen it. If they are murmuring under their
poverty and sickness, they see those born to comfort
and luxury giving up all—imprisoning themselves
within hospital walls—to wait on them; and advice from
such a quarter is more appreciated. Few Catholics
leave the hospital without having approached the sacraments. No distinction of creed is made in this hospital,
and Protestants are as tenderly cared for as the rest,
and freely allowed any ministration of their religion.
' Whether the postulant be Catholic or Protestant,
Mahometan or Jew, he is God's work, made in his
Creator's image; and the gate opens to him freely,
without a question as to his religious faith. He is not
asked to violate his conscience that he may receive
relief. He is not required to purchase his life at the

price of his apostacy. The name of charity is not desecrated by association with sectarian intolerance. It is not made a bait to corrupt or a sword to persecute wretches broken down by disease to incapacity of resistance, and powerless to help themselves.'*

This is a pleasing contrast to another hospital which, though standing in a Catholic country like Ireland, denies admission to any priest within its walls even to visit the dying, and has more than once turned out a patient in his last extremity because he would not die without the consolations of his faith. In a city where such fearful bigotry can exist an hospital like the Mater Misericordiæ is doubly needed. The hospital 'has no grant from the State or permanent income from any other source. It is dependent entirely on public benevolence for support. During the past year a sum of 3,818*l.* was voluntarily bestowed, and every shilling received has gone directly to the relief of the patients. The Sisters of Mercy are no charge whatever on the Mater Misericordiæ Hospital, being supported out of the funds of their own community. Of the 3,818*l.* received last year, 1,851*l.* was realised by a bazaar. One thousand pounds has been lodged towards the creation of a fund for the completion of the unfinished wing of the building. Nine years ago that wing was erected to the height of twenty-one feet, but the work was necessarily stopped for want of funds.' The hospital being now out of debt, efforts are being made to complete this wing. In it 'a fever ward, which is much needed, will be supplied, and it is hoped that by

* Speech of Right Hon. Judge O'Hagan.

the addition of more than two hundred beds the hospital will be enabled to accommodate three hundred
patients.'

The Mater Misericordiæ and also St. Vincent's
Hospital have been founded upon the medieval system.
They are the property of a religious order, which is
alone responsible for their management, and to whom
alms for their support are committed.   In modern times
hospitals have fallen under the management of ' com-
mittees ' and ' boards of directors,' or ' governors.' The
Sisters of Mercy, feeling the magnitude and importance
of their undertaking, and considering the large sum of
public money committed to their keeping, have resolved
to amalgamate the two systems.   They have, therefore,
called to their aid a committee or ' council' of the leading Catholic gentlemen of Dublin, to whom the accounts
of the hospital are thrown open, and whose advice and
co-operation are gratefully received.   It is from their
first annual report that the above quotations are taken,
and the council further add: ' Annexed to this report
is a statement of the receipts and expenditures for the
past twelve months.   We cannot conclude without
expressing our admiration of the good order and cleanliness of the hospital.   The admirable manner in which
it is kept, and the clear and accurate system of accounts
have given us the greatest satisfaction, and reflect the
highest credit on the Sisters of Mercy.'

When we reflect that so large a portion of the funds
was contributed by the Sisters of Mercy themselves,
and that the expenses even of their own support are
not charged upon the funds, we must confess that this
challenge of public inspection and criticism is the very

opposite of that narrowness of spirit with which religious are, and often unjustly, accused. Speaking of this hospital, Judge O'Hagan adds: 'The contribution of the Sisters of Mercy was very great indeed. And this they offered that they might open for themselves a new field of labour—made terrible by mephitic vapours and the groans of tortured men—and bringing them into fearful contact with pestilence and death. And, since the hospital was established, they have been its only nurses. They have ministered, with their own hands, to its suffering inmates—repelled by no form of disease, however loathesome, and declining no office, however mean, so that they might mitigate a pang or speed a soul more peacefully to heaven! And all this they have done gratuitously, not merely receiving no stipend for their services, but maintaining themselves from their own resources, and not taxing even for their food the funds of the hospital in which they toil unceasingly to the extent of a single farthing. Surely this is admirable, and not less admirable too the rule by which they open their doors, at all times and under all circumstances, to every human being who needs their help, without let or hindrance. Suffering is the sole condition of its own relief. It requires no passport from wealth or rank. It is subjected to no cold and jealous scrutiny. There is no fear that a human creature shall perish at the door, whilst those within deliberate on the propriety of his admission.'

The Cardinal Archbishop of Dublin, speaking of the Mater Misericordiæ, said : ' I recollect that when it was proposed to commence this hospital there was a difference of opinion about the merits of the plan according

to which it is now partially erected. Some said that
the proposed building would be too expensive, that it
would be too grand for the poor, and that it would be
better to erect an humble and less ornamental structure,
which would be more in harmony with the miserable
normal condition of our poor. Having been consulted
on the question, I declared in favour of the present
plan. We have palaces for guilt—we have palaces for
force—we have palaces for legalised want, in which
what is called pauperism is dealt with according to the
principles of an unfeeling political economy. Why,
then, should we not have at least one palace for the
poor, in which poverty would be relieved in a true
spirit of charity and according to the dictates of the
Gospel? Such palaces are met with under the name
of Alberghi or Ospizi de Poveri, in Naples and Genoa,
Rome and Paris. Why should not Dublin show its
respect for true poverty by imitating the good example
given by other cities? The Sisters of Mercy, acting
according to the spirit of their institute, determined to
adopt the plan best calculated to elevate and ennoble
poverty, and they have been most successful in erecting
an hospital which does credit to their good taste, and
is a great ornament to the city.'

In the conception and progress of this great work
there presided a guiding spirit—one of those rare
characters from whom 'great' actions may be expected
—and it is her principle, which was here strenuously
carried out, that those who labour for God's glory should
strain every effort to let their work equal, even if it
cannot excel, the deeds of those who toil for an
earthly reward.

The third branch house of the Sisters of Mercy in Dublin is connected with one of the most important institutions in Ireland—the Prison Refuge at Golden Bridge.

It was in Ireland that the problem how to reform our female criminals was first solved, and it is mainly owing to the Sisters of Mercy that the solution was accomplished. The reformation of a female prisoner has long been acknowledged to be a harder task than that of a male—indeed, many have deemed it impossible. She has sinned more against the instincts of her better nature, the consequences of her crime have had a more hardening effect upon her, but, above all, the absence of *hope* has a fatal effect on her character. And this despair is really not much to be wondered at. If a poor woman endure her sentence patiently, and keep the prison rules, she goes out at the end of her imprisonment with very little prospect for the future, save that of fresh dishonesty. What is to become of her? She has *no character*. Who will employ a discharged prisoner? The sharp witticism of Dr. Whately, that he who employed a convict servant would soon have no spoons left in the house but himself, is an article of faith to the vast majority of people, and nobody feels himself bound to risk losing his plate, or his other household gods. For men there are a dozen modes of hard, rough out-door employment to which they can turn; but take away from a woman domestic service, charing, and laundry work, and there is nothing left to her but wretched needlework, at which even respectable women can hardly earn their bread. It must seem almost like a mockery to speak

to a poor prisoner of the mercy of God, when the
mercy of her fellow-creatures is so sternly withheld.
For many years past the Sisters of Mercy have been
permitted to visit the female prisoners at Mountjoy
Prison, the principal and strongest prison in Ireland,
and one which is now too familiar to us, from its
association with the Fenian prisoners.

Here the Sisters exercise a most beneficial influence
over the miserable inmates. They instruct them together in class, and it is a rule that no prison official
shall be present. Yet this class often consists of wild,
desperate women, with great physical strength and
easily-roused passions. The matron of Mountjoy described to us once how standing in a prisoner's cell,
with an immense bunch of keys in her hand, she
suddenly perceived that the woman was about to spring
upon her, in which case the keys would have been
sent with all their force against her head. Just in
time the matron, a strong, vigorous woman, knocked
her assailant down, and thus saved her own life.
Among such as these the Sisters move fearlessly, and
have never had to suffer. Even the wild din of
tongues issuing from those kept all day, and many a
day, in enforced silence, is hushed by the uplifted
finger or the gentle tones of a Sister of Mercy. Great
good was therefore to be expected from placing these
women for the concluding part of their sentence in a
refuge under the sole care of these Sisters. The pro-
position was made to the superioress in April 1856,
and in a few days only she was ready to begin the
work.

Before passing to the Refuge, I must say a word

about Mountjoy Prison, although I do not wish to
reckon it among the ' Irish homes' that I have visited.
It stands at the north of Dublin, in an open, airy
situation. It is a prison for men and women, the two
compartments being of course entirely distinct. The
head matron of the female prison is a person of very
superior attainments. A lady by birth and education,
she does not content herself with merely doing her duty,
but throws all the powers of her mind and heart into the
work. She evidently desires the real reformation of the
prisoners, and gives her cordial co-operation to the
efforts of the Sisters of Mercy. Her subordinates are
carefully chosen, and are influenced by the excellent
qualities of their superior. It is a dismal occupation to
take a walk through Mountjoy; the long white corridors and walls unrelieved by a patch of colour;
narrow iron staircases running here and there to upper
stories and galleries; long rows of cells, with closely
locked doors, and a little window in the middle through
which the matron can peep, or the prisoner make any
necessary want known. Pacing up and down a corridor containing a number of those cells, is a matron
dressed in black, whose countenance and manner show
you she is firm, resolute, patient, and prepared for
emergencies. Here she must stay an allotted number
of hours, till her watch is over, and she is relieved by
another officer.

The next class of prisoners are allowed the luxury
of having their cell door open, and thus seeing all that
passes, in the occasional passage of a matron, or some
other official; yet this slight break in the dread
monotony of solitary confinement is valued, and looked

on as a reward. We went to the school where prisoners attend in detachments for one hour per day.
This is one of their greatest enjoyments, and its deprivation, therefore, is used as a punishment for certain
offences. It was curious to see women of every age,
even to the grey-haired, standing in classes with
spelling-books, like so many children, many of them
able to learn but little, but eager and interested in the
employment, which broke the monotony of their days,
and gave them some new ideas. Women in the advanced classes of prison life work in a common room,
then pass to the laundry, and other employments in
the prison. Through all these stages they must pass,
and behave well in each before they can enter the Refuge; it is intended strictly as a reward for good conduct, and the *hope* of getting there, the *hope* for the
future, is the star that rises on the dark night of their
despair and recklessness, and leads them on to exertion.
The Sisters in their visits to the prison, are able to
learn the character of the women, and this is an
immense help to them in the management of the
Refuge.

I visited the chapels of the prison, both Catholic and
Protestant. The male prisoners are on one side, the
female on the other. There are three chapels in
Mountjoy, Catholic, Established Church, and Presby-
terian, and each has its chaplain. The Catholics are
so numerous as to require the services of two priests.
We need hardly say that the Catholics in Mountjoy and all Irish prisons are in an overwhelming majority over the Protestants; yet for the small minority
ample religious provision is made, while in England

for the large masses of Catholic prisoners, because they
happen to profess a faith different from that of the
State religion, in many prisons very little or no religious provision is made. The most affecting sight in
Mountjoy was the infant school. There are collected
together the poor little creatures whose mothers are in
jail. Some were sleeping in their cots, others toddling
about the floor, others a little older learning their
letters. They were clean and nicely cared for, and
looked happy enough; many of them very pretty, and
all with the innocent baby faces which appeal to every
heart. Poor little beings, what a strange fate is theirs!
there for a brief space sheltered from the storm, but
soon to go out and make experience of life in its
roughest, bitterest aspect. How soon from many of
them the innocence of childhood will be snatched!
Perhaps raging in some of the cells above, or in the
' punishment cells,' tearing about like wild beasts, were
the mothers of some of them, to whom their future
training would be committed. I know not how any
one could look at these rosy, smiling faces, without
shedding tears; it is at least a merciful arrangement
which permits their being cared for during these few
years, and taught holy lessons which may linger as
fragments in the memories of some.

Nothing strikes a visitor to Golden Bridge Refuge
more than the un-prison life look of the place. It is
a striking contrast to the great formidable-looking
military barrack opposite to it. A wooden gate leads
into the domain, and on each side of the gate is a
building, that on the right a disused Protestant church,
on the left the schools; for the Sisters add on to their

prison work schools for the poor children in the neighbourhood.

Golden Bridge is a little way out of Dublin, on the
Inchicore Road, but it lies in the midst of a large
and poor population. The house is by no means suited
for the purpose, and immense pains, contrivance, and
perseverance were needed to enable the Sisters to
receive prisoners there at all—out-houses, lofts, and
sheds have been converted into dormitories and work
rooms, while money has been collected, and large, fine
laundries built. But what cannot be done by the right
person in the right place? and fortunately for the
prisoners the order of the Sisters of Mercy possessed
among its members one whose qualities of head and
heart rendered her pre-eminently suited for the undertaking. I cannot speak of Mother Mary Magdalene,
or Mrs. Kirwan (as she is generally called), as I would,
because she is still among us, and to those who have
done, and are doing great deeds, praise sounds like an
impertinence; it is sufficient to say that she has made
the Refuge what it is—a success; she has 'redeemed
multitudes of women, and redeemed them permanently
to virtue, society, and God.' She has touched 'seared
consciences, and softened flinty hearts.'* Hundreds of
women who would have spent their time in Mountjoy
Prison in a state of chronic rebellion and passion,
engendered by despair, and gone out worse than they
came in, more ready to sin against society and to
break the laws of God, have struggled through their
prison life, done well at the Refuge, and are now

* Speech of Right Hon. Judge O'Hagan.

earning their bread respectably, the past forgiven and forgotten. And though these latter are rare, there have been more consoling cases still where the repentance has been of that depth and fervour which reminds us forcibly of the great pattern of penitents, to whom much was forgiven because of her great love and contrition. Many of the prisoners are not fallen women, and one of them who had unhappily lost her good name, although indeed she had been more 'sinned against than sinning,' wept with many and bitter tears over her lost innocence, humbling herself in spirit infinitely below her companions. 'Ah! Rev. mother, if I were but like the others!' she would say, and thankfully accepted the hardship of her lot as a deserved and salutary penance.

A girl, whom we will call Mary, was left an orphan at twelve years of age with a little brother. They had an aunt who offered to take the girl provided she deserted her brother. This she refused, and the two children wandered about the country all but starving. At last they stole some trifling thing and were sent to prison for a short time, but long enough for the tide of evil to flow over them. They came out much worse than they went in. Mary lost her innocence, and was again and again committed for theft; at last she fortunately received a sentence for seven years, and after spending nearly four in prison came to the Refuge. There she learnt to sorrow truly for the past, and her conduct was so satisfactory that the Sisters placed her in service in Dublin, in the house of one of those charitable ladies who are willing to help on the good work by giving these poor creatures a trial. Here she re-

mained two years, and at their close received an offer
of marriage from a respectable bricklayer well able to
keep her; but she would not accept him till Mother
Magdalene had seen him and approved of the match.
This being done, all seemed going well, when one day
Mary appeared before the Mother flushed and agitated.
'I want you, ma'am, to tell Dennis everything about
me; I could not deceive him; I could not marry him
unless he knows all, and I don't know how he will take
it.' Mary went out and in came Dennis, not at all
over-pleased to find there was any hitch in his love
affairs. 'What do you know of Mary?' said the superioress.—'Everything that is good, ma'am,' answered
Dennis warmly; 'what have you to say against her?'—
'Nothing,' replied the nun; 'and what she has now bid
me do raises her in my estimation, but she wishes you
to know she was once a convict at Golden Bridge.'—'I
know that, ma'am,' said he with much feeling; 'the
housemaid at Mrs. —— found it out and told it to
me, thinking to turn me from Mary, but I have never
spoken to her since, I thought it was so mean; and as
for Mary, I think more highly of her than ever.' They
were married, and at a year's end Mary died in giving
birth to her first child. Almost her last thought of
earth was to see again the loved face of the nun who
had indeed been a true friend and mother to her.
Dennis came afterwards to Mother Magdalene weeping bitterly over his loss. 'Oh, ma'am,' said he, 'she
was a wife for a prince, beautiful and so gentle; all the
people in the house we lodged in respected her, though
she spoke to no one but me. After our marriage she
could not rest till she had told me the history of her

life, but I never cast a thought on it after.' Another girl in her early youth had been betrayed and deserted; she wandered about with her baby begging; falling into the hands of an abandoned woman she was persuaded to desert her baby, and take to theft and evil courses. She allowed the tempter to take the baby from her arms, and then she followed her bad counsel; but a perpetual remorse haunted her, and she strove to drown it in reckless sin. She came to the Refuge; repentance began to do its work, and her sorrow was deep and overwhelming. She behaved very well, and on leaving was respectably placed in America. Friends, home, honest earnings, a good name were again hers; but still she heard that feeble wail, still she felt the last pressure of that little burden on her bosom, and though she went thankfully, patiently about her work, she said there would be a shadow over her to the end of her days.

Strange and romantic indeed are many and many of the histories which have come to the ears of the Sisters in this Refuge; these lives have often been tragedies acted in secret, and would outdo the plot of any sensational novel. One who knows the Refuge well thus wrote of its inmates and others like them:—

> Did each her dark wrongs unfold,
> Well might our blood run cold—
> Love believed,
> Love deceived,
> Anguish and wrath;
> Sad mothers bemoaning them,
> Brothers disowning them;
> Cast away,
> Fast they stray
> Down by sin's path.

Not harshly abusing them,
No, nor ill-using them,
    Saddening some,
    Maddening some,
    Makes them amend.
Instruct them to pray instead,
Earning pure daily bread;
    Bear with them,
    Share with them—
    He will befriend.

Poor outcasts! for peace they sigh,
Sure 't were release to die.
    Who shall say,
    Such as they
    Mercy ne'er found?
'T were hard all their woes to tell,
Christ alone knows it well;
    Judge no more,
    Once before
    He wrote on the ground.

Placing out the prisoners when they leave is the chief care of the nuns; it is the completion of their work, without which all the previous labour would be wasted; and it is not easy. A prisoner who has done well during her prison term has earned money which makes her a prize for the moment to her 'pals' and former evil companions. A girl who had been convicted of sheep stealing and committed to prison in Cork, there made acquaintance with two bad women, and on her being sent to Mountjoy, made a bargain with her *friends* to call for her as soon as her sentence should have expired. When sent to the Refuge she was found to be deceitful and cunning, and little hope was entertained of her reformation. But a change passed over her, and she came to Mother Magdalene to tell her story, and asked to be saved from her prison acquaint-

ances. She was sent to America, where she was found
to have respectable friends; and when at the appointed
time the two women came faithfully to fulfil their
pledge (for when did Satan ever forget · *his* appoint-
ments?) it was with no little jubilation of heart that
the Sisters told them she whom they sought was gone
away. The enquirers seemed greatly astonished at the
news. In America this girl did well, and wrote grateful
letters. Against dangers such as she was exposed to
the nuns have to guard many, and they have to provide
employment for their charges suited to their characters
and capabilities. Many emigrate, and as the Sisters
of Mercy have convents in most of the colonies, they
are sent to these by the Sisters from the Refuge, and
thus find friends and helpers in a strange land.

Mother Magdalene's influence over the prisoners is
unbounded: a result not so much to be wondered at,
because she is one of those beings on whom the gift of
influence has been bestowed; and the intellectual and
the refined cannot resist its spell. And all the powers
of a mind fitted to shine pre-eminently in the most
accomplished circles are exerted to win the confidence
and direct aright the character of these poor outcasts.
One of them was sent to service at a great distance
from Dublin; she behaved very well and remained a
quarter; at its end her wages were paid, and she was
allowed a day's holiday. She took a return ticket for
Dublin, and presented herself at the convent. She
had exactly one hour to spare before she had to return
to the station, and the price of the ticket had swal-
lowed up nearly all her earnings; but she was quite
contented, having accomplished the object of her

journey, which was, she said to Mother Magdalene, ' to have a good look at you, ma'am;' and when remonstrated with by the Mother for spending her money on so transient a pleasure when she might have done other things with it, bought a useful book for instance, replied, ' And sure ma'am, I mean to do it again.' After all was it so very transient? If there are ' sermons in stones' what lessons may not be read from the faces of those we reverence—lessons which may linger in the memory and aid us in the hour of trial.

For a long time the two employments of the prisoners were washing and needlework, but Mrs. Kirwan constantly regretted that she was not able to vary these. Some women are not suited or strong enough for laundry work; and then the long monotony of ' stitch, stitch, stitch ' is very trying and very hard for them, and tends to keep up that dwelling on self, and reverting to the past, which it is the aim of the Sisters to prevent. In the course of 1866, Mrs. Kirwan ventured on a little experiment, and is attempting the weaving of lindsey. No manufactories of this fabric exist in Ireland, all lindsey, as well as most other articles of wear, is imported; and the people who blame the Irish for not exerting themselves, would be the last to purchase home made goods. Mrs. Kirwan's experiment is a very courageous one, for it cannot be made without much expense. A manufactory had to be fitted up, looms purchased, and weavers engaged for a certain time to teach the art. When I visited the Refuge several looms were in operation, worked by the prisoners, and various bales of lindsey manufactured by them were ready for inspection; it seemed

very well made, and as good as what would be seen in
a London shop. If this experiment should succeed,
it will not have to trust entirely to the mercy of the
public, for the Dublin Sisters of Mercy, with their five
branch houses, and the various institutions under their
charge, are consumers of a great deal of lindsey, which
might be supplied from their own looms. At all events
the employment has had an excellent effect on the
women; the work interests them and they labour away
with good will. Passing through the laundries we
saw two pretty little children whose mothers were
among the prisoners. When a prisoner with a child
is sent to the Refuge, the child comes also, and the
mother can see it at the intervals of her work, and this
must have a humanising and softening effect on the
poor creatures. It must be remembered that the
whole cost of this Refuge is by no means defrayed
by the Government; it allows only five shillings per
week for each convict. Out of this and the small
profit arising from the prisoners' labour, every expense
has to be met. The erection of the laundries cost a
large sum : the Sisters borrowed it at the usual rate
of interest, and have to pay off the principal. All
this anxiety, responsibility, and burden falls on them,
in addition to the heavy cares of the Refuge itself.
There is an erroneous idea in Ireland that institutions under Government do not need further help—on
the contrary they often need it more than others, for
it would be a grievous thing if the help that Government offers had to be refused for lack of the necessary
funds to meet it. After the Golden Bridge Refuge was
in operation, a Protestant one was opened which contains

about a dozen prisoners. The Government extend the same help to it as to the Catholic, and in this respect there is no cause for complaint; and as far as the Refuges are concerned, all creeds are treated by Government with perfect justice and fairness. Before leaving the Refuge I visited the schools, divided from it by a long strip of grass land. Several hundred children attend this school, and as the population around is extremely poor, an industrial school is added to the literary ones. The Protestant church on the other side is an absurd object, being utterly empty and disused; there would be no difficulty in the Sisters purchasing it, except that by law a building belonging to the Established Church must remain as it is, whether there be a congregation or not, and when it is not of the slightest use to any mortal.

CHAPTER IV.

On the opposite side of Dublin to Portobello, near the beautiful cemetery of Glasnevin, is the Blind Asylum for boys and men. The door was opened to us by a Brother in the Carmelite dress, but both dress and Brother were so dirty we thought he had come to the door by mistake. He showed us into a small parlour, where we found a poor little blind boy, whom his father had brought, waiting in hopes of admission.

Presently in came the superior, but alas! there was little improvement in his appearance from that of the porter. He was, however, most pleasant and good natured in his manner, and quite willing we should see the institution. We went first into the shop where the articles made by the blind are arranged. Few are sold on the premises, for the asylum is quite out of Dublin, and I should imagine has few visitors. They are bought, however, by shops, and thus employment is afforded to the boys. There was a great array of brushes, mats, and baskets of all kinds, and they looked very well made. Two workmen are employed in the institution to teach the blind and superintend their work. We were then shown into a large, desolate-looking sort of barn, absolutely bare of furniture, except that at the extreme end was a piano. A gentleman was seated at it, and a few of the blind boys were standing round him taking a music lesson. We went to the basket department where we found other blind boys making coarse baskets and hampers, and this our guide told us was all that was to be seen.

The whole place was very dirty and disorderly, the blind inmates were dirty and untidy, and had an un-cared-for look, as if in the hands of those who did not understand their management. We noticed with pain the contrast between the blind boys and girls ; the latter so thoroughly trained to exert their faculties and do all they can to help themselves. They walk about with an air of freedom and confidence, feeling sure they will be guarded from all danger. The blind boys, even those who had been ten years in the house, stumbled here and there, literally *groping* their way, and showing very plainly that their capabilities had never been drawn out, or their education as *blind persons* attended to. And of course it is not every-one or every religious order that is suited to this important work. The teachers must themselves not only learn but possess qualities suited to the task. No doubt the Carmelite brothers have the kindest and best intentions towards their afflicted charges, and we heard from good authority that the moral training of the institution is excellent, but they do not give a visitor the impression of being suited for the difficult and arduous task entrusted to them. We came away wondering that in the diocese of Dublin such an asylum was suffered to exist without reform.

Not very far from Glasnevin, on the Cabra Road, is an institution which forms a striking contrast to the one we have just mentioned. It is the Home for Deaf

and Dumb Boys under the charge of the Christian
Brothers. The building is a large and handsome one,
standing on rising ground, with a large open space surrounding it. Fortunately we arrived there just before
school broke up, and found the large schoolrooms filled
with silent and attentive scholars. The Brother ac-
companying us questioned the different classes as we
passed along. The question was written on the black
board with chalk, and the boys answered on their slates
with remarkable celerity. It was curious to see how
they watched their teacher's face, and how one word or
a sign was sufficient for them; the rest was read from
the countenance of the Brother. From the schoolrooms we passed into the workshops, where different
trades are taught the boys, each superintended by a
skilled workman. We visited the tailor's department,
and then the shoemaker's, and in these a certain number of boys learn to make their own clothes and shoes.
From thence we passed to the bakery, where some of
the boys help to make the bread of the establishment;
and, lastly, we visited the printing office, where the
foreman showed us specimens of very fair printing
indeed done by the deaf-mutes. There is always
plenty of employment for them in this line, as the
Christian Brothers, who are a numerous body in Ireland, publish their own school books and have many of
them printed here. By the time we had seen the shops
the boys had finished school, and rushed out into the
playground where they ran about and occasionally
made an uncouth noise. They never, however, said
the Brother, play with the joyousness of other boys.
They are cheerful and happy, but have a gravity

beyond their years. The Brother showed us the large garden, well-planted with flowers and vegetables. Here a few at a time can always be trusted; they seem to have no turn for running over the beds or doing any mischief. Few have any taste for gardening, but they have a great belief in the efficacy of fresh air, and when they complain of some slight illness like to be allowed a walk in the garden. There they will be seen pacing up and down the gravel paths like grave old men, and after a little while they return to school 'quite well.' The trades which the boys are taught are made quite a secondary object as compared with the school work. They were, in fact, added on after the asylum had been for some time in the hands of the Brothers. For these religious were not content with looking after and teaching the boys, they *studied* them, and they found it would be an excellent thing to create some employment which should fill up spare hours and interest them, besides giving them assistance towards earning their bread when they leave. Playtime is not to them the entire relaxation it is to other boys, and the most common temptation to deaf-mutes would be to plot and conspire among themselves if left too much to their unoccupied thoughts. For the freemasonry of a deaf-mute is unlimited. The most vigilant teacher, well trained in the language of the deaf and dumb, can never be a match for boys who can carry on their conversations in silence and with the utmost celerity. The trades were introduced, and a most excellent effect has resulted from them. The boys are occupied, interested, happy, and contented, and try to prepare themselves for earning their own bread. 'But school

work is by far the most important for them,' insisted
and repeated the Brother; 'to be able to communicate
with their fellow-creatures is the main point for them.'
Reading, writing, arithmetic, history, geography, and
in some cases a little drawing, are generally the whole
of their attainments; and a course of ten years is
usually required before this can be fully acquired. It
is difficult for those not acquainted with deaf-mutes to
understand the immense labour required to teach boys
to whom sound has no meaning.

After passing through the dormitories, which are
large, lofty and airy, we entered a small room called
the study, where the elder and more advanced boys
come to read in the evenings. I was surprised on
taking up the books to see in what simple language
they were written; and then we discovered that when
the deaf-mute has learnt to read, the world of literature is by no means open to him. A new word to him
conveys no meaning. He can read 'banner,' for instance, as well as we can; but till some one shows him
by signs what it is he is none the wiser, and therefore
his progress through the world of words is necessarily
slow. I asked if the boys were inclined to be religious, and was answered in the affirmative. They soon
acquire a settled conviction that there is not much
chance of happiness for them in this world; that most
of its enjoyments are shut out from them, and that
they had better try and secure the promises of the
world to come. They are always eager to approach
the sacraments; have a very lively faith in the unseen
world, and often talk of heaven as the place where
they shall for the first time 'speak and sing.' Their

fault is generally violent temper, which vents itself oftener in spite and revenge, not being able to express itself in outspoken fury. The care of deaf-mutes is a far more arduous and depressing one than that of the blind; and we felt a deep admiration when we saw these excellent Brothers, many of them young, clever and superior men, devoting themselves to this laborious undertaking for the sole motive of the love of God.

The blind are after all beings like ourselves, help-less by a certain deprivation, and cut off from many of the pleasures of life, but with their other senses sharpened to an extraordinary degree, often proficients in certain arts, and able to enter into and understand all that passes around them—affectionate relations, true and faithful friends. The deaf-mutes are a race apart, a people within a people, cut off from their fellow-creatures by a mysterious and impassable barrier. It is extraordinary to recollect how many centuries were suffered to pass away before any attempt was made to alleviate the condition of a deaf-mute. They were ' separated from both God and man by a law more immutable than that which divided the leper from his nation.' Far too little known is the noble man who though he ' worked no miracle, yet taught the deaf to hear and the dumb to speak.' M. Sicard, inventor of the language for the deaf and dumb, was born in 1742 and died in 1822. M. Carton, from whom we quote the above words, remarks on the ' infinite toil and trouble' with which the deaf-mute must be taught. He says, ' it is the labour of a life, one-half at least of which must be spent in learning how to give what the other half is devoted to imparting.' The grave necessity for a deaf and dumb asylum may easily be perceived when we learn that the census of 1863 gives 5,653 as the number of deaf-mutes in Ireland. The Cabra Asylum receives two classes of inmates : first, the children of the poor; and, secondly, the children of those who can afford to pay a small pension for their support. Little difference is, however, made between the two classes; the second have a separate dormitory, a few extra comforts, and do not work at the trades; in all other respects they are on the same footing as their poor companions. Their common misfortune has levelled almost every distinction of rank. For the support of the poor boys, the Brothers are quite dependent on alms ; and as this is the only Catholic institution in the three kingdoms, it ought to be better supported than it is, and either enlarged or similar ones set on foot at other places.

There was perfect cleanliness and order in all parts of the establishment, and a large allowance of fresh air. We took leave of the kind and courteous Brother and left the ' Home for Deaf-mutes,' heartily wishing that the blind boys could enjoy the privilege of being under the care of the excellent and intelligent Christian Brothers. Their superior capability for the work over a single house of Carmelite Friars is obvious. Many hundreds of them are banded together under one superior-general, who can, of course, choose the subjects most suited for each particular work ; added to this, every Brother is specially trained for the work of educating the poor, and taught to study their characters and to raise their tone. If their attention were once drawn to the care of the blind, no doubt

we should soon have an asylum for boys equally good
as that for girls.

Upon the Glasnevin Road stands another large and
handsome building under the charge of these same
Brothers. It is an orphanage for boys, principally
supported by the Association of the Brothers of St.
Vincent de Paul. It seemed to us to be in excellent
order and well managed, and, no doubt, is of great use
in providing a refuge for homeless and orphan boys.

About half a mile farther out of Dublin than the
Home for the Deaf and Dumb Boys, we find a similar
institution for girls, under the care of the Sisters of
St. Dominic; they have also a school for young ladies.
The building is not nearly so good a one as that for the
boys, but at the same time it is well adapted for its
purpose. The course of instruction for the deaf-mute
girls is the same as for the boys. Needlework, of
course, is added in this school. After having been a
few moments in a deaf-mute school, the silence becomes
oppressive. What a hum and murmur and stir of life
would be heard among the children of any other school!
but here these young creatures stand silently in their
places, while their speaking eyes follow us about with
an eager questioning glance, as if we could bring them
news from the world from which they are for ever shut
out. The communication of the deaf-mutes with each
other and their teachers is a mixture of talking on the
fingers and making signs. Their prayers are entirely
in the latter. We asked the Sister in charge to let the
children say a prayer before us, and accordingly they
said, or rather *acted*, the Paternoster and Ave Maria.
We were much struck by the extreme reverence of

their manner and the depth of meaning in their gestures. 'The Lord is with thee,' every head was bowed
low upon the breast, a mute confession that the Highest
had come down to the lowly, the Creator to the creature. The information the Sister (a fair, bright-looking girl of nineteen) gave us about the children tallied
with that of the Christian Brothers ; the same faults,
difficulties, and virtues characterise each sex. The
Sister told us that when she first was put in charge
over the children she could not imagine why the priest
who came to hear the children's confessions always sent
for and consumed a quantity of lucifer matches. At
last she asked the children why he wanted them.
'Why, Sister, he wants to *burn our sins*,' was the instant
reply ; and then she found that all the children who
could write preferred making their confessions in writing instead of using their peculiar language. A young
deaf-and-dumb postulant was teaching in the school.
The Sisters trust she will persevere, and that others
among the deaf-mutes may have a similar vocation.

In my walks in the Glasnevin direction I often turned
into the cemetery and wandered about its numerous
alleys. A more beautiful cemetery I do not think
could be found, thickly planted with trees and shrubs,
the paths and graves most beautifully kept ; many of
the monuments are graceful and in good taste, and
there are few of the hideous erections which disfigure
the London cemeteries. Within the cemetery rises a
'round tower,' but not 'of other days,' for it is a modern
erection and a memorial to Daniel O'Connell. Near it
is the grave of 'the Liberator,' a vault with an iron
gate, to which you descend by steps, and through which

the coffin is plainly to be seen. Offerings of flowers, *éternelles*, and laurel wreaths, freshly gathered, were lying around. And no wonder. Surely there are faithful souls enough to keep tokens ever fresh and green before the grave of him whose great heart beat only for Ireland, without thought of self; who has lain down to rest worn out by the long conflict for his loved country, but victorious, even in his death, and leaving behind him an immortal name.

CHAPTER V.

OF late years many of the foreign orders have found their way to Ireland. The Irish orders had borne the brunt of the battle, had pioneered the way, and now willingly welcomed fellow-labourers into the immense and increasing harvest-field which lay before them.

The Sisters of St. Vincent of Paul, or Sœurs de Charité, were accordingly invited to Dublin about a dozen years ago, and they immediately responded to the call. Their costume excited much attention, for the Irish Sisters of Charity and Sisters of Mercy had always worn black bonnets and cloaks when in the streets, and the white 'cornettes' of the French Sisters was a novel sight. So strong an impression did it make on the Irish mind, that in Dublin the Sisters of St. Vincent are generally spoken of as the 'white bonnets.' The Sisters took possession of a large but ancient house in North William Street, standing in a somewhat forlorn situation on the banks of a canal. It had already been the home for many years of two communities of enclosed nuns, both of whom had migrated to more suitable quarters, and the convent chapel had become the parish church. This, however, was no obstacle to the establishment of the Sisters of Charity, for, according to their holy rule, ' their chapel ' was to be ' the parish church.' The grated choir of the religious still remains, and is used by the Sisters, who to the eyes of those who know them in other countries look strangely out of place, for 'their grating,' said their holy founder, 'was to be no other than the fear of God.' Joining on to the old and dingy-looking convent of the Sisters, now stands a large handsome building in red brick, which forms the Orphanage of the Sisters, and contains over a hundred orphan girls of various ages. This building was raised and furnished by funds principally provided by the commercial young men of Dublin. The order of the Sisters of St. Vincent seems to be a favourite one with them, and they determined that a suitable orphanage should be added on to the convent. With great zeal and energy they organised a large bazaar and raffle, took the whole management into their hands, and realised so large a sum of money, that the Sisters were able to buy the ground, and then build the Orphanage. It is well built, and the arrangements are excellent. Two large schoolrooms are divided off by folding doors, which when occasion requires can be taken down, the rooms thrown together thus forming one really magnificent room. We visited the large dormitories, the lavatory, and linen room, and, finally, the industrial school department, where the orphans are taught needlework and artificial flower making. They also do the work of the house, under the direction of the Sisters, and are thus trained for servants.

Besides the Orphanage, the Sisters teach the parish day schools, and visit a large number of sick and poor. Happening to go there one Sunday, I found the Sisters busy at work in a Sunday school, which was well filled, especially by a class of girls who were not able to receive instruction in the week.

At no great distance from North William Street, the high road leads us to the quiet suburb of Richmond, consisting of green fields and lanes, with detached houses and cottages next them. Before the high green wooden gates of one of the houses we paused, and the door being unlocked by a porter, we made our way up the short avenue to a small neat villa, with a garden on one side, and large grounds at the rear. At the extreme end of these grounds, on rising ground, stood a large, newly-built house, with windows from which it would not have been easy for anyone to make their exit, and this, we were told, was the asylum, containing sixty lunatics, under the charge of the Sisters of St. Vincent de Paul. I expressed my surprise at finding the Sisters of this order in charge of such a work, having always been accustomed to see the white cornette surrounded by little children, or bending over the sick bed of the poor.

The superioress replied that the Sisters were not often called upon to take charge of the insane, and that at the present moment she believed there was only one other establishment of the kind among their many thousand houses; but that there was nothing foreign to their spirit in their doing so; for their holy founder had an especial compassion for the insane, and would have rejoiced to see his daughters called to their service. And what a service it is!

What a scene presented itself to my gaze when, accompanied by the Sisters, I went through the house! What a motley crowd all gathered together under the

ban of that common misfortune which had shut them
out from the happy homes and busy world in which
they had once had their share! Those who are tract-
able are allowed to be in the Sisters' house and the
grounds, the reception parlours only being shut off from
them.

An elegant-looking girl, with magnificent coils of
hair wreathed round her head, was playing and singing
at a piano; a nun in her habit was walking about
the grounds; a young lady of three-and-twenty was
amusing herself with a doll; another was seated under
a tree surrounded by dozens and dozens of pieces of
paper of every variety, shape, and hue—'her corre-
spondence;' and various other poor creatures were
scattered here and there, while one or two Sisters were
employing themselves in their neighbourhood, keeping
a quiet but vigilant guard.

We walked through the grounds to the asylum, and
after seeing the various parts of it, the Sisters unlocked a door, and we found ourselves within the
portion set apart for those who cannot be at all trusted
alone. We had so sooner entered than a woman flew
at me, and seizing my wrists with an iron grasp, implored me to rescue her. She had written to the Lord
Chancellor and Dr. Cullen, but her letters were in-
tercepted. The Sisters were not unkind, but they
would have it she was mad, and kept her here among
all these insane people, and it was all a conspiracy
against her. At last the Sisters prevailed on her to
release me, but she followed us about wherever we
went in that portion of the building, repeating in a
vehement manner her piteous story. There were

terrible cases in these rooms: wild, haggard-looking creatures, with their grey hair streaming on their shoulders, talking incoherently to themselves; one keeping up a perpetual moaning and weeping, and others talking incessantly and in the wildest way; and with these some of the Sisters have to pass the livelong day. We saw the bedrooms for cases like these so arranged that they cannot hurt themselves, and can tear nothing else *but* the bed clothes in pieces. These latter are very frequently found in shreds in the morning.

Close beside the Lunatic Asylum, divided only by a high wall, stood a convent of the Presentation order, built some forty years ago, and inhabited by a community of nuns who taught their poor schools, and prayed in peace. It was a terrible blow to them when the Lunatic Asylum was built. Solitude and silence fled from their pretty chapel, their quiet cells, their pleasant grounds. They could not even be at peace when they wandered to the little cemetery at the extremity of their enclosure, where some of their dearly loved companions reposed, and where they had marked out their own graves.

The Presentation nuns are, as we have before remarked, an enclosed order; each house is independent of another, and the nuns at Richmond soon found that novices would not venture within their walls for fear of their strange neighbours. Meanwhile, the lunatics had increased in number, and applications for admission had constantly to be refused. The committee who manage the asylum had to contemplate further building, and so after some years of this trying life for the

Presentation nuns, and many negotiations, an arrangement was effected. The committee purchased the
convent and grounds, and the community removed to
one of the other suburbs of Dublin. It was a great
sacrifice; many of the nuns had grown old in these
walls; every spot had its association in their eyes; here
they had peacefully lived, and here they had hoped to
die. Their chapel was particularly dear to them. It
had been built by a benefactress, and was certainly an
elegant and devotional one. However, they had the
consolation of knowing that their departure would help
on a good work, and that at the place to which they
were going poor schools were very much wanted, while
the children who had attended their schools at Richmond would be able to find instruction in neighbouring
ones. The day succeeding their departure, and on which
the Sisters of Charity took possession of their new domain, was September the twenty-seventh, the anniver-
sary of the death of St. Vincent de Paul. Benediction
was given in the little chapel, at which many of the
patients chose to be present. It was a strange and painful sight to see the places just vacated by the nuns
filled by these wild-looking creatures, attired in every
variety of costume. After Benediction, we walked
through the new grounds, and visited the nuns' cemetery, a pretty, peaceful spot. The names and ages of
the departed are inscribed on a stone tablet let into
the wall surrounding the cemetery, while a little cross
stands over each grave. We observed that many of the
Sisters had attained great ages; none had died young,
and one had reached the good old age of *ninety* years.
We asked the Sister of Charity with us if she now

would choose her grave among the vacant spaces. 'It would be of little use to do that,' she answered, smiling; '*we* must never cling to any spot on earth; orders might come from my superiors any day, and I should pack up my little blue bag, and be off.'

While standing in the cemetery and walking in the grounds we could fully appreciate the late sufferings of the nuns. Distinctly borne upon the air that still autumn day came the wild shouts and shrieks of the unfortunate inmates of the asylum. Near the convent their words could be heard distinctly, and too often these are of a nature at which the hearers shudder. We went over the empty, deserted convent and saw how it was to be adapted to its new purpose. We found that some of the nuns' cells had actually looked into a piece of ground at the back of the asylum, where the poor patients too much afflicted to mix with their more peaceable companions were allowed to take the air. At that moment two were in it leaping, dancing, and howling exactly like wild beasts. It was a sickening sight. 'One of those,' said the Sister with us, 'is a young lady of good family and fortune, handsome and accomplished. She is an excellent musician, and in her lucid intervals spends much time in music; but, when her paroxysms come on, she is in this state. But,' added the Sister cheerfully, 'she will be cured, no doubt.' She then went on to tell us that, as a rule, those violently afflicted are often cured. The quiet delusions are the most obstinate, and generally incurable. When the new buildings are ready the Sisters will receive three classes of inmates, at different rates of payment. They have a number of strong country girls as servants

to help them in the house work. They have no other
assistance, and in all the years they have managed the
asylum, have never required it. No men have ever
had to be called in to quell the violent outbursts that
will occasionally occur. The asylum is under the medical care of Dr. Fitzpatrick, whose skill and care, supported as it is by the devotion of the Sisters, has won
success for this institution, and has led to its being able
to send out a great number of cures. No words can fitly
describe the arduous nature of the task the Sisters have
undertaken for the love of God. One Sister observed
that, had she known before she entered the order that
she would ever be called upon to take care of lunatics,
she did not think she ever could have joined it. Now
that it is her appointed work she goes through it fearlessly and cheerfully. The great difficulty is to make
the patients eat ; a disinclination for food is a constant
accompaniment of madness. 'The food is poisoned,' or
' they are dead, and don't require any food,' and a dozen
other delusions are urged in answer to any entreaties. The
struggles of the Sisters at meal times with their patients
are most wearing. Dressing and undressing also are
times of woe. Not only will the patients refuse to help
themselves, but they will throw obstacles in the way
of their attendants, and be far more troublesome than
the most refractory child. Then in petty spite the insane are often ingenious. On Sundays when the Sisters
come down in clean cornettes of snowy whiteness, the
result of much starch and ironing, it is thought a great
amusement to launch a cup of coffee at their heads, and
lo! the work of some hours is undone. It is the harder
because the rule of the Sisters of St. Vincent enjoins

that they wash and get up their own cornettes. Then, what patience is required to listen to the constant rambling, the extraordinary stories, to soothe the wild delusions, to quiet the restless maniacs! Much can be done, say the Sisters, by moral influence. Incessant vigilance is required to foresee a coming storm and allay its violence. The patients have ingenious ways of hiding themselves in distant corners of the large grounds, so that, when the dinner bell rings, the Sisters may have to hunt for them. The trial of their incessant noise and restlessness must be very hard to bear, but the worst trial of all is the language which will pour forth from the lips of the violent. It is a strange phenomenon, of which no satisfactory solution has yet been given, that in insanity the mind turns to the very opposite of the direction which it took while in the exercise of its faculties. The fond wife turns against her husband, the mother forgets her child, and so, from the lips of those who were formerly gentle, refined, and earnestly religious, there flows forth foul and blasphemous language, which sickens the hearts of those compelled to listen. Religion has great influence over them: it has a softening and soothing effect on many; and then there are cases where a long lucid interval occurs, during which they can approach the sacraments. Cases which the Sisters have received from other asylums where religion formed no part of the system, were always the most difficult to manage. A beautiful account of the working of the insane asylums in Belgium, under the charge of religious Sisters, gives many examples, which the experience of the Sisters of St. Vincent bears out, of the wonderful results of

religion on the insane. Watchful care can often per-
ceive when fits of violent insanity are coming on, and,
' in these circumstances, confession is often made and
the Holy Communion received : the viaticum, as it
were, of the dolorous way through which the stricken
spirit has to pass.'* In incurable cases, lucid intervals
often occur before death, and then the Sisters are at
hand to discern the first dawn of returning reason—to
husband the precious hours—to bring to the fainting
spirit all the succours of its holy faith before its weary
journey be ended, and it has gone where there shall be
no more mists or shadows, or humiliation of the body
and intellect.

As we passed through these melancholy rooms and
grounds, bright even as the latter were with flowers and
shrubs, and watched the Sisters at their task, firm, vigilant, alert, gentle to all, bright and cheerful in manner,
and above all, perfectly calm and fearless, we wondered
at the wonderful versatility of the order of St. Vincent
de Paul—how it models its subjects for every variety of
work, enabling them to watch over every form of suffering, and to pass from one employment to another
with the greatest ease. I had last seen the superioress
of this asylum, as a Sister, in charge of the immense
' lingerie ' of the military hospital of *Val de Grâce*, in
Paris. There she had sat tranquilly among sheets and
shirts, sewing on buttons and counting out towels. Life
had flowed by her in quiet routine, and she had loved
her community well. At the instant call of obedience
she went out to another field as widely different as could
be well conceived, and here she was moving about

* *The Month*, July 1864.

among the lunatics as tranquilly and as calmly as when in her linen store, glad and joyful to be doing the will of God. 'It is not a work that any one would choose,' she observed; 'but, after all, the insane are the *most forsaken of all God's creatures.*' And I felt how true these words were, no matter in what rank they may be born—how lovable and charming they may have been —their family are afraid of them, want to hide them out of sight, and get rid of them; and as I quitted this 'home for the forsaken,' I felt that I had witnessed to what heights the self-abnegation of a Sister of Charity can attain, and rejoiced that in Ireland true-hearted women had been found who would devote themselves to the care of these afflicted and lonely beings. Though the Sisters of St. Vincent are a French order, a great number of Irish and English ladies have, of late years, joined their ranks. Some of the ancient names of England have sent daughters to swell their numbers. At the asylum the community is entirely of Irish and English Sisters. In North William Street, the superioress only is a Frenchwoman.

In Mount Street, near Merrion Square, Dublin, I found a house of Nursing Sisters, or ' Dames de Bon Sécours,' a branch of the well-known order in France. These Sisters are trained to nurse the sick; they leave their convent and go to the houses of either rich or poor, performing the work of a nurse, and doing all they can with both body and soul of their patients. They return to their convent from time to time for both bodily and mental rest. This has been found a very useful order in Ireland, and Protestants as well as Catholics often ask for the Sisters' services. When I visited the house, the whole community, with the exception of the superioress and one Sister, were out nursing. As the house is simply adapted for their residence when resting from their labours, there is, of course, nothing observable about it. The chapel, which I visited, is merely a large room fitted up with great care for the purpose.

Dublin abounds in pretty suburbs. Turn in what direction you will, you soon come to shady lanes and green fields. From the Drumcondra Road many of the former branch out; and one pleasant Sunday afternoon, when the first leaves of autumn were beginning to fall, we turned our steps towards High Park Convent. This convent, as its name denotes, stands in the midst of a small but exceedingly pretty park, which visitors see to advantage, having to walk some distance through it from the porter's lodge to the convent. The house of the former owners of the place has been converted, with additions, into a convent, and creepers grow over the front of the house, and a prettily-laid-out garden is on one side. Some hundreds of yards from this house stands a large and rather gloomy-looking building, which is used as an asylum for penitents; it is quite separate from the convent, but the penitents and the Sisters in charge of them come up often in the day to the convent chapel. At the rear of the convent is a low range of buildings, formerly out-houses, but converted with much ingenuity into habitations for human beings. The entrance to these was locked, and, on being ushered within them by a courteous nun of the Good Shepherd, we found ourselves in the midst of a number of reformatory children, who, at that moment, were in the playground. This reformatory is under government inspection, and contains about forty children, most of whom had the bold glance and the hardened manner habitual to children who have been early accustomed to sin—who have lost their innocence before they knew its value—who have been taught to curse instead of to bless—to mock instead of to reverence. Here they are undergoing the sentence of the law for some offence or other—a regiment of miniature prisoners, defiant and cunning and hard to manage, with the bloom of childhood rudely rubbed off, and with no womanly steadiness and self-respect to take its place. They formed a great contrast to the penitents whom we afterwards saw —the voluntary prisoners who, knowing their own degradation, and having tasted the bitterness of sin, have willingly entered these sheltering walls, and are trying to regain their good name, and to make their peace with God. We asked the Sister which of the two works was the most trying. She said the reformatory was by far the most arduous; the penitents were in all ways more amenable to rule and easy to manage. She told us sad histories of some of the reformatory children. One of them had come from a family of thieves—father, mother, brothers, sisters, and even grand-parents having followed the trade. She told us of others whose parents drove them out to steal—of parents waiting like harpies for the day on which their child's sentence expires, to drag it into fresh crime, utterly ignoring and defeating the efforts of the nuns to provide honest employment for it in the future. Such are some of the trials and discouragements with which the religious have to contend. To counterbalance them they have the comfort of knowing that many of the children improve during their detention; the kindness shown them softens their hearts, and they go out really reformed. Some do well afterwards; and, even in those on whom time and anxiety have been apparently wasted, there is hope that the good seed may be lying dormant and some day may bear fruit. They have, at all events, been taught what is right; their detention has been a time for learning good—not of increasing evil—and those to whose charge they have been committed can feel they have done what they could. We saw the refectory and schoolroom of the reformatory. They are well contrived in buildings which we should have thought it impossible could ever have been converted into useful rooms; but new buildings are greatly needed: neither air nor space are sufficiently allowed in the present ones, besides which room for additional children is very much required.

One great difficulty in this reformatory is the want of work; employment is absolutely necessary for the children; needlework is their only resource, and even this is hard to get. As the Government allowance for each child is by no means sufficient for all the expenses, the Sisters would be glad to get any work which would bring in a moderate profit, but they have not been able to procure such. The work we saw was exceedingly well done; we were shown some coloured shirts, requiring plenty of neat, strong work, which were supplied from a shop in Glasgow. The owner of them said he would give some more. Yes, and well might the canny Scotsman promise a supply, seeing that he paid for the making the liberal sum of half a crown per dozen, or twopence halfpenny each. The penitents are chiefly employed in laundry work, and fine large laundries are attached to their asylum.

It was the hour for vespers when we left the reformatory, and all the penitents were assembled in the chapel. Their quiet, subdued appearance and reverent manner was refreshing after seeing the poor children. The system of this asylum differs from that at Donnybrook. The women remain two years and then are provided with situations; some few, however, who wish to remain for life can do so.

The Sisters of the Good Shepherd are a French order; there are two distinct branches of them in Ireland, differing only in their form of government. The Sisters at High Park are independent of any other house, receive and train their own novices, and are entirely under the control of the bishop of the diocese.

On the road to High Park we passed the College of All Hallows, a fine extensive building surrounded by large grounds. It was a generous thought for Ireland amidst her many home wants to provide a college for missionary priests, and it has been nobly carried out. The idea of its foundation originated with a single priest, without money and influence, but with a great deal of faith, zeal, and perseverance. Around such a one others always gather, and so from a small beginning All Hallows has attained its present fair proportions, and it now receives a large number of students, and sends out priests every year to foreign missions. The chapel and library are well worth seeing.

The nuns of the Sacred Heart have also given their services to Ireland. This order was founded in France immediately after the French Revolution, and the nuns make an especial vow of devoting themselves to education. They educate both rich and poor; and in Ireland they have three convents. I was only able to visit the one near Dublin. These nuns had formerly occupied the house at Glasnevin, now the property of the Sisters of the Faith, and on removing from thence had purchased the house and grounds belonging to the late Mr. Dargan, near Stillorgan. The house is not sufficiently large for the purpose, and when I visited the convent workmen were busily employed in raising additional buildings. The grounds are magnificent, and were laid out by Mr. Dargan with admirable taste. It was at this residence that the Queen came to visit Mrs. Dargan when in Ireland, to mark her sense of the great services Mr. Dargan had rendered his country. From the tower of this house there is a magnificent view extending over several counties. The nuns have a boarding school for young ladies, and a day school for poor children.

I took a delightful drive along the western side of the Phœnix Park to visit the convent of the Sisters of St. Joseph at Mount Sackville. The park quite surpassed my expectations of its beauty ; it is indeed a park for a city to boast of, and I think the most enviable part of the Viceregal office must be the possession of the Lodge situated in the midst of this lovely domain. As we neared Mount Sackville, we had a fine view of the Strawberry Beds on the north bank of the Liffey, the favourite summer resort of Dublin residents. The house chosen for the convent stands in an excellent situation, with a lovely view on all sides, and fresh air in abundance. The Sisters of St. Joseph are a French order, and have many houses in France and the French colonies. They can undertake all works of mercy; but their house in Dublin, when I visited it, was intended only for a young ladies' school. The nuns received us most kindly, and courteously showed their little chapel, and their large garden, and gave us all the information we wanted. Their habit is picturesque, being of dark blue, with white coif and black veil.

I have already spoken of the religious institutions in the neighbourhood of Dublin, at Merrion, Black Rock, and Stillorgan. At Booterstown there is a convent of Sisters of Mercy, a branch from Baggot Street. Here are large poor schools and an orphanage.

At Kingstown is a convent of the Sisters of St. Dominic, built on an eminence, with very fine grounds, and commanding a magnificent view of the bay and mountains. This order has a school for young ladies and a poor school of eight hundred and sixty-seven children.

An orphanage managed by ladies, and called St. Joseph's, is well worth a visit. Some of the ladies who superintend it live in their own families, and give to it what time they can spare; others live altogether with the children. The latter seemed particularly well-trained, bright, and intelligent. Their singing was very good; one little creature had an exquisite voice, and was besides so exceedingly pretty that she especially needed a safe shelter and a careful training to prepare her for her future life.

I believe the plan of keeping the children till they are quite grown up is in operation at this orphanage, and that so far the result has been satisfactory.

The orphanage stands in a good situation adjoining fields ; there is no wall around the garden, and all is free and open, forming a strange contrast to its neighbour a quarter of a mile off, the celebrated ' Birds' Nest,' whose dismal playground shut in by high walls and locked dormitory, denote its true character—a prison for Catholic children.   The girls of St. Joseph among their other accomplishments are taught to bake bread, a most useful preparation for domestic service. The bread seemed to us excellent, and the elder girls take great pride in making it so.   The children looked thoroughly happy, and evidently every effort of the cheerful beaming superintendent was directed to making them so, and bringing them up to be useful and happy in the future.

CHAPTER VI.

NOTWITHSTANDING the arrival of so many foreign orders, and the rapid increase and growth of those of native birth, Ireland is still putting forth new blossoms of good works and devoted lives. A new religious congregation of women has recently been canonically erected by the Cardinal Archbishop of Dublin, under the title of Sisters of the Holy Faith, and closely connected with it is an excellent and charitable work known as St. Brigid's Orphanage. To speak of it rightly brings me to a painful subject, and one on which I would fain not touch, but that it is impossible to avoid it; I mean the disgraceful practice of what is called *souperism*. In looking into the past history of Ireland we have seen the various efforts made to draw the poor Irish, and especially their children, from their ancient faith. But as years have passed on, and at the present day when some of the rooted prejudices of our fathers have been torn up, and when the Irish Catholics have made such great efforts to educate their own children, in spite of difficulties, we should have imagined that this form of persecution would have vanished away, and been among the things that were. On the contrary, it is lively and rampant to the present day; more rancorous,

more bitter, and more unprincipled than ever. ' Souperism,' indeed, may be said to have attained its full
maturity at the very time when the dictates of mere
humanity would, we should have thought, have silenced
it for ever. The time of the Irish famine ! We know—
nay, rather, alas ! we do not rightly know that lamentable history.   Sitting at home by our comfortable
English firesides, we did not fully estimate the sufferings of that slow, lingering death by starvation.   We
can hardly realise the scenes witnessed at pleasant
country houses in Ireland when the lawn would be
covered by gaunt hungry forms, strong men wasted to
a shadow, women with dying children in their arms
calling out to the mistress of the house, ' Don't be
afraid, ma'am; if you have nothing for us, tell us so and
we will go quietly away.' At such a time as this, when
the brave and patient people were in the throes of their
strong agony, the detestable (may we not say dia-
bolical ?) system of *souperism* put forth a new and
strong development.

The agents and helpers of this society, which is
called by many names, and has various branches, were
not ashamed to tempt the starving man to sell his soul ;
were not ashamed to snatch the child from its mother's
arms, promising food and shelter at the price of that
child's faith.   No one can ever forget the efforts that
were made in England to assist the Irish in their dire
distress.   Government did much, and private charity
was not behindhand. Crowds of Protestants gave relief
to the poor Irish, neither asking nor caring whether
they were Catholics or not, and numbers of generous
hearts in England sent large alms to their suffering

fellow-creatures with no thought of anything save of
their misery. But there were others whose course was
very different, and who took advantage of the misery
of the poor to tamper with their consciences. And
deep was the injury they did to Ireland. Not on
account of their converts—for after all their pains and
their expenditure, the numbers are very small, and
those whom they have perverted are precisely those
whose loss is little felt—but on account of the bitter
feeling against England which their proceedings tend
to keep up in the minds of large classes of the Irish.
At the time of the famine much might have been done
to cement a cordial feeling between the two countries,
if help and sympathy had been given with universal
generosity. When Irish people are doing their utmost
to relieve the wants of their poor, giving up their
patrimony, and devoting their whole lives to the cause
of education or the works of mercy, or when good
undertakings are being raised up and supported by
the pence of the poor, what effect must the proceedings
of a body like the Irish Church Missions produce
on them? Here they see 26,000*l*. sent from England
annually, for no other purpose than to try to undo
or to mar the efforts of their whole lives. They see
starving Protestants neglected in order that starving
Catholics may be tempted. They see ladies and gentlemen, when they find themselves unable to turn the
poor man from his faith, bribing him to give up his children to be brought up in one which they must know
that in his secret heart he disbelieves, and they see
this work wrought by English gold and too often by
English hands, supported by noble names, patronised

sometimes by the very rulers whom they are bound to
respect; and then at the same instant they are told
that in England truth and honour are valued beyond
all other possessions.   The latter assertion must seem
to them a mockery, and the whole proceeding must
tend, and does tend, to estrange them from a
country from which they have a right to expect better
treatment.   The progress of the soupers with the
adult poor is very slow; they only succeed in obtaining
the nominal conversion of handfuls of them, who are
unable to resist the tempting offers made to them.   A
story told at the time of the famine may be taken as
a fair illustration of the way in which adult converts
are made.

A poor man sorely tried by hunger made up his
mind to 'turn souper.' He went into a Catholic
church and looking at the altar with its Tabernacle
said, 'Good-bye, God Almighty! when the famine's over
I'll come back to ye.' Dr. Forbes, in his 'Memorandums in Ireland,' says, 'the conversion movement
originated in the year of famine,' a fact which of itself
would be enough to throw suspicion upon it. In truth,
so unsatisfactory have the adult converts proved, so
addicted are they to the practice of what is called
'jumping' back to their ancient creed, to sending for
a priest in their last moments, and otherwise disappointing their patrons, that the efforts of the soupers
are now more exclusively directed to another branch
of mischief more costly, but far more sure of success
—the perversion of children.

A bad Catholic in Ireland can always sell his
children if he only apply at the right quarter, and

orphanages of various kinds and under various names have been raised for the sole purpose of receiving these Catholic children.

So pressing and increasing became this evil that it was determined in Ireland to make a strenuous effort to resist it, and St. Brigid's Society took its rise for this purpose, placing itself under the patronage of a well loved Irish saint. Its object was to receive such children as were in danger of losing their faith, and the founders of the charity were determined not to relax their efforts till five hundred children should have been rescued.

The mode of management of this institution is almost *unique*, and could not be carried out in any country so well (if indeed practicable at all) as in Ireland. Instead of placing the children in an orphanage and thus incurring the expense of building or renting a house with its inevitable cost of management, the children of St. Brigid are placed with respectable peasants in the country, who are paid for each child's board and clothing. These families are carefully selected, and are bound by certain rules in regard to the children, such as that they shall be kept clean and tidy and sent to school.

Generally, several children are placed in one parish, which seems to keep up an emulation among these foster-parents. At certain times the managers of St. Brigid's go to the place where the orphans are and hold an examination, and prizes are given to the parents, consisting of ten shillings for each child that proves to have been kept up to the standard which the managers have laid down for it. The plan has answered admirably; the work of St. Brigid's has been visibly blessed; funds have flowed in and helpers have come forward; and, in 1866, when the tenth report of the society was put forth, the managers were able to state that 622 orphans had since 1857 passed under their care. It is curious to look at the subscription list of this charity; there is but one sum which would be reckoned in England as a large subscription; but as the amounts decrease in size they increase in number, till at last it becomes evident that the mite of the poor man and the hardly-won money of the middle class have been largely given to aid in this good work. This work was set on foot by a lady named Miss Margaret Aylward, whose early exertions in behalf of the poor were rewarded by six months' imprisonment on most unjust grounds. After her release other ladies gathered round her, and by degrees a religious community has sprung into being. These Sisters, besides undertaking the large amount of work which the management of such a widely-scattered family as the children of St. Brigid must entail, have opened in various parts of Dublin six poor schools, for besides the orphanages the 'soupers' have started poor schools, where clothing, food, and other bribes are freely given, and the Sisters of the Faith found that additional schools to the existing ones were needed to combat this evil. After the labours of the day the Sisters retire to a beautiful convent at Glasnevin, surrounded by extensive grounds, through which the little river Tolka takes its way. Glasnevin was in early ages the home of saints. St. Columba 'came to the little monastery of Glasnevin near Dublin and found himself to his great delight in the company of St. Comgal,

St. Canice, and St. Kieran.' It is therefore a fitting
site for a religious house, and suited for those whose
special mission is to sustain in Ireland the faith that
these great saints sought to plant.

It is chiefly in Ireland that children could be safely
placed in country villages and left to the guardianship
of the peasants. In many parts of England and
Scotland immorality is as rife in the country as in
towns; in Ireland, whatever may be the faults of the
people, the innocence of children is safe among the
peasantry. In Ireland only would one remarkable
result of placing the children among peasants be
attained. Many of the people insist on adopting the
orphans, some before their time ' on the books ' of
St. Brigid's is expired, and others as soon as the
managers announce that they must remove the children and place them out to earn their own living. The
report of St. Brigid's for 1865 states that twenty children were thus adopted ; in 1866, twenty-seven. The
managers of St. Brigid's rejoice greatly over this fact,
not on account of their release from responsibility and
expense, but because the poor orphan has now found
what St. Brigid's could not give him—a *home*. And
this leads me to say a word on the vexed question of
orphanages, and the relative merits of the system
of St. Brigid's, and that of the more usual one of
bringing up the children in large masses under the
care of religious. It is in Ireland chiefly that a
discussion of this question is useful, for the plan of
St. Brigid's has never yet been tried on a large
scale in England. In England the present plan of
orphanages is a necessity, and it is certain that in

Ireland the existence of both systems is also a necessity. There are some cases which can only be properly
dealt with in regular orphanages.

As regards St. Brigid's, the benefits seem to be as
follows: First, economy—no slight recommendation
when people have to contend against the lavish out-
pouring of English wealth on the wrong cause; the
Sisters of the Faith maintain 256 orphans, and manage
six day schools, with an income of 1,903*l*. Secondly,
their system tends to provide the children with homes
and friends of their own, and thus to prevent them from
ever being such waifs and strays of humanity as poor
orphans often run a chance of becoming. Even in the
cases when the foster-parents cannot adopt them, they
have a great affection for them, and always look on them
as bound to themselves by a certain tie. Thirdly, they
are more fitted for the rough path in life they have to
pursue. The child in the orphanage is brought up too
tenderly; her life flows on in an easy routine; she is
under the care of kind and gentle teachers, striving to be
just in all their dealings with her; food and clothing come
to her without any trouble. It is true she is taught to
work for the general good, but not for her own individual
wants and needs, and all this produces a tendency to
helplessness. When she goes out of the peaceful convent, and hears rough words, and meets the petty injustice, thoughtlessness, and selfishness which those who
live in the world must meet, she is dismayed, frets to
get back again, and finding that impossible, often gives
up the struggle in despair. On the other hand, the
advocates of the old system plead that in Irish country
cabins you cannot train the children in proper habits

of cleanliness, order, and industry; you cannot fit them for domestic service; you reduce them to a lower level, instead of raising them to a higher; that if well brought up in orphanages they will be able to provide for themselves, and so gain friends, and have homes of their own. It will be seen that the arguments on both sides apply principally to girls; indeed, for boys I think it is a matter of indifference under which system they are brought up, but for girls it is really an important question. The report of St. Brigid's states that the children placed out in the world are doing well, with a very few exceptions. The greatest fault to be found with the old orphanage management—and this equally applies to England—is that it does not train orphan girls to be good servants. The want of good domestic servants is becoming a serious evil, and the tendency of girls of the lower classes to reject this mode of livelihood, and adopt others of 'more freedom, more independence,' is certainly injurious to them, and it is but natural to expect that orphanages would do something to stem this evil. Yet the complaints of those who take servants from these institutions are all but universal, and cannot, therefore, be considered as the prejudices of a few. The great cause, we believe, arises from sending out the children far too young. The French orphanages, which *do* train good servants, keep their girls till they are twenty-one. It is the custom in our orphanages to send out the girls at fourteen or fifteen, before the character is formed, the principles strengthened, or the habit of steady exertion has been formed. At eighteen or nineteen a girl may wish to see the world even if it cost her some trouble, may be tired of living a dull and monotonous life, and of being treated like a child, but she will have overcome these feelings when four or five years younger.

The managers of St. Brigid's are able to record with thankfulness that not one of their children has been sent to a reformatory or prison, or even brought before a magistrate.

Touching anecdotes can be told of the affection and gratitude of the orphans. A little boy, when placed out to service, came to the Sisters with his Christmas box of four shillings. Another, in announcing a rise in his wages, said, ' Then I can support my poor mother, and I'll pay for two of the orphans too.'

As an instance of the affection of the foster-parents, the following may be given: A little boy, after being four years on the books, gave signs of idiocy: it was necessary to send him to the union, as he could not be a permanent burden on the orphanage; but when the nurse heard of it, she said she would adopt him. ' Is he of any service to you?' was asked. ' What service could the poor boy be to me? But he is a loving child, and if he must be put off the books, I'll keep him, I'll be a mother to him.' Such, then, is the history of St. Brigid's, ' a simple story of a good work silently, laboriously, and successfully carried on.'

There are many charitable institutions in Dublin under the management of seculars instead of religious. The most remarkable of these is the Night Refuge for women and children. It is situated in the worst and most wretched part of Dublin, 'the Liberties,' and therefore easily to be found by the miserable class of people for whom it is intended. This admirable institution was founded by an excellent priest, the Rev. Dr. Spratt, and has continued for many years under his care. He has been fortunate in securing a building well suited for the purpose, an old warehouse containing three floors, and surrounded by a large yard. In this yard are large wooden doors which unclose at five in the evening, and remain open till nine o'clock, to admit homeless wanderers. The first floor of the Refuge contains the very poorest class who apply for admission, the homeless and the starving, to whom a great charity is done; the beds consist simply of a mattrass and rug laid in a sort of open wooden box, one close beside the other. A greater charity still to our minds is given to the inmates of the second floor; here are iron bedsteads, not so close together, and a greater air of comfort is apparent; it is meant for the bettermost poor who may be reduced to utter penury. I call it a greater charity, because the misery of this class, when brought to extremity, is greater than that of the very poor. The loss of shelter to them is shameful, as well as hard, and they are often driven into sin for want of it. The third floor is much smaller than those below, a sort of loft in fact. Here we find an altar and crucifix; here night and morning prayers are said, in which the inmates may join; and here once a year mass is offered up, and that solitary occasion is the feast of *Christmas*. Could a better day be found than the birthday of Him for whom in a whole city there was no room, and whose birth took place in a poorer place even than a night refuge?

Every night the inmates of the Refuge receive a piece of dry bread, and in too many cases this is the only food they taste in the day. The funds do not allow that even this poor relief should be given on the week day mornings, but it is bestowed on Sundays, as there is so little chance of the poor people getting any elsewhere. All the inmates must leave the Refuge at eight in the morning, and the doors are then closed till five in the evening, when the ' refugees ' begin to flow in; the matron takes her place at a table, and inscribes in a book the name and occupation of each comer. It is left to her discernment to know who shall be sent to the upper dormitory. Persons in every kind of employment have sought refuge here. Governesses, dressmakers, seamstresses, domestic servants, some more, some less respectable, have implored shelter in these charitable walls; and the mercy extended to them does not end with giving them rest, shelter, and food, their case is enquired into, and, if possible, means are devised for giving them a fresh start, and taking them out of the wretched class of mendicants. Many a poor creature has been saved from despair, many a wounded heart comforted by this kindly charity; and many sins prevented—who can count up the sins avoided by the poor inmates for even *one single night?* Every evening the Rev. Dr. Spratt comes himself to the Refuge, and sees that all is going on well. Here he is truly like a father amidst his children, a wretched and miserable crowd, dirty and footsore, homeless and friendless, cold and hungry, but still the children of that heavenly Father who rejects no one, and whose example His faithful servant is thus following. This good priest is also responsible for the whole expense of the institution, and has of course to beg for it the alms

of the charitable. Like every other work of charity it is
capable of being imposed upon; but we imagine that
the *simplicity* of the accommodation would prevent
any but those in real need from availing themselves
of it.

A brief record of the numbers admitted each week
to the Refuge appears in the *Freeman's Journal.* I
extract the following at hazard :—

'THE NIGHT REFUGE.—Weekly return of admis-
sions into St. Joseph's Night Refuge, Brickfield Lane,
Cork Street, Dublin, of homeless women, girls, and
children of good character, who there received nightly
shelter and partial support for the week ending March
21, 1867 : Servants, 229 ; children, 68 ; children's
maids, 28 ; cooks, 23 ; laundresses, 31 ; plain workers,
44 ; shirtmakers, 24 ; dressmakers, 9 ; school teachers,
7 ; bootbinders, 10 ; petit dealers, 27 ; factory girls, 36 ;
knitters, 42 ; travellers, 29 ; shopwomen, 7 ; scourers,
38—total, 651.'

In Mecklenburgh Street, Dublin, is a penitentiary
containing thirty-three women under the charge of a
matron. It does not differ from the ordinary aspect of
such institutions, except in the circumstances of its
foundation. Bridget Burke was a poor widow, who
after her husband's death became a domestic servant.
While in this employment she began to take a lively
interest in the fallen of her own sex, and rescued one
after another of them from evil courses. A good man
about the same rank in life as herself helped her, and
at last proposed to her that they should take a house in
which to receive penitents. 'But,' exclaimed Bridget,
'sure we have no money.'—'Let us have confidence in

God,' he answered; 'let us place it under the protection of the Blessed Trinity.   They knelt down together and prayed.   On rising, Mr. Quarterman said, ' Here is a penny.'   Bridget gave another; a third was contributed by her daughter, and with this sum they commenced their undertaking; they began to collect, and most of their funds came from the poor, chiefly domestic servants, and so the work prospered and grew into its present form.   Many of the poor creatures rescued by Bridget, after a probation, found employment, and did exceedingly well : some married; and touching stories are told of the gratitude that many evinced to the charitable woman, who out of her own poverty had thus aided them in their dire necessity.

Not far from the convent of North William Street is a building with somewhat of a conventual appearance, although it is unfortunately not under the care of religious.   It is an asylum popularly called the ' Old Maids' Home,' and intended to receive respectable single women when age and failing health have made them unable to earn their own bread.   The building is well adapted to its purpose; and there is a little chapel attached to the house, where mass is daily said ; a chapel that would be pretty if it were only clean. This institution proved by no means a pleasant sight; from one end to the other it was extremely dirty, untidy, and forlorn looking.   The infirmary, in which were several sick women, was fearfully close, and was in terrible need of ventilation.   The matron seemed a most unfit person for the charge.   She was far too old, bent, feeble, had lost all her teeth—in fact was almost decrepid.   It is impossible she can rightly manage such an institution; none of the inmates looked comfortable or cared for. I wished for a fairy wand to be able to put the institution under the charge of the Sisters of Charity, or the 'Little Sisters of the Poor,' and then to behold the change that their arrival would create. Soap and water, fresh air, and a wholesome atmosphere would attend their footsteps, and the poor inmates' faces would brighten, and peace and content reign in the house.

There are various confraternities and guilds in Dublin, in fact far too numerous to be noticed at any length. Bands of men and women join together for prayer or good works and meet at certain hours. One great use of these confraternities is the high tone they tend to keep up in their members; any member guilty of a serious offence would be disgraced before his fellow-members and expelled from their company. The Confraternity of the Sacred Heart were most under my notice, as they came for their devotions to the church of St. Francis Xavier, Gardiner Street, near which I happened to reside. A number of men, apparently respectable mechanics, met the first five evenings of the week, at eight p.m. They did not need any priest to direct their devotions, but performed them among themselves, if not very melodiously, at least very fervently. It was a picturesque sight to see the group with their lighted candles at the bottom of the nave, while the rest of the large handsome church, with its side chapels, was hidden in gloom, lighted only by the dim rays of the altar lamp. This church on Friday and Saturday evenings is also a sight worthy the attention of a tourist. It is literally filled with people waiting their

turn around one of the fourteen confessionals.   There
may be seen people of every rank, of every position
in life, but notably the poor, in earnest attentive groups.
It is a moving phalanx.   The people who were there
before seven gradually move on, confess, and depart;
they are succeeded by others, and it is long past ten
o'clock before the numbers begin to thin.

On Sunday morning the scene is equally remarkable.
The masses commence at six, and continue every half-
hour till noon; often three or four masses are going on
at different altars at the same moment.   At all these are
crowds of communicants, and a priest has to descend to
the communion rails, placed in the nave, to communicate
the mass of people, who would otherwise obstruct the
way. This is not peculiar to St. Francis Xavier's; the
same scene might be witnessed at the Cathedral in
Marlborough Street, St. Dominic's, and many of the
other large churches in Dublin.   The most ordinary
spectator could hardly fail to be struck with the fervour
and devotion of these crowded congregations.   There is
little ceremonial in Dublin except at the Cathedral
Church, where the offices are grandly performed; but
elsewhere beauty of ceremonial is little regarded, and
certainly it has not been by 'appealing to the senses'
that the faith of the Irish has been sustained.   The
beauties of architecture, rare paintings, stained windows, good church music, incense, and gorgeous
vestments, were for centuries unknown to the Irish
people; but without any of these things their faith
was fervent and clear, and their devotion intense and
fruitful.

CHAPTER VII.

DROGHEDA is easily reached by rail from Dublin—the
line running a great part of the way along the coast,
and giving the traveller pleasant sea views. The great
lion of the place is, of course, the viaduct which spans
the River Boyne, at a height of 90 feet. The railway
passes over it, and it is a curious sight, when standing
on *terra firma*, to watch the progress of the train over
the perilous height. Viewed from the railway station,
Drogheda is a most picturesque town, divided in two
parts by the River Boyne, the ' nun-faced river,' broad
and clear, with a crowd of shipping lying on her waters.
The town has a singularly twofold character, standing
in two counties, two ecclesiastical provinces, and two
dioceses. The busy part of the town lies in a deep
valley, and the descent from the railway station is a
sharp one. Half-way down, my attention was attracted
by a pretty Gothic building, surrounded by shrubs and
flowers. On enquiry, I found it to be the poorhouse,
and then the mullioned windows and pretty ornaments
appeared a great mockery of the misery within. Climbing a steep and dirty lane behind the poorhouse, I
gained the heights commanding a good view of the town,
and found myself on the spot from which the batteries

of Cromwell first opened on the devoted city, and from
whence he directed the siege.   At no great distance
stands St. Mary's Protestant Church, an ugly modern
building, which occupies the site of the Church of St.
Mary of Mount Carmel, that fell the first day that
Cromwell's cannon began to play upon the town.   In
the churchyard still stands a fragment of the old walls,
covered with moss—all that has survived the batteries
of Cromwell and the ravages of time.   Descending a
long flight of steps leading from St. Mary's, I found
myself in the streets, and found also, alas ! that the
enchantment lent by distance had vanished, and that
Drogheda was a very dirty old town.   It was raining,
and the streets were literally a sea of black mud, and it
was a relief to make a temporary halt at the Imperial
Hotel, where cleanliness, comfort, and civility reigned
supreme.   Leaving the centre of the town, and climbing the hill on the north side, I came to St. Peter's
Church, also modern and Protestant, but of better
architecture than St. Mary's.   It occupies the site of
the ancient St. Peter's Church, and the principal scene
of the horrors of that most horrible siege, when ' there
was no mercy for man, or woman, or child.'   ' The
grey old veteran of a hundred fights and the little child
of a year old ; the fair-faced Leinster woman, singing
her Irish song as the tall Tipperary grenadiers strode
up the hill ; the brilliant young English cavalier and
the wild Wicklow chief ; the grave alderman at the
Thorsel ; the circumspect gunner at the Millmount ;
priest of hoary head, and lady of high degree—all alike
doomed to mingle their blood in a stream full enough to
flow from the steps of St. Peter's Church to the river

wharves.'* For four days the carnage raged, till the
Parliamentary soldiers were able to report that it was
finished and ' none spared.'

Drogheda seems to abound in Catholic churches. I
went into three, and learned there were several others.
The town is now well supplied with religious orders:
Augustinian, Dominican, and Franciscan monks have
each their church, in addition to those of the parishes.
Passing along the streets we saw a poor woman standing
at the door of one of the houses. It opened, and a
white cornette, the well-known head-dress of the Sisters
of St. Vincent, peeped out to answer the call. I speedily
made my way to the same portal, and was kindly welcomed by the superioress. It happened to be a Saturday, ' our busiest day,' said the good Sister, ' on which
I am transformed into a banker's clerk. We have
under our care a home for factory girls, whose Saturday
afternoon is free, and who come to pour their wages
into my hands, and insist on their accounts being kept
for them.' In the same street with the convent another
house has been taken by the Sisters, in which between
forty and fifty factory girls are lodged. Here the homeless and friendless, and those whose own homes are scenes
of temptation, may take refuge. Here they are lodged
and boarded, and have firing, candles, and soap for 3s. a
head per week—and the institution is entirely self-supporting, although the wages and board of two servants
have to be paid out of the funds, for the factory hours
do not allow the girls time to do their own cooking and
cleaning. I made enquiries about the bill of fare, and,

* *Dublin Review*, January 1866.

although I found meat (always a rare luxury with the
Irish poor) was not tasted more than twice a week, it
comprised soup and potatoes for dinner, porridge for
breakfast, and the dearly-loved comforts of butter and
tea. The house is large, roomy, and airy. Two Sisters
sleep there, and at half-past four every morning, no
matter at what time of year or in what weather, have
to traverse the short distance from the home to the convent, and join the community at meditation.   At half-
past five they return to the home to read morning
prayers with the girls, who must be at the factory by
six.   At eight they return to breakfast, and must be
at the factory again at nine.   From one to two is the
dinner hour, and at six the day's work is over.   Their
evenings till nine o'clock are free, but the Sisters have
evening classes for them, to which they persuade them
to come.   The superioress herself superintends the
class for needlework, which she is very anxious they
should attend.   Their occupation is rough and hardening enough, and she is desirous that they should learn
the art so necessary for a woman's own comfort and respectability, and so likely to render them better wives
and mothers if they marry.   At nine o'clock there are
night prayers, and the doors are closed for the night,
and no one can stay out after that hour.   This little
community, therefore, consists of girls who wish to lead
a steady respectable life, for the wild ones would not
submit to these few wholesome restraints.   Their love
and confidence for the Sisters is strong.   On Saturday
afternoon, as we have said, they bring their money to
' Mother,' as they insist on calling the superioress, and
require her to manage it for them.   She has first to

deduct the 3s. due to the house, and then to enter the balance remaining to each girl, and to advise as to the disposal of it.   Then she has to decide on the respective merits of various bonnets, shawls, and gowns, for they are never happy till their purchases are exhibited to and approved of by the Sisters.   The girls are a light-hearted set—living in the present and thinking little of the future.   ' I cannot help laughing sometimes,' said the superioress, ' at the very sound of their merry bursts of laughter.'   Nevertheless their life is a hard one, and disease and death overtake them sooner than other women.   The exposure to all weathers tells upon their constitutions.   The sound of the factory bell must be obeyed to the instant, no matter whether it be through rain, snow, or wind ; and they often arrive at the factory wet to the skin, yet obliged to work for four hours without changing clothes or shoes.   The Sisters desire to add on to the home an asylum for them in sickness or premature old age; but, for this purpose, funds are needed.   I have rarely seen a charitable work which appealed more to my sympathy than this.   It is so completely helping the poor to help themselves—keeping up in the girls a spirit of honest independence while giving them at the same time the protection and guidance they require at their age and in their position—guarding them from continual and terrible temptations to sin.   Besides the factory girls there are a few young dressmakers' apprentices, from the country, serving their time, and thus under safe protection while away from their own homes.   An interesting story was told us in connection with this home.   A travelling pedlar, with his wife and three little girls, often passed through Drogheda, and stayed a while in the town. The three children then went to school at the Presentation Convent, and in all their future wanderings never forgot the lessons they received from their kind teachers. While they were in Dublin the father died, and the mother, unable to support her children, was tempted to sell them to the ' soupers.' A clergyman of this school offered to take the three children off her hands provided he might bring them up Protestants. While the poor mother was wavering, the children themselves took the matter in hand, ran off to a priest, told their tale, and assured him that if they could only get back to Drogheda the Presentation nuns would take charge of them. The priest paid their fares, and the little group presented itself at the doors of the Presentation Convent. A consultation took place between the good nuns and the Sisters of St. Vincent: the result was that the three girls were received into the home. The two eldest go to the factory, and earn their own support; the youngest attends the Presentation school, and the expenses of her support are shared by the nuns and the Sisters. The Sisters of St. Vincent have a large night school, which is well attended. They also visit the poor of half the town, and this is a more than usually arduous task, for the people are miserably poor, and there is a very small proportion of the wealthier classes. Many manufacturers make money in Drogheda, but when it is made they hasten to spend it in pleasanter localities.

Close beside the Sisters' house stands the old gate of St. Lawrence, the only one left of the ten gates which once guarded the town. There is a portion still remaining of the West, or Butter Gate, but no vestige of the others.

St. Lawrence's gate is entire, and an excellent specimen of mediæval architecture, consisting of two circular towers of considerable height, pierced with loop holes. A short distance from the outer side of the gate we found ourselves at the door of the 'Sienna Convent,' so called because it is dedicated to St. Catherine of Sienna. This convent is one of the second order of St. Dominic, and the nuns are enclosed. The convent at Drogheda has a long and eventful history attached to it. The last victim put to death at Tyburn under the penal laws was Oliver Plunkett, Archbishop of Armagh, who suffered July 11th, 1681. In his letters from Newgate he spoke with his usual tenderness of the relations who would have to mourn his loss, and among the others he spoke of his niece, 'little Catherine.' The little girl grew up, inheriting some of her uncle's zeal and devotion, and at an early age entered a Dominican convent in Brussels. When it was decided to make a new foundation of the order in Ireland, Catherine was appointed prioress, and Drogheda was fixed upon as the scene of her labours. A mud cabin in the outskirts of the town was the first convent; from thence they removed to a small house in Dyer Street, a narrow and wretched *locale*. They dressed as seculars and were not known to be nuns, but were notwithstanding faithful and loving children of St. Dominic. By degrees, as the clouds of persecution began to hang less heavily over the land, the nuns began to build a house ostensibly as a school for young ladies; they devoted themselves to education for the twofold object

of supporting the community, and concealing their
religious profession. All appearance of a conventual
building was carefully avoided, and a plain, solid looking house of grey stone was completed. It is surrounded by a large garden, and thus removed from the
bustle of the streets; being also built on the heights
overhanging the town, it commands a fine view of the
Boyne and adjacent country. On one occasion, while
the penal laws were still in force, the house was visited
by government officials 'searching for nuns.' Catherine Plunkett had by that time gone to her rest, and
the prioress who held her place received them. Her
dress, appearance, and composed manner removed all
suspicion from herself, and when the officers asked her
if there were any nuns in the house, she replied with
true woman's wit, ' They are no more nuns than I am.'
The officers were satisfied with the reply, and withdrew.
At length brighter times began to dawn, and the nuns
were able to put on their habit, and some of the
older religious of the convent now can well remember
that day of joy. Like so many of the ancient Irish
convents, this house is full of traditions of saintly lives
among those whose consecration to God was unknown
to the world around them, and who, by perseverance
under terror, hardship, and difficulty, won for the
daughters who were to come after them a peaceful
heritage. And a benediction has rested on the house.
Gradually precept after precept of their holy rule has
been put in force, although the difficulty of uniting its
strict observance with the care of a large school is very
great. There is also a poor school attached to the
convent. When St. Dominic framed the rule for the

second order, he did not contemplate the union of active duties with the precepts which he imposed. The nuns have resumed the singing of the Divine office in choir, and as the ' vesper bell' sounded before my visit was concluded, I went into the exterior chapel to be present at the service. Vespers were followed by compline, and it was a striking and picturesque sight. The choir was filled with religious in their habits and scapulars of white serge, the professed nuns with black, the novices with white veils. The community possesses among its members several voices of great power and sweetness, and the chanting was very lovely. While the ' Salve Regina,' which concludes the compline office, was being sung, the nuns came down from their stalls, and passed in procession before the Prioress, who sprinkled them with holy water, according to an ancient custom of the Dominican order.

Sienna Convent possesses another object of great interest, which often brings strangers on a pilgrimage to its doors. The head of the martyred Archbishop Plunkett was placed in this convent by one of his successors in the see of Armagh, to whom it was granted from Rome. The mangled remains of the Archbishop were after his death given to his friends, who interred them close beside the grave of Father Whitbread and four other Jesuits, also martyrs at Tyburn, ' under the north wall in St. Giles.' The head and arms from the elbow were placed in a separate case. Two years afterwards the precious remains were removed to a Benedictine monastery at Lambspring, Germany. The head was placed in a silver shrine and sent to Rome, and was for a long time preserved in a Dominican convent there. But it was fitting that the relic should belong to the country for which the Archbishop had laid down his life; and Sienna Convent, founded as it had been by Catherine Plunkett, was undoubtedly the most fitting place for it. It is kept in a little oratory opening from the reception parlour, enshrined in a little ebony temple, with four silver pillars. The skull is of a dark brown colour, but quite perfect, and the features are plainly to be recognised, and give evidence that some of the existing likenesses of Dr. Plunkett are very good ones. With mingled feelings of many kinds, I stood and knelt before the relic. Here was the silent record of Ireland's past; bitter persecution met by undaunted courage, faith, and patience to the end. Standing by me were the white-robed nuns, records of Ireland's present putting forth daily new strength and vigour, and giving promise for the future. An old gray-headed bishop, whom English justice could not spare, was yet more honoured in his death, his memory more cherished and reverenced, than were ever any of her proud and prosperous men. And he too was the *last* on whom Tyburn's cruel work was done; he was the witness and the seal of that long list of victims—the noble, the talented, and the holy, some in the flower of their days, some in declining years, both English and Irish—who had offered their lives for the faith.

After taking leave of the kind and courteous nuns, I pursued my way to the cemetery outside the town, bearing the curious name of the ' Cord,' it is supposed because it was originally the burial-place of a convent of Poor Clares in the olden time. This, how-

ever, is simply a tradition: no traces whatever exist
of the convent. From the cemetery I had a magnificent view of the Boyne, the viaduct, and the south
side of the town; I found myself standing exactly
facing the spot on the opposite heights which I had
reached in the morning, and on which Cromwell's
batteries had been placed. An old labouring man was
passing through the cemetery, and was very willing
to answer any questions. 'Yes, it had always been
supposed that there were nuns on this spot; and that
walk,' said he, pointing to a path shaded by trees, 'was
for many years called the "nuns' walk."' After
returning to the town, and passing once more through
St. Lawrence's Gate, I turned to the right, and made
my way up streets built on rising ground to Magdalene tower, the only vestige yet left of the Dominican monastery existing before the siege. The
tower is very beautiful, and I should have been glad
to get close to it; but it was so surrounded by hovels
of the dirtiest description that it was impossible. While
I was walking about, trying to get the best view I
could, a man came up whose costume was a curiosity;
it consisted of a mass of rags, and the wonder was how
they all managed to keep together. There did not
seem to be half a yard whole among them; but there
they hung, dirty but picturesque, and crowned by
shaggy locks and a tattered hat, from beneath which
shone out two large bright Irish eyes. To him the
humorous lines might certainly have been applied—

> And if my poor parents should want to discover me,
> Sure it won't be by describing my clothes.

He looked at me, his face lighted up, and he wanted

to know if I were going to sketch the 'tower.' I said
'No,' but I wished I could see it to better advantage;
whereupon he volunteered to pilot me through one
of the hovels to the foot of the tower. This offer I
declined, but I was struck by the lively interest the
poor fellow took in the old ruin: the siege, and
Cromwell, and the monks were all pat on his lips; the
history of the past was a vivid and familiar thing to
him. He did not beg, but seemed to regard my investi-
gation of the 'ould tower' as a personal compliment to
himself. On the south side of the town stand the
large schools and convent of the Sisters of Mercy.
This, to my regret, I had not time to visit; but I learned
that the education of the poor girls, and the visitation
of the sick of all on this side of Drogheda, was undertaken by this community. I did not leave Drogheda
without driving to see the celebrated ruins of Monasterboice, about three or four miles from the town.
They have been so often described in Irish travels, that
I will not dwell on them, or endeavour to describe the
round tower, the two ruined churches, and the wonderfully sculptured crosses to be found closely grouped
together in this lonely spot. On my journey to and
from Monasterboice, I had a specimen of the Irish car-
driver, who, on my asking him if he had spent all his
life in Drogheda, replied, 'Sure, havn't I been to
England?'—'How long did you live there?'—'Sure
and thin I went one day, and came back the next,'
said he, with a twinkle in his eye, as if quite aware of
the absurdity of the proceeding; 'I went over to Liverpool, and thought it was a mighty bustling place, and
then I came back.'

CHAPTER VIII.

VERY beautiful is the view which Newry presents from the main line of railroad, as the traveller looks down on it, lying on the banks of the river, with mountains rising in the distance; and it is very curious to watch the train apparently climbing up the hill as it wends its way from Newry to Goragh Wood, the junction station. There is a great confusion of stations at Newry: you can alight, if you please, at the main line station, and walk or ride less than two miles into the town; or you can get out at Goragh Wood, cross the line, and be conveyed in another train to the town. In Newry itself there are two stations, and the line runs through them to its terminus at Warrenpoint. I had reason to remember well the railway arrangements at Newry. I took my ticket at Drogheda, and saw my luggage labelled for Goragh Wood. On arriving at my destination no luggage was to be seen; the van of the train I had left was open, and I spied my possessions and pointed them out; but the train was late (I doubt its ever being otherwise), the guard shut the van, and the train was gone. On arriving at Newry, I poured my griefs into the ear of the station master, who telegraphed up to Goragh Wood for particulars. Profound silence ensued. No answer whatever came back. He then proposed telegraphing to Belfast, and while he was doing so I went out for a short distance into the town. On my return, I was informed that there was *nobody at the other end of the telegraph*, and so he had written by the post! Unable to go on to Warrenpoint as I had wished, I betook myself to a hotel in Newry, which turned out to be an ' Orange ' one, for at Newry one has entered the north, and finds oneself between the two contending armies. The next morning was Sunday, and I had an amusing illustration of the way in which the poorer Irish answer a question. Being too late for the eight o'clock mass at the Cathedral, and finding the next mass was at ten, I asked the chambermaid if there were not one at another church. ' Yes,' she said, ' at the old chapel at half-past eight, if you can only find the way; go straight up the street, and then ask.' I set out, and soon after passing the Cathedral asked a bright-looking servant girl, in her Sunday best and prayer book in hand, the way to the old chapel.

' But sure there's no mass there,' was the reply ; and do what I would, I could get no other answer. Seeing a postman the other side of the street I crossed over and asked my way of him. ' But sure there's no mass there,' was his reply ; and as he had evidently no intention of directing me further, I gave it up and retraced my steps to the hotel. The idea of answering the question simply, and leaving me to find out my own mistake, never occurred to either of my informants. Newry is a bright, clean, cheerful-looking town, with some large fine streets and good buildings. It seems also busy and stirring ; there is access every half hour by train to Warrenpoint, the port of the town, and an

exceedingly pretty sea-side place, only less lovely than
its little neighbour Rostrevor. Warrenpoint is greatly
frequented in the summer, and a great number of
lodging houses have been built to supply the demand.
On Sundays the whole ' aristocracy' of the town hasten
to their favourite place of resort. The Cathedral of
Newry is nothing more than a large handsome parish
church, with good proportions, and well lighted. It
was filled with a large attentive congregation, both
at the four masses and in the evening. Until the year
1830 not a single convent existed either in Newry or
even in the whole of Ulster, so virulent was the spirit
of the Orange party. In that year, however, it was
determined to break ground, and a community of
Poor Clares from Dublin came to Newry and took
possession of a house in the High Street, a close and
narrow one in the heart of the town, and having for
their neighbours a Unitarian chapel on one side, and
an Orange Lodge on the other. The little band of
defenceless and innocent women were housed, and
their chapel arranged in one of the front rooms of the
house. They were not suffered long to remain in
peace. The Orangemen assembled outside the convent, broke every pane of glass in the front of the
convent, then threw into the house a quantity of
stones, and tried their best to break down the iron
grating which guarded the door; in this latter attempt
they did not succeed. Then one more unmanly than the
rest fired into a cell window, and the ball passed close
to the head of the nun who occupied it, grazing her
cheek. As the chapel windows were completely destroyed, the nuns were anxious to remove the Blessed

Sacrament into the back of the house, but for some time it was impossible to get a priest into the house, and when one did come on the following day he had to creep in disguised. During the whole of this outrage, which far exceeds anything which the Fenians have done in the late rising, and which took place less than forty years ago, the police never once interfered, not a hand was put forth by the guardians of the law to defend a community of educated, refined, and Christian women from injury, insult, and danger of life. For many months the windows remained unrepaired, and the community lived in the rear of the house, fearing further attacks.

The grounds of St. Clare Convent are very extensive, and a sharp hill rises at the end of them, which has been well planted and laid out with trees and flowers, and from thence there is a lovely view of the town outspread like a map, the river, and the mountains. There, on more than one bright summer's morning, I sat gazing on the fair landscape, and listening to one who, undeterred by stones and missiles, came in the bloom of early youth to link her fate with the nuns of St. Clare; and who now, in the evening of a life thus spent in devotion to God and His poor, can look back, and witness to the wonderful changes wrought in the position of the Catholic religion even in a part of the country where it naturally could least expect to flourish. The proper place for the nuns' cemetery would have been at the summit of the hill; but so great was the virulence of the Orange party that even the graves of the dead would not have been safe in a spot to which easy access over the walls at night could have been obtained, and the dead were therefore buried in a vault scooped out of the middle of the hill. But now they might safely rest in the open ground, and no angry strife would be waged over their resting-place. The Unitarian chapel has long since been closed, and its buildings thrown into the convent; the Orange lodge has been razed to the ground, and on the site are rising up the walls of fine large poor schools in the place of former ones too small and ill-ventilated, in which the nuns have for many years instructed poor children. The nuns of this order are enclosed, and no secular can visit any part of the convent, except the chapel and grounds, without the bishop's permission. This being, however, obtained, I went over all the convent, the refectory, kitchen, and dairy; the bright-looking community room with piano, pictures, and books; the library with well-filled shelves; the long rows of cells: all was very simple and poor; there were none of the beauty and ornament which is so fittingly introduced into conventual buildings. The adverse times through which the community passed have prevented all this; but there is a peculiar charm attached to the dwelling-place of those who have bravely fought and gained great and important battles, and this has been essentially the case of the nuns of St. Clare at Newry. A large number of poor children attend their schools, and for many years they were the only Catholic girls' schools in Newry. The chapel is open to the public, the choir of the religious being separated from the rest of the church by a *grille*. The entire relics of one of the martyrs of the Roman catacombs was recently presented to this

convent, enclosed, as is the custom in Rome, in a wax
facsimile of the Saint richly dressed. It is the object
of great admiration and respect to the poor, many of
whom come long distances to visit it, and the chapel
is hardly ever empty. So successful has the mission
of the Sisters of St. Clare proved in Newry, that it
was thought advisable that another religious order,
and one whose members were able to visit the poor,
should be brought in; and in 1855 a foundation of
Sisters of Mercy was sent from the convent at Kinsale,
and a house taken for the nuns on the opposite side of
the town to that on which St. Clare's convent stands.

In course of time, a large and very fine convent was
built almost facing the ' Model Schools,' a pretty
Gothic building. The convent is in the Italian style,
one which, though not so pleasing to the eye, is
generally found to be more adapted for conventual
purposes. The chapel, though only a large room, is
very devotional and pretty; a fine painting by Carlo
Dolce, ' Our Lord showing His Wounds to St. Thomas,'
hangs upon the wall, and several other paintings are
very good. A large garden divides the convent from
the House of Mercy and poor schools; attached to the
former is an Industrial School on a large scale, and
which has so high a reputation for the excellence of
its work that orders come from all parts, even the
colonies, and the girls are therefore kept in constant
employment. The specimens I was shown were wonderfully fine work. The Sisters have a great deal to do
on Sunday, having several confraternities to manage.
These consist of girls of different classes, and also
women, a sort of ' mothers' meeting.' They meet in

the different schoolrooms, and are each superintended by a Sister. On entering one of these rooms, where a class of rough looking girls was assembled, the sound of weeping reached our ears, and several of the pupils were seen to be ' drowned in tears.' The cause of the grief turned out to be the approaching departure of some of the Sisters who had been instructing them, and who were going the next day to make a foundation of their order in Lurgan, a town about twenty miles off. Many of the girls who attend these classes are from the factories, and these Sunday associations tend to keep up an *esprit de corps* among them. Their conduct, their piety, and zeal would put to shame many who have leisure, and every opportunity of serving God. Out of their scanty wages they put aside money to be spent in helping those who are poorer than themselves.

The Sisters have a branch house at Rostrevor, about seven miles from Newry, and two from Warrenpoint. This lovely little spot has been often described by travellers in Ireland. It is, I think, one of the loveliest sea-side places that can exist; it stands in the midst of rich woods, with mountains rising on all sides, and the beautiful bay of Carlingford lying at its foot. As yet it is unspoiled by tourists; for though it has its ' season,' the accommodation is not large, and the place is so quiet that none but real lovers of scenery would care to spend much time in it. There is a handsome Protestant church in the centre of the town, and a little farther on a Catholic one, which is in its way a little gem, both exteriorly and interiorly. Adjoining it is a small convent with two large schoolrooms, built in

the same style as the church, and the two together
form a striking object from the road, framed as they
are in a landscape of such extreme loveliness: when I
visited the spot the convent was yet unfinished, but
the Sisters had been there more than a year, and were
lodged in a house or rather large cottage opposite the
church, and formerly the residence of the parish priest.
Everything here was on a very small scale, the chapel
being of the tiniest description, and the school being held
in a *cow house*, and one which from its size and ventilation was not at all good enough even for cows. Yet in
this wretched place, filled with dirty ragged children,
often coming in dropping with wet, in this stifling atmosphere the Sisters of Mercy have gone on patiently
doing their duty. The visitation of the poor in these
country villages often entails a great deal of fatigue,
as the Sisters have to traverse long distances and rough
roads, and to encounter all kinds of weather. Attached to the Sisters' house are a nice garden and
several fields, from which lovely views may be obtained
of the bay and the opposite shore. The work at Rostrevor is overshadowed and made more difficult by the
existence of *souperism* in an aggravated form within
its borders. Every effort is made by a certain number
of people to draw away the poor from their faith by
giving them food, clothing, and other rewards; and to
cope with this renders the work of the Sisters cruelly
hard. A lady of this class once made her way, not
without great apprehension as to her safety, into the little
convent. She was courteously received by the Sister
in charge. She asked her if she had *ever heard* of the
Redeemer, or knew that such a book as the Bible

existed. The Sister begged her visitor's pardon for laughing heartily at the questions. ' I have read of such things in books, madam,' she said, ' but could not have believed that any educated person could really have believed us ignorant of that knowledge which is the foundation of our faith.' Against bigotry and gross ignorance such as this the Sisters have to fight their way with the weapons of patience, gentleness, and forbearance.

The pleasant town of Carlow on the banks of the ' goodlie Barrow,' and lying in the county called the ' garden of Erin,' is easily reached by rail from Dublin. Its principal object of interest is the cathedral, which is so closely connected with the memory of the celebrated Dr. Doyle, Bishop of Kildare, whose exertions for the cause of religion in Ireland are so well known. The cathedral is a very fine building, with a tower of one hundred and fifty-one feet in height; the west front is richly decorated. In the interior the very striking monument to the memory of Dr. Doyle, representing the Bishop reclining in sleep with Ireland kneeling by his side, is one of Hogan's best executions. Close by the cathedral is a pleasant park, well planted with trees, and overlooking the river Barrow as it rolls along. In this park stands St. Patrick's College consisting of a centre and two wings. Both ecclesiastical and lay students are educated here ; and the library and the chapel are both well worth seeing.

There is a large Presentation convent at Carlow, with flourishing poor schools. The Sisters of Mercy have also a convent here, and it boasts of being the third foundation made by Katherine McAuley in her lifetime. Mrs. McAuley went to Carlow April 10, 1837, where a temporary abode had been taken by the Bishop for the Sisters. As the Presentation nuns had already the charge of the poor schools, the Bishop begged Mrs. McAuley to allow her Sisters to take charge of middle schools, and to this she consented. In due course of time a convent with its House of Mercy was built. It is a pretty 'home-like' looking convent, surrounded on all sides by a large, well-planted garden, and shut in by high walls from the road. The middle schools are exceedingly well managed, and the children were particularly intelligent and well taught, and had good manners, a point of no little importance with a class of children naturally inclined to 'airs.' Middle schools, well managed, are certainly a great want of the present day, and to provide them is a great charity. We are all of us as particular about our *castes* as any Indians that ever lived, and no one can expect that a small tradesman or farmer will send his children to the same school with the bare-footed little ones of the peasant. And the children of this class, removed from the rough simplicity of the poor, a little inflated with comfort, a little set up above their neighbours, run a terrible risk of serious evil. But when girls of this class are well educated, as those at Carlow assuredly are, they grow up steady, sensible women, with immense power of doing good to their own families and to others, in their hands.

The Sisters of Carlow have also a school for little boys, which is situated at some distance from the convent, unfortunately for the Sisters who have to go there in all weathers, and unfortunately for me, too, since I

had to wait some time ere a beaming face, whose sunshine
even the trials of life in Eastern hospitals could never
overshadow, returned from it to welcome me to her
convent home ; and, moreover, was unable to visit this
school, as I should have liked to have done. The Sisters
have a large number of poor and sick people to visit ;
the House of Mercy adjoining the convent was full of
inmates; the building is well adapted for the purpose,
and all seemed to be in perfect order.   I much wished
I could have stayed longer at Carlow, have visited the
old castle, and rambled over some of the surrounding
country, which looks so tempting when viewed from
the town; but the exigencies of a return ticket and
press of time obliged me to hurry back to Dublin.

I was unlucky enough to enter the fine old city of
Limerick the day before the annual races, when the
streets were thronged by a motley crowd, and there
was no slight difficulty in getting accommodation.   A
kind friend came some distance to meet me for fear I
should miss seeing any of the ' lions.'   So we saw the
huge stone on which the treaty, so soon to be broken,
is said to have been signed.   We stood on the bridge
of the Shannon, the ' king of island rivers,' as it lay
rippling in the sunlight, and I tried to fancy the boat
with the dying monk :

> Through the low banks where Shannon meets the sea,
>   Up the broad waters of the river king,
> (Then populous with a nation) journeyed he,
>   Through that old Ireland which her poets sing:
> And the white vessel, breasting up the stream,
> Moved slowly like a ship within a dream.

I suppose almost everyone knows the story of the
Italian monk who cast the bells for his own monastery

in Italy, from whence he and his brethren were driven by some invading army; and how, long years afterwards, when sent on an embassy to Ireland, he heard the sound of the bells he had so loved from the towers of Limerick cathedral:

> The white-sailed boat moved slowly up the stream;
>   The old man lay with folded hands at rest;
> The Shannon glistened in the sunlit beam;
>   The bells rang gently o'er its shining breast,
> Shaking out music from each lilied rim,
> It was a requiem which they rang for him.*

The cathedral when reached is disappointing, being heavy and gloomy looking. I was disappointed also with the new Catholic cathedral, which, though a fine building, is cold and uninteresting. On the outskirts of the town is a very handsome church belonging to the Redemptorists, and a pretty little one near the railway station is that of the Dominicans.

In the good old times a Dominican priory had existed in Limerick, but its inmates had been driven away, and their convent had fallen into a picturesque ruin. Within the enclosure which surrounded this convent a house had been built, and when Mrs. McAuley was induced, in 1838, to make a foundation of her order in Limerick, this house was given to the Sisters. She thus describes it in one of her letters: 'There is a very nice old convent enclosed by the walls of an abbey—a beautiful ruin. There is a most simple, beautiful tomb just opposite to the cell I occupy; a holy abbess and a lay sister are deposited there—a very large weeping willow hanging over the grave.

* Bessie Rayner Parkes.

It looks delightful and excites me to meditation of the most consoling kind.' This convent was situated in a very wretched part of the town, but that the Sisters cared little about, and were only glad to be among the poor. The work increased so rapidly that a large addition to the original convent, together with a House of Mercy and poor schools had to be made. Even these latter seemed to me insufficient for the number of children who flock to them. I thought the infant school was overcrowded; but the education and management of the children were apparently very good. Besides the schools attached to the convent, the Sisters have four others in different parts of the city, and altogether more than 3,000 children are instructed by the Sisters of Mercy in Limerick. There are two branch houses belonging to this convent in Limerick: the first is St. Vincent's Orphanage, a fine large building in the Gothic style, built a little way out of the town. It is on the same plan as the other orphanages that I have mentioned, and was filled by a crowd of clean, healthy, contented-looking children. An almshouse for old widows is also connected with this branch house; and the chapel, and indeed the whole pile of buildings, is exceedingly pretty. This house receives 130 orphans and 16 widows. The most interesting institution in Limerick, and one of the most remarkable I think in all Ireland, is the second branch house of the Sisters of Mercy at the workhouse infirmary. The workhouse is built in an excellent situation, about half a mile out of the town. In the year 1856, the guardians took the enlightened step of asking the Sisters of Mercy to undertake the charge of

the infirmary, and they readily responded to the call.
A workhouse infirmary, though under the same roof,
is always a distinct department from the rest of the
workhouse, and with the infirmary only the Sisters
have to do.   There are various wards for both men
and women, and nearly 1,000 patients can be received.
A workhouse infirmary is a familiar spot to me.   I have
visited one often, and certainly I never left one without
a sad heart, after having witnessed the discomfort,
dirt, and neglect (to use the mildest words), in which the
patients were left.   But in the Limerick infirmary a
changed scene met my eye—floors clean and fresh, beds
with spotless linen and white coverings; the medicines,
books, and little comforts the patients require close at
their side; the Sisters of Mercy with pleasant faces and
kind words moving about in lieu of the ' pauper nurses ;'
an indescribable air of comfort and repose in the whole
place.   Wardmaids and wardsmen assist the Sisters in
the rough work of the infirmary, but their vigilant care
superintends all; they see that their patients are properly fed, that the doctor's orders are carried out, that
they are treated as the poor in a Christian land should
be treated, and not as in other workhouses, far worse
than a pack of valuable dogs would be.   And then the
Sisters care for the souls of their patients and try to
turn the time of their illness to good account.

It must always be borne in mind that the class
of poor who enter an infirmary is very different
from those who come into an hospital; the latter are
the respectable labouring poor, servants, &c., and
often the lower middle classes who are reduced in
circumstances; the former are the pauper class, the

lowest, most wretched, most ignorant, most neglected
of the population, and therefore most needing instruction and elevating influences.   Among this class of
sufferers the Sisters of Mercy in Limerick go about
consoling, teaching, and helping. They bring back forgotten truths to the minds of some; they teach others
sublime lessons which they have never before heard;
they lead the sinner to repentance, they soften the
hardened, deadened heart; and God's special benediction rests on them as they pursue their course; for not
only are they doing a great work, but they have won a
great victory for their country, they have broken down
a tremendous barrier, have gained the outposts of the
great barren desolate field of workhouse poor, neglected and oppressed. Their example has been already
followed in three or four other towns; and may we not
hope that the time will come when the workhouses of
Ireland shall be in their hands? The Sisters took me
into two small wards equally as good as the others,
and rather more comfortable on account of their size;
these were the 'Protestant wards.' One, I think, had
four, the other six, inmates, while the whole number of
patients at that moment was over 600. So careful
are the guardians that the feelings and consciences of
the Protestants shall not be interfered with by their
Catholic fellow-patients, that this arrangement has
been resorted to. Here the Protestant clergyman can
visit them, hold services, &c., whenever he pleases.
And this is done in Ireland to a minority of ten
among 600, and I thought of certain English workhouses, where the Catholic poor are counted by hundreds, yet where their feelings and their consciences

are utterly ignored; where a priest can only enter
when he is sent for to an especial case, and may not
speak to any other Catholic in the ward; where Catholic visitors are allowed no entrance, and Catholic
books are confiscated; where no provision is made for
the administration of Catholic services; and I asked
myself where was the boasted justice of Englishmen,
and when would this disgrace be wiped off from our
country.   The expenditure of the Limerick infirmary,
under the new management, does not exceed that of
the preceeding, although the comfort of the patients has
been greatly increased.   The reason for this is very
obvious, as the recent disclosures respecting London
workhouses will abundantly demonstrate.   The comforts that should have gone to the patients went to
the nurses, and the process is now reversed.   The
Sisters practise the most careful economy in all details, and waste of all kinds is rigidly prevented.   If
there be ever any apparent increase of expense in this
infirmary, it arises from the fact that more poor
consent to enter it since the Sisters have been in
charge.   Some, perhaps, will cavil at this, but surely
every poor man has a right to relief and comfort in
the hour of sickness; the infirmary at least of a poorhouse should be made such as he will not shrink
from entering.   As it is now rather a fashion to abuse
workhouse guardians, a tribute should be given to
the wisdom and humanity of the Limerick Board in
having had the courage to break through existing
customs and make these excellent changes.

They must, I am sure, be rewarded in seeing their
infirmary a model one in Ireland, and knowing that

they have pioneered the way for others to follow, in bringing about a reform which must work an immense good in the country.

I visited the convent of the Good Shepherd in Limerick, which is a foundation from the well-known house of this order in London. The Sisters have an asylum for penitents under their care and also a Government reformatory for children. The asylum was begun many years ago in Limerick by a lady, who, unable from pressing family duties to enter a convent in her youth as she wished, devoted herself to good works, and especially to the raising up the fallen of her own sex. The asylum for penitents prospered under her care, and many souls were rescued. When middle life had come, and those of her relations whom she had brought up had gone to give themselves to God's service, she resigned her work for penitents into the hands of the Sisters of the Good Shepherd, and went to serve her novitiate as a Sister of Mercy under a superioress whose childhood and youth she herself had trained; and when her vows were made, and, as old age was creeping on, it would have seemed time to rest in her loved community, she gave up her native land, and those who were dearest to her heart, and set out on a long and arduous journey to a distant shore to found a convent of her order. There she now rests from her labours, far away from her own green Ireland, one of those heroic souls of whom the world knows nothing, who neither sought nor cared for fame, but for whom is reserved an exceeding great reward.

The Convent of the Good Shepherd is a large and handsome one ; the asylum can receive more than seventy penitents; the management seemed to be the same as that in High Park; the women are employed chiefly in washing, and there are magnificent laundries. The penitents here are not expected or urged to remain for life and the greater part do not, but some who desire to remain can do so.   Among these were a few who had entered the asylum when it was under the management of the lady I have spoken of; and when her name was mentioned they blessed it with deep gratitude.

The faces of the reformatory children here were a great contrast to those in Dublin; I could have fancied myself in an ordinary school, and on entering their room we were received with the same pleasure and interest that the arrival of visitors generally excites among ordinary children.   It was a great comfort to hear the nuns say that they were not at all bad children, but had been generally committed for some very slight offence, and had been led into that principally by poverty and neglect.   The Sisters had good hopes of sending them out thoroughly improved by their detention.

There is a convent of the Presentation order in Limerick, with schools for 500 children; and at Laurel Hill, near the city, a convent of 'Faithful Companions of Jesus,' a French order for the education of the upper classes.

CHAPTER IX.

Notwithstanding all I had heard of the beauty of Cork, it quite surpassed my expectations. The weather was perfect—a ' St. Luke's summer ;' and from the kind and hospitable ' Irish Home ' in which I was living, at the summit of one of the heights which surround Cork, we saw the grey autumn mist hanging over the city gradually disperse before the sun, and the river, the churches, the steeple of ' Shandon,' and the quaint picturesque houses lie glittering in its rays.

The surrounding scenery of Cork has been often described in better words than I could hope to use. The river Lee, with its rich variety of landscape, lies outspread before the spectator's delighted gaze as the train or the steamer transports him from Cork to the Cove. A line of railroad runs on each side of the river, with stations at the various pretty villages which ornament the banks of the Lee.

The Ursuline Convent, at Blackrock, is a large and handsome building, and forms a conspicuous object in the landscape. It was founded by the Ursuline Nuns who came from France in 1771, and is one of the chief places of education in Ireland. The river joins the sea at Queenstown, or the Cove of Cork; its magnificent harbour and the view from the heights, of sea and land, with islands dotted here and there, the wind-

ing river, and the shipping, are exceedingly beautiful;
and then there are the ' Groves of Blarney,' with the
stone which so few have courage to kiss, great as the
promised result may be ; and the castle ' once strong
and aincient,' as the song declares, but now—

> Sure you're nothing at all but a stone
>   Wrapt in ivy. . . . .
> Bad luck to that robber, ould Crommill,
> That plundered our beautiful fort.

My first visit to Cork took place immediately after
the erection of the statue to Father Mathew, at the top
of Patrick Street, immediately facing the bridge, and
the town had hardly recovered from the excitement
consequent on the fêtes of the occasion.   There, in the
midst of the city in which he was born, in which so
much of his great work was wrought, stands the image
of the man whom his country can never forget—the
simple, self-denying, warm-hearted Irish priest, whose
one thought in life was to rescue his countrymen from
the dread curse of their existence.   I went to the
church in which he used to minister, but there was
nothing of any note to be recorded of it ; then to the
cemetery which he laid out and arranged, and in the
centre of which he now lies.   It is at some little distance
from the town, and might with ordinary care and pains
be as beautiful a cemetery as that of Glasnevin ; but
it had, when I saw it, fallen into a terrible state of
neglect.   The only tomb apparently properly looked
after was that of Father Mathew himself.   It consists
of a broad slab of granite laid upon the ground, a cross
in the centre, and an iron railing surrounding it.   There
is hardly an hour in the day when a ' pilgrim ' may not

be found kneeling by the grave of him whom many reverence as a saint. But the rest of the cemetery was in sad confusion—trees and shrubs growing as if in a forest; while weeds, nettles, and long grass choked up the passage to and from the graves. Perhaps by this time matters may be all put straight, otherwise it would be a disgrace to the enlightened city of Cork.

One of the great 'lions' of Cork now is the Church of SS. Peter and Paul, worthy in beauty if not in size to be the cathedral of the diocese; it is, however, only a parish church, but a very large sum indeed has been spent on its decorations. It is the work of Mr. Welby Pugin, son of the great architect of that name, and it is one of which the city has every reason to be proud. The elevation of the building, the roof and the apse, are most admirable, while pillars of different coloured marbles, and the richest carving in stone for the altars, delight the eye.

It formed a great contrast to another church which I visited in Cork, and one of the oldest, strongly resembling a well-constructed but weather-beaten barn of enormous size, with great ugly galleries, and an altar raised on high steps so that it could be seen by all. This church fulfils the object for which it was built, that of containing as many people as possible. These two churches struck me as remarkable specimens of Ireland now and Ireland fifty years ago. Then space and a roof to shelter them, and an altar which they could see, and a floor to kneel on, was all the Irish hoped for, dared to expect. Faithfully and patiently through long years of trial they worshipped in these humble temples, while the cathedrals that their fathers built were neglected and disused by those who could not value them. Now the time has come when once more the beauty of architecture, marble, and gold, and gems can be brought into the service of the sanctuary, and buildings may rise up to vie with those which sprung from the love and devotion of olden days. Connected with the ' barn-like' church, I heard of a confraternity which interested me greatly. It was for young girls from the time at which they make their first communion till they are twenty-one, and thus it lays hold of the girls who have left school, a class which, at the present day, is not nearly so much attended to as it ought to be. These girls meet at the church at two o'clock every Sunday afternoon, are divided into classes, and receive instruction, or rather keep up the instruction of their school days. The priest in charge of this association, a specimen of those devoted self-sacrificing men of whom the Irish priesthood can furnish so many examples, gives them a short address, and there is, I think, some singing. All simple enough, but tending to sustain a bond of union and keep holy lessons alive in their hearts. All the members are bound to go to the sacraments once a month, and a high tone of conduct is kept up amongst them. Serious offenders are punished by expulsion, which is looked upon as a terrible disgrace. ' And what do you do with those who misbehave,' said I, ' because there must be some ?'—' If possible,' was the answer, ' I try to persuade them to go to England.' The reply smote upon my heart, for I knew well how many of the Irish girls in England who are so hard to manage, so difficult to reclaim, were those who, in their own country, had began by being a little

wild, and having taken the first downward step, and
rubbed off the bloom of their youthful innocence,
when thrown into the whirl of one of our great wicked
cities hurry onwards with rapid pace to ruin.   There
is some difficulty in getting teachers for this confraternity.   Many ladies do not like to give up the best part
of a Sunday afternoon for a work requiring patience
and skill ; besides which, the teacher's duty binds her
to look after her pupils in the week, to see why the
absentees did not make their appearance, and to visit
those who are ill.   A story was told me in connection
with this association which would not form a bad plot
for a novel, and was certainly a little ' romance in real
life.'   A young girl once offered herself as teacher in
the confraternity.   She was poorly clad, and stated
herself to be a seamstress ; but there was a grace about
her appearance and manner which convinced the priest
to whom she spoke that she was of gentle birth.   It
turned out to be the case ; she and her sister were
well born, but, losing father and mother in their infancy, were left, with their fortune of 20,000l., to the
guardianship of an uncle.   He sent them to be educated at a convent in France, and there one sister
died ; and when the other, at the age of seventeen,
returned to Cork, she found her uncle flown and herself penniless.

She went out as a governess, but finding that mode
of life intolerable, gave it up, and earned her bread
by needlework.   She was received as a teacher ; the
priest watched her narrowly, and was perfectly satisfied with her conduct and patient industry.   One day
she came to tell him that one of her pupils was seriously

ill, and had no one but an old mother, almost too infirm to work, to nurse her; might she go and help her? He gave permission, and Ellen (as I will call her) nursed the young girl till she died. Then the poor mother wailed bitterly; her last, her only one, was gone, and she was left alone to starve and die. She, too, had seen better days, but misfortune had come heavily on her, and her only son, a bright and clever lad, had chosen to go to California, telling his mother to be of good heart, for he would come back to her a rich man. But seventeen years had flown by, and not a word had come from him; so he must have been dead long ago; and now her girl was gone, who used to help her with washing, and enable her to keep out of the dreaded union. Then Ellen bade her be comforted, for she would fill a daughter's place, live with her, and work for her till life should end. And in a Ruth-like spirit she toiled hard for the old woman's support, watched tenderly over her, and hoped when that task should be fulfilled to become a nun. One day a letter came to the priest who directed the confraternity bearing a foreign postmark; it proved to be from the long-lost son of the old mother, who had truly enough become a rich man, and had acres of lands and flocks of sheep, whose letters home had all gone astray, who had thought his mother dead, but had heard of her from a former member of the confraternity, married in California, who told him he had a mother and sister in Cork. So Robert (as I will call him) wrote to the priest to beg him to break the news to his mother, to give her money from him, and to entreat her and his sister to take ship and come out

to him, where they would live in peace and plenty the
rest of their days. When the old woman heard the
news she fell down in a fainting fit, but on her reco-
very expressed herself eager and willing to undertake
the voyage, and see her only child again before she
died, provided Ellen would take the place of the sister
he expected, and accompany her on the voyage. And
to this Ellen consented, intending, as soon as she
should have delivered the old woman safe into her
son's keeping, to seek admission into the convent of the
Sisters of Mercy at San Francisco, who were greatly
in want of fresh sisters. So the pair set off, and
arrived safely in California, where, as my readers will
of course foresee, Robert fell instantly in love with
Ellen, and besought her to be his wife. His position
would have insured her every comfort that money
could buy in California. But Ellen's heart was too
firmly anchored ; to love the poor and to serve her
Lord was her sole ambition, and steadfast to her word
she speedily entered the convent. Already a true nun
in heart she fulfilled her duties admirably. Soon after
her profession she was sent into the hospital. An
officer, mortally wounded, was brought in, and Ellen
had to wait on him. He was a confirmed infidel,
and was ready to die as he had lived, unbelieving and
blaspheming ; but beside him Ellen prayed, and beside
him she laboured. The conquest of this soul was
given her, and he died penitent, blessing the name of
Him whose love had so inspired the feeble words of
a Sister of Mercy.

The Christian Brothers have a large establishment
in Cork, and I have purposely omitted mentioning the

schools of these Brothers in Dublin, because it was in Cork that I first became acquainted with them. The order of the Christian Brothers is a French one, and was founded by the Ven. J. B. de la Salle, towards the close of the seventeenth century. His rule and constitutions were adopted in 1817 by a small body of men in Ireland who, from the year 1802, had been devoting themselves to the care of poor schools, and living in community. From that time the order in Ireland has made rapid progress; they have now seventy establishments in the country, and have about 30,000 children under their care.

Our Lady's Mount at Cork is a large house built on one of the hills that surround the city; a wide lawn gradually slopes down it to the entrance gate, where stand the schools, and in a few minutes after passing them you find yourself among the poorest population of the city. The schools are very fine, space and air abound in them, perfect order and cleanliness prevail, and the manner of the boys is very good. There are eight class rooms in this school, the boys advancing by different gradations. There is a great mixture of ranks among the boys, a barefooted little fellow with scanty garments standing next to one evidently of a better grade; indeed, the education given in these schools is of so excellent a character, that parents above the very poor are eager to procure it for their children. ' The knowledge communicated in the schools embraces not only reading, writing, arithmetic, grammar, geography, and bookkeeping, but also an acquaintance with such branches of mathematical science as are suited to the taste and talents of the pupils, and to the

stations of life which they are destined to occupy.
Geometry, mensuration, drawing, and mechanics, are
special objects of attention.'

The occasion of the erection of Father Mathew's
statue brought to Cork several 'special correspondents'
and reporters of the London papers. One of these
gentlemen was persuaded to visit the Christian
Brothers' schools. He began by asking what books
they used, and on being told 'our own,' looked the
scorn he was too polite to express. The books were
given to him, and he was requested to examine the
classes himself in his own way. Thus he gradually
advanced through the school, becoming more and more
surprised as he went on. ' Really this is astonishing,'
said he, to the friend who accompanied him, and at last
on reaching the last class he relinquished his task as
examiner, fairly confessing the boys were beyond him.
He was then taken to the drawing school, the walls of
which were hung with framed drawings of various
kinds. The visitor, imagining them to be selected for
the boys to copy, said they were very good—some evidently were by a French artist—and it was with difficulty he could be made to believe that they were the
productions of the boys. But when at last the fact had
dawned upon him, and he realised what well-educated
intelligent lads the Brothers could turn out, a brilliant
idea seized him. ' What do you do with them here?
send them to *London*; with such acquirements they
could get excellent situations there.' And then he was
informed that even in the benighted city of Cork it
was quite easy to place the boys in positions in which
they can do well. So he departed a little wiser than

he came; but I never heard that the British public were ever informed of the result of his visit.

In the chapel belonging to the Brothers the superior showed us a silver lamp for the altar, the present of one who had attended the schools a barefooted, ragged little urchin, and who was now a prosperous tradesman, never forgetting in the hour of his prosperity the kind teachers of his poverty-stricken childhood. He was by no means a solitary instance of the rewards the Brothers often meet amid their toil and discouragements. The Brothers' house is spacious, and very simply furnished; the chapel is a very pretty one, and there is a library well stocked with books. By rule the Brothers are obliged to devote a certain time to study each day.

This house possesses a peculiar interest, as having once possessed among its members the brilliant and talented Gerald Griffin. Here he died, of typhus fever, in June, 1840, and his body rests in the little burying-ground half-way down the garden, which divides the house from the schools; a small green plot of grass, with iron railings around, and large trees overhanging it, and a few graves marked with a headstone and a cross in the centre. With varied and mingled feelings we stood by the grave of one whose life, though brief, had contained so deep a lesson. Nothing, perhaps, can more clearly describe the true vocation of a Christian Brother than Gerald's own letters, written from this very spot. To a friend in London he writes: 'I was ordered off here from Dublin last June, and have been since enlightening the craniums of the wondering paddies in this quarter, who learn from me with profound amazement and profit that o, x, spells ox; that the top of a map is the north, and the bottom the south, with various other " branches;" as also that they ought to be good boys, and do as they are bid, and say their prayers every morning and evening, &c.; and yet it seems curious even to myself that I feel a great deal happier in the practice of this daily routine than I did while I was roving about your great city, absorbed in the modest project of rivalling Shakespeare, and throwing Scott into the shade.' It is a curious task now to read the records of Gerald's early life; to see the young man of twenty, full of the ardour of youth and genius, struggling in the great arena of London life, thirsting for fame, and often not able to earn his daily bread; how he went about from manager to actress and from actor to critic, burning with eagerness to see a play of his performed on the boards of a London theatre. ' The object of my life for many years,' he calls it; and when a piece of his actually did appear he is thrown into ' buoyant excitement of mind and heart.' What a cup of bliss then would have been the furore about the ' Colleen Bawn;' but, happily for him, the fame he sought for did not come. He attained a certain amount of success, but was so wearied with the struggle that he turned away to a settled profession, and then his views changed; he began to think that fame, after all, was not worth the pursuit, and a few years after beheld him a Christian Brother, happy and radiant and full of peace, and eager only to devote his fine talents to the service of God. But it was not to be; the soul that seemed fitted to do so much in the future was not to linger

on the earth : his early presentiment was to be fulfilled.

> In the time of my boyhood I had a strange feeling
>> That I was to die ere the noon of my day ;
> Not quietly into the silent grave stealing,
>> But torn, like a blasted oak, sudden away.

In his community life Gerald had been as much
loved as he had been by the family and friends he
had left. Even after the lapse of so many years, the
superior of the house could not speak of him without
deep emotion, and he had not yet ceased to mourn
the loss of one so richly gifted, both by nature and
grace.

Besides the schools at Our Lady's Mount, the
Brothers have two others in different parts of Cork.

Just opposite their gate is a convent of the Irish
Sisters of Charity. They have large poor schools for
girls, and also one for infant boys, and they are of
great assistance to the Brothers in preparing the boys
well before entering the boys' school.

Attached to this convent is a Magdalene Asylum,
the finest of the kind I have ever seen. The plan of
management is the same as that at Donnybrook, but
the general arrangements of the house very far excel
those of the latter. Each inmate has her own little
cell, and this renders the house a very suitable one for
women who were of a rather better position in life
than those who generally fill such asylums. It greatly
increases the difficulty of reclaiming persons of this
kind, if they find they are to be in constant contact
night and day with those who are naturally rough,
coarse, and unfeeling. The first germs of their re-

pentance are often weak, and they frequently give up
the struggle in despair, and run back to evil courses.
In the Cork asylum, as elsewhere, the penitents have
to work for their own support. There is a large
workroom, and magnificent laundries. We were much
struck by the quiet manner and modest demeanour of
many of the women, giving evidence of the improvement which had been wrought in their characters.

The convent of Sisters of Mercy in Cork bears the
poetical name of St. Marie's of the Isle; it is built on a
piece of ground called the Island, and formerly the site
of a Dominican abbey. This convent is the fifth
foundation made by Mrs. McAuley, and is one of
the most flourishing of the order. It is built in the
Gothic style, of brown stone, with bright coloured
limestone quoins, windows, and door-ways, and is a
beautiful and picturesque building. The interior is
equally good, and altogether it is a worthy successor
of the convents of bygone days. The whole expense
of its erection was borne by the people of Cork,
and it is certainly a great ornament to the city. Adjoining it are large poor schools, an orphanage, and a
large House of Mercy. There is a numerous community, and all their works seemed to be in a flourishing condition. There are several branch houses belonging to this community, one of which has charge of a
hospital, which we visited. A large house has been
devoted to the purpose, and the hospital is managed
on the same plan as that in Jervis Street, Dublin.
The size of the house does not admit of good accommodation being given to the Sisters; but this they
accept and make light of with their usual cheerfulness.

A little way out of Cork, at Sunday's Well, is a
lovely little church, belonging to the Vincentian
Fathers. The interior is remarkably graceful, and it
is the work of Mr. George Goldie.

An institution in Cork interested me very deeply.
It was situated in Mary Street, and was a home, or
rather a training school, for workhouse girls. A certain
number of ladies in Cork visit the workhouse regu-
larly, and, in common with all other workhouse visitors,
were grieved to the heart at the state of workhouse
girls. Indeed the condition of these girls in all the
unions where the system of district schools does not
exist is perfectly appalling, and it is extraordinary that
no steps to remedy such a state of things have been
taken. A number of orphans and deserted children
are always found in the workhouse school; when they
become old enough to go out to service, they are sent
to it; but, as a rule, they never stay. They do not
want to stay; the restraints of service are very irksome,
they like the workhouse, and back they come, not back
to the schools, which are, I believe, in Cork very well
managed, and where only a certain amount of evil can
be learnt; but they return to the adult wards to
mix with women of all ages, of all classes; to hear
language, to learn evil, which we cannot even contemplate. Here the habits of idleness strengthen; they
dawdle through their little task of work, with no care
for the future, no incentive to exertion; the worst
passions of their nature are allowed to grow up un-
checked, and if they ever do leave the workhouse, it is
certainly to swell the criminal class of the country, or else
they are sent out to the colonies in emigrant ships, with

the worst possible results. To take the lowest ground, they are from first to last an enormous expense to the union. Yet such is the immovability of workhouse guardians, that the excellent efforts of the Cork ladies were only supported by a portion among them, and seem in great danger of being shipwrecked by the senseless opposition of the rest.

Two years ago it was determined to try the experiment of training workhouse girls for service, and after an infinity of trouble the guardians consented. They took a house in Mary Street, in a very dilapidated state, so that a large sum had to be spent on repairs. It was plainly furnished, a matron engaged, and girls drafted in; but every possible obstacle that can be imagined stood in the way of its success. The girls hated to be taught, and had brought with them the bad habits engendered by workhouse training, inveterate idleness, and a tendency to cunning and deceit. A very short time only was allowed for training them, and the girls always felt that if they chose to go back to the workhouse they had only to turn restive and the thing was accomplished. Many of these girls had been trained from infancy in the workhouse, some even born there; they knew no other home, cared for no other life, for it is the remarkable characteristic of workhouse girls that they have no ambition to rise; then there were the guardians wanting to see the results of the plan, fearing the expenses; good people shrugging their shoulders and prophesying the work would be a failure. Notwithstanding all this, the ladies and their matron worked on; in these two years *seventy-seven* girls passed through the house; *forty* of these are doing well in situations, nineteen were failures, nine had not sufficient health for service, and nine were in the house when it closed. For it is closed, and the good work stopped. The immediate cause of its closing was the ruinous state of the house, from which it became absolutely necessary to move, while there was difficulty in finding another. While the matter was pending, some of the guardians strongly opposed the reopening of the home, asserting that the good done by it did not compensate for the expense to the ratepayers. The financial state of the home was as follows:—Entire cost of home, 730*l*. 10*s*. 2*d*.; value of clothing on hand, 48*l*.; clothing in store at the workhouse for use of home, and charged to its account but never drawn, 74*l*. 17*s*. 3*d*.; cost of utensils, 47*l*. 17*s*.; bedding, 31*l*. 14*s*. 6*d*.; furniture, 31*l*. 11*s*. 5*d*. All the above articles were available for use, and should therefore be deducted from the 730*l*. 10*s*. The repairs of the house were 90*l*.; therefore the actual expenses of the home for two years were 406*l*. 10*s*., and for this sum the result has been obtained that forty girls have been taken from the pauper class, and are earning their bread respectably. It is quite certain that if they remained in the workhouse all their lives they would have cost a great deal more than 400*l*., and even if this were not the case, is not such a change as regards these unhappy children worth some expense. To deny them the opportunities which it is now certain that they are ready to avail themselves of, is surely worse than the slave trade. It is difficult to believe that the Cork guardians can persevere in their opposition; we trust soon to hear that the home is reopened and in a flourishing

condition. I was much struck when I visited the house
with the excellent good sense with which it was managed.   For instance, the matron's bedroom was fitted
up simply but nicely, as a lady's would be, in order
to teach the girls how to set a bedroom in order.   Her
meals were served with the same care, and the girls
taught to wait on her.   The ladies of the committee
would sometimes order their luncheon to be prepared
at the home in order to teach the girls how to wait, and
how to use the common articles of civilised life.   These
things may seem too trifling to repeat, but they would
not appear so to those who understand what a workhouse girl is, and how completely the ladies have had
to train young barbarians.   ' Their entire surroundings
in the workhouse are different from those of everyday
life, their daily routine there in no way fits them for
life outside, and a girl of fourteen or fifteen years of
age, reared in the workhouse, is as unlearned in the
experience of life as a child of five years old in the
general population.   It is only when a girl leaves the
workhouse that she learns the use of such simple domestic implements as a knife and fork, or knows prac-
tically, at the cost of her mistress's temper and pocket,
that an earthen bowl is more brittle than a tin por-
ringer.   Children in the workhouse never, or very
rarely, see the commonest articles used in a kitchen.
As to the way of setting out, or the appendages of the
simplest table, they are mysteries to them.   Beef,
mutton, poultry, fish, &c., were all things they read of
or saw in pictures ; but, if all were placed before them,
it would be very problematical if they could distinguish
one from the other.   Soup or porridge they could

understand—it was their daily food—but if they were starving, and given the materials to make it, they could not do so.'*

The ladies feel certain that if they had a large house, and were able to take in a greater number of girls, the expenses would be in comparison lessened, and the results equally satisfactory. ' The expense individually would be less than the dreadful experiment of emigration, and the guardians would have the consciousness of knowing that, as Christian gentlemen, they had helped the poor females under their care (many of whom are orphans) to make themselves respectable and useful members of society at home, instead of paying thousands of pounds to send them out to certain destruction.' It is very satisfactory, but not surprising, to find that the girls placed out in service come to the matron or the ladies for advice and help.   Surely it is not possible that such a work as this, in the heart of generous Ireland, will be suffered to perish.

There are two Presentation Convents in Cork, one of which is that built by Miss Nagle, whose grave is to be seen within its enclosure.

The picturesque town of Kinsale is comparatively little known to tourists, lying as it does out of the beaten track.   Did such a lovely sea-side place happen to lie on the English coast it would long since have been overrun by visitors, and much of its beauty destroyed. Stucco villas and a grand ' parade ' would have broken in upon the calm and repose that now hang over the little town, full of memories of the past.   Irish chief-

* Report of the Mary Street Home.

tains, and Spanish invaders, and Parliamentary soldiers have each in their turn held Kinsale in their power, and stirring deeds have been wrought within its walls. Now it is quiet and deserted—the quaint old houses rising in tiers on the side of a hill, while a river slowly wends its way towards the little bay. A promontory, once occupied by a fort, now in ruins, juts out into the harbour. Charles Fort is on the opposite side, and beyond is the broad Atlantic and the ' Old Head,' looked out for as eagerly by the Irishman returning from America as the Land's End or Needles are by English eyes. Kinsale abounds in pretty walks, and there are many points on the different hills in the vicinity of the town from which beautiful views of the forts, bay, Bandon river, and surrounding country can be gained. I was living in one of the pretty country houses in the neighbourhood, a true and pleasant ' Irish home,' with a lovely garden, shaded by large trees, the sea almost at one's feet, and a tremendous hill to ascend or descend in coming or going to the town, but up and down which the horses trotted complacently, as they were used to it all their lives, and desired nothing better. The Convent of Sisters of Mercy at Kinsale forms a conspicuous object, being erected on the summit of the hill above the town, and consisting of a large pile of buildings in the Italian style. The church is large and handsome, with a beautiful choir for the religious on one side of the altar, shut off by a grating, while the rest of the church is open to the public. The schools attached to this convent are very fine ones. No pains or expense have been spared on the buildings or on their fittings, while equal care has been taken with the training of the children. There are several large school-rooms and various class-rooms opening from them, and the whole arrangements and training of the children are very good. They are under government inspection, and they are another instance of the excellent results that can be attained in schools to which women of education and ability, actuated by the highest motives, devote their full attention and energy. Besides the literary schools, there is a large industrial one, in which the girls are taught needlework, and also lace-making. There is a large poor population at Kinsale, and it is very necessary to enable the older girls to do something towards their own support. The needle-work was very good, and some of the specimens of lace quite beautiful. A House of Mercy and Orphanage are also connected with this house, both on a small scale, the Sisters not having possessed sufficient land to build as largely as they would have desired. The land, however, now, has been obtained, and a large orphanage will be built, and also, I believe, an hospital. The Sisters have a large number of poor and sick to visit, and often go considerable distances; they also visit the poorhouse. The convent at Kinsale was founded from Limerick in 1844, a lady of Kinsale having devoted herself and her fortune to the good work. A few Sisters were sent from Limerick to make this foundation, and in twenty-three years their numbers have swelled to nearly two hundred, enabling them to send out a large number of filiations. They have sent foundations to various towns in Ireland, to England, California, and the United States. Ten years after the convent had been founded, two Sisters of

Mercy from Dublin arrived at its door.   Soon after
their entrance the great bell of the convent was rung,
and the whole community, to their astonishment, were
begged to assemble; and then the visitors told them
that Sisters of Mercy had been asked for by the English government to nurse the soldiers of the Crimean
army.   The essential point was to provide a suitable
superioress for the little band to go forth on this new,
untried, and difficult mission.   Would they give up
their Mother under whose auspices their convent had
risen up, and was then flourishing, and sending out fresh
branches, for this arduous and perilous undertaking?
Without this leave and the permission of the bishop
the superioress could not go.   The sacrifice was a
hard one, but it was generously made; and the Rev.
Mother, with two Sisters, set out for Dublin, and
from thence to London.   Other convents contributed
Sisters.   Cork sent two, as also did Carlow, Charleville,
and Dublin; Liverpool gave three, and Chelsea one;
and the fifteen Sisters went out in December, 1854, to
their hard and trying labours.   In rather less than two
years they returned, but *not all.*   Some were left behind,
far away from quiet convent cemeteries, where they
had hoped to rest, never to be seen again till the

> " resurrection morning
> Has just begun to break."

CHAPTER X.

'St. Luke's summer' unfortunately came to a sudden close the very day that we quitted Cork for Killarney. It began to rain, and there seemed no intention of its ever leaving off; and so it was amidst driving clouds of rain and gusts of wind that I caught the first glimpse of the mountains of Kerry, and entered the far-famed town of Killarney. The season was over; the hotels were empty, and the town wore a deserted aspect. 'Doing' the Lakes was utterly out of the question—

> It rained all day, and it rained all night;
>   It rained when morning broke;
> It rained when 'the travellers' went to sleep,
>   And it rained when 'they' awoke.*

We amused ourselves with a visit to the beautiful Convent of Sisters of Mercy, built some little way out of the town, and commanding, I believe, a very fine view, but on the occasion of our visit this was hidden from our gaze by the blinding rain. We went into the poor schools, which were very fairly attended in spite of the weather. There is an industrial school for lace making attached to this convent, and also a House of Mercy; while the Sisters have heavy work on their hands in visiting the numerous sick and poor. This convent seems to have excited particular ad-

* F. W. Faber.

miration in Dr. Forbes, who says, ' There was a singular air of calm and solemnity in this house, and the Sisters, though looking cheerful, as busy people generally are, had something in their bearing which inspired at once reverence and awe.'

The great ornament of Killarney is the cathedral, the only one I have seen in Ireland worthy of the name. It is one of Pugin's happiest conceptions. The tower is not yet built, and this of course greatly detracts from the beauty of the exterior; but within, the great height of the roof, the noble pillars, the sense of space and grandeur, made one think of some of the beautiful cathedrals of old, of our own and foreign lands. Our first visit was paid about eight o'clock in the evening; it was a pitch dark night, not a star was to be seen, and as Killarney is guiltless of street lamps it was with some difficulty that we groped our way to the cathedral. We were amply rewarded. The only light was cast from one or two lamps burning before the altars, throwing flickering gleams of radiance here and there, and leaving the stately pillars and great spaces beyond wrapped in gloom. Here and there was the form of a worshipper enveloped in a cloak and drawn together in the extraordinary fashion which Irishwomen only can adopt. Now and then they prayed out loud in a low sort of moan, an Irish habit anything but agreeable in a small church, but which here, coming as it did from distant corners, had a very curious weird-like effect; then the moan ceased and there was utter unbroken silence, and the darkness seemed to deepen. Presently appeared a light, borne by a man who clumped over the church and peered about with his candle,

evidently looking for some one; but not finding the
object of his search, he knelt down and prayed. In a
few minutes in came three or four other men quite of
the working class, to whom the first comer administered
a sharp rebuke for their want of punctuality; they
were succeeded by some others and fell to their devotion very heartily. They turned out to be the confraternity of the Rosary who meet in the cathedral every
night. Wishing to be in Killarney itself, we had taken
lodgings, being tempted thereunto also by the excessive
cleanliness and sweet face of a young woman who
wanted to let her rooms. The lodgings were spotlessly
clean, and snowy linen lay upon the beds. I had
ordered a fire in my bedroom, and on returning from
the cathedral we were dismayed to find the room choked
with smoke—peat smoke, too, which fills your eyes and
gets down your throat without any mercy. ' And sure
I am *so* sorry!' said the pretty landlady; ' it is the first
fire that has been lit since the summer, and it is just
that the jackdaws have built a nest on the top of the
chimney.' So both for the jackdaws' comfort and our
own we begged to have the fire put out as soon as possible. It was a pleasant sound when the house grew
quiet to hear from the upper rooms a chorus of little
voices saying their ' ora pro nobis,' as the pretty young
mother was putting a brood of little ones to rest.

The next morning we started for Kenmare, telling
our landlady we should be away one night or it might
be two; but as it depended on the weather, she might
expect us back the next day. And the next evening
accordingly we did come, and found everything neat and
clean; but our hostess's face grew sorrowful—' Oh!

sure, ma'am, we thought you said you *might not* come till to-morrow, and the first thing to-morrow morning my husband was going to see about the jackdaws!' It was an Irish trait—truly a vexing one. During our absence we had left all our luggage in this woman's keeping, although we knew nothing of her, having an instinctive trust in the goodness of her face, and our confidence in Irish honesty was not misplaced.

The weather was kind enough to hold up for a little as we pursued our journey along the mountain road which leads from Killarney to Kenmare. I wonder whether a more beautiful drive than that one can be had anywhere, and I strongly doubt it. To me the memory of it will certainly be ' a joy for ever:' on the one side, the lakes lying in their deep valleys; on the other, the richly wooded heights rising above our heads, decked as they were that day in their autumn tints, every variety of brown, red, gold, and orange; in the distance the great purple mountains, from which the clouds rolled away sometimes in great black masses, and sometimes overshadowed with gloom, and every now and then a transient gleam of sunshine broke over them like a smile; while between us and the lakes lay a tangled mass of underwood, and shrubs, and rocks in wild fantastic confusion, as if nature, weary of painting the landscape, had thrown them carelessly from her hand. And then we came to a little lake lying by itself in silent beauty with the great mountains watching on all sides; and as the miles drew on we came more into the heart of the mountains, and a wild rocky waste spread itself on either hand, and the rain began again, or rather a sort of thick falling white mist which made

all surrounding objects look ghost-like and strange.
The rain cleared away again, and the sun came fully
out, as we began a sudden descent, and found ourselves
looking down on the valley of Kenmare. In the midst
of the valley lay a beautiful pile of buildings, such as in
an English village would be at once taken for church,
parsonage, and schools. They are, however, in fact, a
church, schools, and convent bearing the title of Holy
Cross. Arrived in Kenmare, we were not long in
paying the convent a visit, and were received with affectionate hospitality. Our frontispiece gives some idea
of the beauty of the church and convent, although the
size of our pages has not allowed us to give any view
of the surrounding landscape. The whole has been
raised at the expense and under the constant superintendence of the parish priest, Archdeacon O'Sullivan.
Spacious cloisters surround the building, one of which
leads to the choir of the religious, which occupies the
left side of the sanctuary.

The interior of the church is very beautiful, and
contains several good painted windows ; the east
window is especially excellent, representing the Cru-
cifixion. The ancient and beautiful custom of the
' sanctus bell ' has been introduced into this church.
The bell is so placed that it can be rung from the altar,
so that all absent from the church may know the exact
time when the greatest act of Christian worship is
accomplished. There is a fine organ in the church,
and the music is particularly good. The nuns take
great pains with their choir ; they happily possess
several first-rate musicians, both vocal and instrumental,
in the community, and they make it one of their duties

to render the music of the sanctuary as worthy as possible of divine worship, and also carefully train some of their school girls to play the organ and conduct the choir in country churches.

This convent is one of the most interesting in Ireland; it seems so completely to fill the place of the religious houses of by-gone days, when the convent was the refuge for all who needed help or sympathy; when

> The Abbess listened, prayed, and settled all:
> Young hearts that came, weighed down by love or wrong,
> Left her kind presence comforted and strong;
> Thus strife, love, sorrow, good and evil fate,
> Found help and blessing at the convent gate.*

Most of the religious houses we meet with now have been called into being by the exigences of the times; and their presence in large crowded towns seems to fit in, as it were, with the manifold wants of the present day; but the abbey of the Holy Cross rises in such a valley and amidst such beauties of nature as the monks and nuns of old loved to surround themselves with. Great purple mountains lie in the distance with their glorious variations of light and shade; a river, called in Irish *Finihé* (bright water),† wends its way through the convent grounds; the quiet nuns glide through their cloisters; and all recalls the vision of olden days when the land was overspread with stately abbeys and priories.

* Adelaide Anne Procter.

† The river takes its rise in a mountain lake which lies beneath an abrupt precipice, some 1,000 feet high. In this lake there is an island called the *Finihé*, or Bright Island, from the exceeding brightness of its verdure and of the wild shrubs and plants that grow on it.

The nuns of this convent are a foundation from the
Poor Clares at Newry, and came to Kenmare on the
feast of St. Raphael, October 1861.

The poverty of the people at Kenmare is great,
arising chiefly from the fact that there is *no work*, the
sad, sad cry which so continually reaches one's ears in
Ireland.   There is no resident landlord in the place,
and what the people are to do to help themselves, as
they are so constantly advised to do in England, it is
hard to see.   The building of the church and convent gave employment to very many for some years,
and the distress has been great since they were completed.   Both men and women, when they can manage
to earn a little, try to save rigidly, that they may get
enough money to emigrate; and the Sisters in order to
obviate this evil opened an industrial school, which
gives employment to several hundreds, and here
needlework of all kinds, and lace making are carried
on; Limerick lace, and Irish point and guipure, with
many other varieties, are beautifully executed.   The
great market for the disposal of the lace is in the
tourist season, when Kenmare is the halting-place
between Killarney and Glengariff; the lace is displayed at the hotel where the tourists stop to dine,
and some who stay longer pay a visit to the convent,
and see the good that is effected.   Many ladies have
been so struck by the sight that they have endeavoured on their return to England to get orders for the
lace there, having taken specimens with them to show
their friends.   Besides the industrial school, there are
the literary ones, which are under excellent management and are numerously attended.   Without having

what is actually called a middle school, the nuns try
to classify the children, giving to each the education
most suited to their position, and of course to their
capabilities. Some of the children are of the poorest
class, and are not only taught but fed and clothed by
the nuns; the breakfast and the little stirabout and
bread given at noon is often the only food of hundreds
of these little ones, while winter's cold and summer's
heat make no difference in their clothing—the same
wretched rags are worn all the year round. Then,
again, there are girls of a superior grade, who are being
trained for schoolmistresses: they receive a solid and
excellent education, their music is carefully attended
to, and their drawing is exceedingly good. I was
much struck by the specimens shown me, which gave
evidence of considerable talent in the children, and
careful cultivation by their teachers.

It would not seem that the mountain wilds of Ireland
were the most likely place for literature to flourish;
nevertheless the convent of Holy Cross, Kenmare, has
done a great deal in this respect. Several works of
considerable importance have been composed by a
member of this community. Of one of these* a com-
petent judge has said, ' the book possesses a profound
interest, and that of a character wholly apart from
polemics.'

The History of the Franciscan Order, and the Life of
St. Clare, are the productions of the same pen, besides
which the writer has found time to send forth a vast
quantity of little books suited for the poor and children,

* The Life and Revelations of St. Gertrude. London: Burns and
Oates.

and has thus supplied many a gap in popular literature. I understand that a work long wanted is now
in progress within the walls of this convent—a popular
and illustrated History of Ireland. It is extraordinary
that such a work has not long since appeared; the field
of Irish history has been far too little explored, and
the books issued on the subject, if learned and accurate,
are, as is truly said, too 'pale in colour and tame in
language,' and thus, though useful no doubt to the
earnest student, have failed to interest the general
reader. In giving, then, a really trustworthy, impar-
tial, and yet popular history of the country, enriched
with good illustrations, a religious of St. Clare will be
doing a good work and furthering a great cause.

The morning after our arrival at Kenmare was Sunday, and the town presented a spectacle well worth
seeing. Apparently the whole population turned out to
mass; the roads were thronged, and every house seemed
to be empty; all were arrayed in their Sunday best
—even with the poorest, soap and water had achieved
some sort of victory, and the poor garments were
tidied up, while with a great number their Sunday
apparel was by no means to be despised. At the eight
o'clock mass the church was filled, and the sermon was
a surprising one indeed to Saxon ears; not that it was
given in the Irish tongue, it was in the vernacular and
listened to with profound attention.

It appeared that a few days previously two of those
miserable beings who, not content with their own ruin,
go about seeking to compass that of the young and innocent, had entered the little peaceful town. The
vigilant eye of the shepherd had marked them out, and

the wolves were to be driven from the flock. The people were forbidden to give them lodging or food, to exchange a word, or hold any intercourse with them. I learned afterwards that the warning would be quite sufficient; the intruders would, as similar ones had done before, find the place too hot to hold them, and would decamp with all possible speed. The people of Kenmare are not perfect, and have their faults in common with the rest of their fellow-creatures; but the social plague-spot of modern days and the dark shadow which hangs over our green English villages can find no resting-place in these mountain wilds. Kenmare is a very widely-spread parish, and the priests have to go immense distances to attend the sick and to hold 'stations.' It was impossible to help laughing at the absurd idea of the 'Parish Church' of Kenmare not being that of Holy Cross. However, such is the case. At the other end of the village stands a commodious building, with plenty of room for a large congregation, and an incumbent paid, out of the funds of the country, to minister in it. His congregation consists of about a score of people. This district suffered greatly at the time of the famine, the people being reduced to the utmost misery, which was immediately taken advantage of by the 'soupers,' who were willing to relieve any who would read Protestant Bibles and tracts, and receive the visits of the 'Scripture reader.' But the Kerry folk stood firm, and would not sell their birth-right for a mess of pottage.

It was certainly very provoking of the rain. On our return to Killarney, it came down in torrents, and seemed to have made up its mind to go on. There were

so many places we wanted to see—so many things we
wanted to do; for to visit Killarney and *not* sail upon
the Lakes is really something to be ashamed of—

> But the merry clouds knew nothing of that,
> And the rain kept pouring on.

Everybody said that when it once began to rain at
Killarney it always went on for a fortnight, and as
what everybody says must, of course, be true, we took
leave of our pleasant landlady, paying her bill of such
a marvellously small amount that an English lodging-
house keeper would certainly have thought her insane,
and went by train to Charleville. It is a sleepy, uninteresting town, with plenty of objects of interest in its
neighbourhood, and a fair, fertile country spreading on
all sides. It is strange now to think of the stir and the
bustle that must have been aroused in the quiet place
by the conflict so recently going on at the town of
Kilmallock, only five miles distant, when the Fenians
attacked the police barracks, and the manager of the
bank was shot down at his own door. There is a strong
contrast between the two towns. Kilmallock is one of
the most ancient places in Ireland, and one considered
of such great importance that it was entirely surrounded
by fortifications. Here the great Earls of Desmond
had their chief power and state, and unfortunate Kilmallock was, in the days of Elizabeth, razed to the
ground. Arising once again in new strength and state,
its beauty excited even the admiration of Cromwell,
who, bent as he was on destroying ' every fortified town
and every castle and habitation of the Irish,' was anxious
to spare this place. However, he speedily changed his

mind, and the fine buildings and fortifications were reduced to ruins, and it is now one of those desolate spots
which never seem able to recover the loss of their former
greatness. Charleville is, comparatively, a modern
town, and has but a brief history attached to it. It
was founded by the Earl of Ossory in 1621, and named
after the reigning sovereign; and it was burnt to the
ground by the Duke of Berwick in 1690.

At the very outset of Mrs. McAuley's career as a
Sister of Mercy she was entreated to found a convent
at Charleville—a lady of the neighbourhood having
offered 500l. and a house for the commencement. She
foresaw great difficulties for the new foundation, and
was unwilling to make it, but, with her usual meekness,
yielded to the entreaties of others, and went there, with
other Sisters, in October 1836. The description of
her journey thither reads strangely when we remember
it took place but thirty years ago. She went to Tullamore, and intended to 'go on by the canal boat to
Limerick, and thence to Charleville. She did not know
what a very slow and inconvenient mode of conveyance
the canal boat was, nor its hours for starting. It was only
when she reached Tullamore she learned it would not
leave until the middle of the night. This arrangement
precluded the possibility of her or the Sisters getting
any rest; and as the boat did not reach Limerick until
late the next night, they all suffered much from cold
and fatigue.' When they reached Charleville, they
found the house so damp that their clothes were moist
when they rose in the morning; and the difficulties Mrs.
McAuley had anticipated came in abundance. But the
Sisters persevered, and won the gratitude of the poor

who were wont to exclaim, ' It was the Lord who drove
you in amongst us !'   The damp house has been long
since deserted, and a spacious convent built in a good
situation fronting the principal street of the town, and
having at its rear a pretty garden, well laid out, with
several fields beyond.   The interior arrangements of
the convent are excellent—the corridors being particularly wide and airy.   The nuns have a pretty choir,
divided by a grating from the rest of their chapel, which
has an entrance from the street, and is open to the public.   Attached to the convent are spacious poor schools,
numerously attended and well managed.   An industrial
school is also presided over by the Sisters, and their
visitation among the poor and sick is very large.
Nothing gives more striking evidence of the marvellous
way in which the Sisters of Mercy spread than these
convents in the provincial towns.   They begin with a
handful of nuns, and a few years later there is a
flourishing community.   Nothing more plainly shows
also the zeal, generosity, and self-denial of the Sisters
than the history of some of these foundations.   The
community at Charleville had surmounted long and
trying difficulties.   The harvest had come after the seed
time, and the community was large and flourishing,
dwelling together in close union and peace.

Nuns for a colonial foundation were asked for, and
the Sisters responded to the call.   Those who were
bound together by the tender ties of nature, as well as
those of a religious sisterhood, were content to part
probably for ever in this life.   In the summer of last
year, a ship sailed from Queenstown, carrying on board
a freight of passengers never before, I should think,

gathered together in one vessel, and whose assemblage gave very evident proofs of the rapid progress of the Catholic religion, and the generous efforts of Ireland in its furtherance.   The vessel contained two Bishops, half a dozen priests, eighteen nuns, and some ladies who intended to join the religious as soon as they were settled in their new homes.   Three communities of nuns made up the party—one of Sisters of Mercy from Charleville, another from Athy, and a third of Presentation nuns.   They were bound respectively for Bathurst, Maitland, and Hobart's Town.   The vessel was surnamed by some the ' holy ship,' and seldom indeed would such united sounds of praise and prayer have been heard as when this vessel made her way through the world of waters.   Those who think that conventual life blunts the affections and hardens the heart would have been surprised to hear the account of the partings on board that memorable vessel—how the Sisters of Charleville clung round their ' Mother,' who had gone to see them off, and how the sacrifice of parting from their convent home, though generously made, had cut deeply into their inmost hearts.

CHAPTER XI.

ORANMORE, on an arm of Galway Bay, is a desolate
looking town ; a number of deserted, unroofed houses
meet the traveller's gaze, and he soon learns that emigration has rapidly thinned the population of the place.
The country round is bare and dreary, except where
the eye catches a view of the coast with its innumer-
able bendings, points of land, and juttings out into the
bay.   The line of railway from Dublin to Oranmore
is considered to be a very uninteresting one, and in
truth, after the pretty suburbs of Dublin have been
passed, and a glance has been caught of the grey
towers of Maynooth college, there are few objects
worthy of notice, and the country is for the most part
flat and ugly ; but the day I travelled on that line was
what the Irish call a ' pet day,' and the whole landscape was bathed in such floods of glorious sunshine
that even great tracts of barren moorland had their
charm.

At Athlone the railway crosses the Shannon, which
even here is a beautiful and stately river.   The train
halts awhile at Athlone, giving the traveller time to
recall the ancient glories of the place, its eventful history, the wars that had raged beneath its walls, and
last, not least, the fatal battle of Aughrim, whose loss
was so disastrous to the Irish cause.

At one station on the line the train also drew up for a considerable time, and I was amused at watching a specimen of Irish manners. A sort of half gentleman, who had evidently been shooting or fishing in the town, joined the train, and was accompanied to the station by three or four young women, with shawls thrown over their heads, and several boys and men, the evident idlers of the town. A great deal of fun and chaff was going on, the traveller giving warm invitations to ' Mary, my dear,' to come with him, which Mary laughingly refused. My attention was specially drawn to one of the group, because I thought I never had seen so dirty a face before; presently the owner of it said something, which fortunately I did not catch, whereupon a storm burst upon his head; ' that he should have dared to say such a thing in the presence of girls,' was the burden of the scolding, and he was abused by the traveller from the third class carriage with vehemence, and called every name of reproach in the Irish vocabulary; his companions and the stragglers on the platform looked on in silent approval. I expected to see an Irish row, but no, my dirty friend took his reproof meekly, and seemed greatly ashamed of himself, if not for what he had said, at least for saying it ' in the presence of girls ;' and I could not help wondering how many men of a similar class in England would have submitted to such a dressing for a like offence. The country round Oranmore is extremely rocky, and the eye grows weary of the continual ' crop of stones.' ' Stones everywhere ; in the walls, the roads, the hills, the plains, and the fields ; all one unmitigated sheet of grey monotony, only relieved by the distant hills of Clare.' Here and there along the lonely roads we came upon a peasant woman in the picturesque costume of the neighbourhood; a red petticoat, beneath which are seen her bare feet, and a heavy cloak of dark blue woollen, curiously draped about the figure and head. It is no wonder the people emigrate, there is nothing for them to do ; the cry of no work is repeated here more sadly than ever, and the poverty is extreme. When in the winter through which we have passed, London was snow-bound for a week, and groups of men went about the streets wailing out in melancholy cadence, ' We have no work to do,' and people's hearts were touched, and those who never gave to beggars sent out money and food, saying they could not refuse that appeal, I used to think of the peasants in county Galway, for the snow was deep on the ground there too, and there the cry, ' We have no work to do,' might be chanted, not for one week, but through many a long month. There is a little Presentation Convent at Oranmore, with poor schools, and a few miles distant, at the village of Clarin Bridge, is a lovely little convent of the Irish Sisters of Charity, called ' Our Lady's Priory.' We are so ac-customed to come upon these Sisters amidst the busy whirl of great towns, that it seemed quite a surprise to find them in a ' village convent,' and one which reminds us again of days gone by, when the convent stood close by the castle gate, and religious were to be found in country solitudes as well as in the heart of great cities. The convent at Clarin Bridge was founded in the year 1844. It is a beautiful little building, standing back from the road, and surrounded by a pretty garden,

shaded by a variety of trees. On one side is the
chapel, and on the other the schools; and though
Clarin Bridge is such a quiet village the population is
large and widely scattered, so that the Sisters have a
large attendance of children, averaging between two
and three hundred. There is also a small industrial
school attached, where lace is made, and we were
shown some beautiful specimens of it; but here, as in
most industrial schools, the great difficulty is to get a
sale for the work. I was much interested at finding
that the Superioress of this convent was the sister of
Gerald Griffin, the ' Lucy ' of whom he speaks so tenderly in his letters, to whom he was wont to pour out
his hopes and fears, joys and sorrows, and whose
example, no doubt, greatly influenced him in turning
from a vain pursuit of worldly fame to a life of devotion and sacrifice. Of her convent life he thus
speaks in his poems :—

> To see that bark with canvass furl'd
> Still riding in that port of peace.

And then he continues :—

> Oh! darling of a heart that still
> By earthly joys too deeply trod,
> At moments bids its owner feel
> The warmth of nature and of God.
>
> Still be his care in future years
> To learn of thee truth's simple way,
> And free from groundless hopes and fears,
> Serenely live, securely pray.
>
> And when our Christmas days are past,
> And life's fair shadows faint and dim,
> Oh! be my sister heard at last
> When her pure hands are raised for him.

And they were parted. Cut off in the prime of
life, he rests in his quiet grave, and his memory is
yet green amongst us. She has lingered on to a
good old age, while those she loved have, one by one,
dropped by her side; patiently filling up the measure
of her appointed task, and waiting for the hour when
those who parted for the love of God shall have their
joyous meeting.

Near the convent is a large school, with house adjoining, belonging to the Christian Brothers; the community is, of course, very small, but their school
seemed to be fully up to the mark required for a
country school; they also have a good attendance, and
some of the boys come long distances.

The Brothers told us various anecdotes of the love
the boys have for learning, and the pains some of them
take to keep up their learning in spare hours, after
they have been obliged to leave school and go to work.
This school and monastery were founded by the late
Sir Thomas Redington, who thus conferred a great
and lasting benefit on the poor of the neighbourhood.
He also gave a large portion of land to the Sisters
of Charity, while their convent and its endowment
for five Sisters was the gift of his mother, Mrs.
Redington.

Around the town of Galway gather many memories
of history and romance. On every side the quaint old
town bears marks of having fallen from a great estate,
while at each turn there is some record or other of the
busy part Galway once took in the history of the
country. Its ancient feuds, the proud names of its
' Tribes,' its mercantile greatness, its victories and its

defeats, its sieges and its surrenders, all flock fast upon
the visitor's memory as he passes through the narrow,
half-deserted streets. But neither feud nor conquest
could rob it of its chief interest—the beautiful bay which
lies spread at its feet. No words can adequately describe the view when one stands on its shores, and the
wild Atlantic, broken only by the dark ridge of the Isles
of Arran, bursts upon the sight. Galway abounds in
religious houses; to it the ancient orders have seemed to
cling, and to raise their heads again within its walls as
soon as ever they could do so in safety. I had an especial
wish to visit the Convent of Poor Clares in Galway,
standing on what is called 'Nuns' Island,' for the history of the order is one of the most romantic of any of
the Irish religious houses. It seems that a convent of
this order was existing in Galway in the year 1511,
but it suffered the same fate as others at the time of
the dissolution, and all traces of the religious who filled
it are lost. From time to time, Irish ladies entered
foreign convents with the hope of being able to make
foundations in their native land, and six Irish nuns from
the Poor Clares' Convent at Gravelines came to Dublin
in 1625; and, says the old chronicle, 'soon after they
had encloistered themselves in the city of Dublin, they
admitted several to this form of life, and their persecution began by search and threatenings in such manner
that it was needful for them sometimes to hide themselves and to send their ornaments (i.e. church ornaments) to some Catholic houses. Yet, notwithstanding,
the sweet savour of their virtues extended itself, and
the manner of their life was much admired, and the
more so because in people's memory there were none

cloistered in that kingdom, and so everybody was desirous to see and hear them.   Amongst the rest, the
Lady Deputy went disguised to look on them, the which
she did through the high grate, as they were in divine
office, and was in great admiration.'   Unfortunately the
Lady Deputy must needs tell her lord what she had
seen, upon which ' the Lord Deputy sent the mayor
with armed men to the convent, ordaining to bring the
Abbess, with some of the religious, to his presence, and
to leave a guard upon the convent and the rest, until
further orders.'   As the mayor came back with the defenceless nuns, ' there assembled great concourse of
people, who took compassion to see them go abroad
barefoot, and feared much that they would suffer greater
harm ; they raised such tumult that the mayor feared
to be stoned, whereupon, directing his speech to Father
Luke Dillon, brother to the Abbess, and some other
lords, knights, and gentlemen kinsmen to the nuns, who
were present there, he said that no hurt should be done
to the gentlewomen, and, therefore, for God's love, to
appease the people.   They did so, by the persuasion
of the same Abbess and other Sisters.   Having arrived
at the Castle where the Deputy and peers, with a great
multitude of people expected them, the Deputy questioned the Abbess how did they dare to put up their
grates, and settle themselves in cloister there.'   The
answers of the Abbess, however, somewhat abated the
fury of this wise ruler, and instead of driving them out
of Ireland as he had intended, he only commanded them
to quit Dublin within a month from that day.   The
order was obeyed, and, as the six novices, though un-
professed, would not be persuaded to forsake them, the

whole set forth on their exile. 'They divided themselves into three companies amongst some noble county
friends of theirs, who charitably harboured them until
a poor house was built for their habitation in a solitary
neck of land, without inhabitants, near a great cave,
not daring any more to settle themselves in any great
town or city or populous place; and there they founded
a convent, which they called Bethlehem, and it was
situated in such a low and shadowy bog as the physicians
wondered how such tender creatures, very delicately
reared, could live therein, for in wet and rainy weather
the water would not only fall through the roof of the
house, but also in several places came up through the
ground. Besides that, all their houses were so low that
their cells and other rooms, except only the choir, were
upon the ground.' This convent was situated in the
neighbourhood of Athlone, on the banks of Lough Ree,
a noble expansion of the Shannon, but where there is
much marsh and bog land; and, notwithstanding the
unhealthiness of the site, the community rapidly increased, and people came from a great distance to see
them. Another Lady Deputy had the same curiosity
as her predecessor, and made the journey to Athlone,
together with the Duchess of Buckingham, for the
sole purpose of seeing and conversing with the nuns.
However, fresh persecution was at hand, and in 1641
the nuns were warned that the Parliamentary soldiers were on their track. For some months they
lived ' in such panic as it were far easier for them to
suffer death at once than to live in the like martyrdom.'
It was now that the people of Galway, confident in
their own superior safety, besought some of the nuns

to come within their walls for protection. Accordingly
a foundation was made, but thirty nuns remained behind
in Bethlehem, being unwilling to quit it till they should
be actually forced to do so. This soon took place, and
they had to fly away in boats to the other side of the
lake, while the soldiers took possession of the convent,
' devouring all the provision, making sport and laughter
of the altars, pictures, ornaments, and sacred things
that were therein. Some of them would put on the
habits of the nuns they found there, and, jesting at
them, would say, " Come, let us say Mass." Lastly,
they set fire to the convent.' The exiled nuns divided
into two parties—one going to Wexford and the other
to Athlone. But a few years later both these convents
were destroyed by Cromwell, and the nuns driven
away. Many of them went to Spain, and were received
into convents of their order, and beautiful records remain of their holy lives and deaths—stories which might
form themes for a poet and subjects for an artist.
One ship touches the Spanish shore, but the aged
Abbess who is on board is worn out, and dies in sight
of land; or again, when Sister Julia Blake, of Galway,
is dying, she is ' so jocund and glad that she caused to be
played on a harp for her and therewith to sing *Te Deum
Laudamus*.'

The Poor Clares, on their arrival in Galway, received
a great number of novices, and soon after sent the following humble petition to the corporation : ' That
your petitioners, *members of this corporation*, did some
yeares sithence forsake the world to serve the Almighty,
and what through the distempers of the times, and
through God's holy will, have suffered great affliction

these seven yeares past, and in their necessity, as bound
by nature, repaired to this toune; shewing, further,
that through necessity, by reason of the tymes, their
parents and friends are unable to furnish their wants,
as in peaceable tymes they have intended; and that
your poor petitioners doe suffer much by the exorbitant
rent they pay, and, notwithstanding their due payment,
are to be thrust out of their dwelling next May, their
lease being then ended; the premises considered, and
taken to your consideration the inconvenience of religious women who want habitation, the convenience
of their residence in this place, the preferment of young
children, though poor, shall be relieved, by God's assistance, in our convent, the everlasting prayers to be
made for you, the glory of God, the preservation of the
town by your petitioners, and their successors their
intercessions, the honour of Gallway to befounde such
a monasterie; the petitioners humbly pray that you
may be pleased to grant them sufficient roome for
building a monasterie, and rooms convenient thereunto,
a garden and orchard, in the next island adjoyning to
the bridge of Illanalltenagh, and for that your petitioners' building will be rather a strength than any
annoyance, hindrance, or impeachment, either to the
highway leading to the other island, or to the safety
and preservation of this corporation, which granted,
they will ever pray.

'SISTER MARY BONAVENTURE,
'Unworthy Abbesse.'

This petition was acceded to, and the island 'was
granted to the community in 1648, and the same

was recorded in chapter and mayoralty book, in the mayoralty of Walter Blake, knight.' Upon this island a handsome convent with cloisters was erected, but all was lost when Galway surrendered, in 1652, to the arms of Cromwell, and the convent was torn down. Many of the nuns seem to have lingered in Galway or its neighbourhood, for a few years afterwards we find two of them renting their own land from the man to whom it had been granted by the Parliament, and farming it. The land afterwards became the property of the crown.

In 1686, a few of the Poor Clares still survived, and still pined after a convent home, and they ventured once more into Galway, and took a large house in Market Street, where they received lady boarders for the purpose of concealing the fact that they were religious. The annals state that on the 1st of May, 1698, the convent was broken into by the military, the nuns turned out, and obliged to disperse among their friends. Undaunted in courage, as soon as this storm had blown over, the nuns returned to their place, and lived unmolested till April 1712, when they were again turned out, and the convent converted into barracks. A kind friend living next door, Mr. Ambrose O'Connor, harboured five or six of them for the moment. When night drew on they had a great longing to creep back to their beloved and deserted choir, there to say their matin office. Mr. O'Connor supplied them with candles, and gave the sentry a douceur to induce him to allow the poor ladies to say their prayers for an hour.

So the nuns crept up to the chapel, and in low tones said their matins and lauds; meanwhile, the soldiers who were sleeping in the cells were shaking with terror, and went next morning to their officers to complain that the choir was filled by the ghosts of nuns saying their prayers, and that they would no longer sleep in a haunted house. The convent was therefore deserted, and after a little time the poor nuns ventured back to it. That same year they sent six Sisters to found a convent of their order in Dublin, but soon after their arrival they were seized and taken to the Judges, and their papers also looked into. Such was the alarm the arrival of a handful of nuns excited, that an order was given that ' all the laws in force against the papists should be strictly carried into execution.' It does not appear that this was put in force as regards the Dublin nuns, but as it had been discovered they came from Galway, orders were sent down to disperse the nuns in that town. However, the religious were warned of it, and putting on secular clothing, they so mixed themselves with the boarders that they could not be discovered. Time went on, and the nuns were in great straits, and reduced to uttermost poverty; and in 1740, ' the times being more peaceable,' two of the nuns actually had the courage to make a journey to London, a formidable undertaking indeed in those days. Sister Sherritt, belonging to one of the oldest names in Galway, was cousin german to Lady Hamilton, one of the ladies of the bedchamber, and through her interest the queen was induced to grant them three acres of land, ' on their own island, to feed a couple of cows.'

No doubt the peculiar character of Caroline of Anspach inspired a hope that she might lend a favour-

able ear to the petition. She was a woman of education,
' a solitary model of refinement in the midst of a gross,
clownish, and corrupt court ;' she was fond of power,
and determined to exercise it. It is also said that ' she
took great delight in making theologians dispute knotty
points in her presence, perplexing them with questions concerning the opposite doctrines of the different
Christian churches.' Perhaps the idea that the nuns
of St. Clare had been unjustly robbed and persecuted
had some chance of getting into her head; at all
events, it must have been a strange sight when they
appeared before her, wearing the poor habit of St.
Clare, in the sight of her regal splendour.

The nuns came back from London in ' great joy,
and soon got possession of the three acres, when they
planted a garden, and built a small lodge for such of
the Sisters as might want to change air, the convent
within the town being close, and filling fast with subjects to the number of fifty at one time.' As time
passed on the funds of the community increased, till at
last they were able once more to build on their beloved
island ; a convent, chapel, and poor schools, all under
one roof, accordingly rose up, and the entire community removed there on the 15th of June, 1825.
Thus, after an exile of one hundred and seventy-three
years, the same religious family, the successors of those
who had been driven out, and who had gone through
such cruel vicissitudes, came back to their old quarters,
to what is so touchingly called all through their annals,
' their own island,' ' their dear island,' to live there at
last in peace and security. Forty years have passed
away, and here the community still dwell ; only that
by their side have risen up the fresh young communi-

ties of modern days. On the other side of the river, which runs around the island, is a Presentation convent, with schools, and the Sisters of Mercy are also in the town.

We went into the chapel of the Poor Clares, and heard them saying office. The community does not seem to be numerous, and many of the Sisters are old, so that their poor school has been discontinued, and, indeed, it is not required in such close vicinity to the Presentation nuns. No doubt in time, as is often the case in these ancient communities, a fresh element of life and strength will spring up; and as active work seems no longer required from the religious, the 'first rule of St. Clare with the straight statutes made by St. Collet' may be practised, as in another 'Bethlehem,' on the 'Nuns' Island.'

And then from the records of the past, from the convent whose rule was made for quiet days in the ages of faith, we went to see the Sisters of Mercy in one of the outposts that they have lately gained in their incessant warfare with the misery and the evil which have sprung up in modern times.

We made our way to the workhouse, which stands a little way out of the town, and where, within the last year or two, the infirmary has been given up to the care of the Sisters of Mercy; the guardians having thus followed the good example set by the board in Limerick. The infirmary is, of course, on a much smaller scale than that of Limerick. I do not think more than one hundred patients can be received; neither is the building to be compared to that of the former, and many of the rooms are not at all suited for sick wards. Notwithstanding all these difficulties the Sisters have done wonders; the infirmary is perfectly clean, everything in order, and an air of comfort pervades the place. We happened to see the dinners served, and the quality of the food, and the nicety with which it was sent up, formed a great contrast to the wretched food and dirty plates I had often seen used in workhouses belonging to rich English unions.

At Limerick the Sisters of Mercy have a little house to live in, divided from the infirmary by a small garden; at Galway they have a set of rooms in the workhouse, and closely adjoining the sick wards. It would be far better if they had large airy rooms at a greater distance from the sick; but it is of no use to talk to the Sisters of Mercy about their own comfort and convenience. It is much better for the patients, they say, that they should be close at hand, and with that they are satisfied. It would be only a repetition of what I have said about Limerick to dilate longer on this work. It is precisely similar, though on a smaller scale, and great is the good wrought to both bodies and souls of the patients by the presence of the Sisters. We were much struck by various little things which showed us with what scrupulous care waste was avoided, while the comfort of the patients was rigidly attended to. The very faces of the bright cheerful Sisters were calculated to cheer up the weary despondency of the poor sufferers. We went into the workhouse girls' school here, and I was dreadfully pained at the sight, they looked so exactly like a set of young savages; perhaps the bare feet gave them a particularly wretched aspect to English eyes, but I had seen plenty of barefooted children in the schools and in the streets of Ireland who were civilised enough;

the uncared-for, wild aspect of these children was most
terrible to behold.   Their playground is a very confined one, and along one side of it runs a range of low
buildings containing the rooms in which are lodged the
unmarried mothers and their babies.   This fact needs
no comment.   How such things can be suffered to go
on in a Christian country is a mystery ; and how the
rulers of a land can allow the prevalence of the workhouse system, calculated to demoralise a large portion
of the population, is also extraordinary.   Retribution
for the crime of such neglect comes heavily on us, but
its warnings seem thrown away.   O'Connell, with his
keen foresight, was convinced of the evil the workhouses would do to Ireland, and raised up his voice
against them, and his prophecy has been abundantly
fulfilled.   The plan of drafting workhouse children
into district schools does not exist in Ireland, and I
believe the poor-law in England and Ireland differs so
much, that the Acts passed in one country do not
affect the other.   There is no doubt that, excepting
only the glaring injustice done to the children of
Catholics in the district schools, their system is a great
step in advance.   In Ireland the formation of district
schools would have less difficulty to contend against
than in England.   The children are all Catholics ; if
there be exceptions, they are so few and so readily discovered that such children could be easily transferred to
some Protestant orphanage, while the Catholic children
could be placed under the care of religious or a staff of
respectable secular teachers, so easily to be found in
Ireland.   Then, instead of training up a gang of
young savages ripe for any kind of mischief, the
orphan and deserted children would grow up to be

useful members of the population. That the plan
would be economical in the end it is certain, because
the present system, as we have seen in Cork, tends to
make the children life-long burdens on the unions;
whereas, if the district school were well managed, the
children would become independent when grown up.
It is a fact, that children sent out from the district
schools in England do provide for themselves. In these
schools, however, the managers see the evil of sending
out the girls at the early ages of fourteen and fifteen,
and some of them are trying to get power to keep
them till eighteen. In Ireland, I believe, if the guardians were energetic the plan of district schools might
be introduced at once.

The Sisters of Mercy have a large convent in Galway, from whence the religious who serve the infirmary
are sent out; they have two branch houses, one an
orphanage, the other a Magdalene asylum. I had not
time to do more than visit the churches of the Franciscans and Jesuits, the latter of which is quite modern,
and a very pretty and devotional one.

And so I took my leave of Galway, a place I had so
often longed to see; the city which, ' once frequented
by ships with cargoes of French and Spanish wines, to
supply the wassailings of the O'Neils and O'Donels,
the O'Garas and O'Kanes; her marble palaces handed
over to strangers, and her gallant sons and dark-eyed
daughters banished, remains for 200 years a ruin; her
splendid port empty, while her " hungry air," in 1862,
becomes the mock of the official stranger.' *

* *Cromwellian Settlement of Ireland.* By John Prendergast.

CHAPTER XII.

THE pretty town of Loughrea, on the northern bank of the lake from which it takes its name, is at some distance from the railway. I left the line at Athenry, and proceeded thither on an outside car. The country was still bare and rocky, and the landscape was not improved by occasional scudding showers of rain; but when it cleared, there were distant mountain views to be caught which enlivened the scene. The history of the Carmelite Convent at Loughrea is one of deep interest, and is another of those wonderful stories connected with the ancient religious houses of Ireland.

During the whole rage of the religious persecutions, the monks and friars had weathered the storm in far greater number than the nuns, having been able to disguise themselves, move rapidly from place to place, and find means of support in a way which women could not accomplish. Consequently though the beautiful old monastery, in the early English style of architecture, built at Loughrea by Sir Richard De Burgh for Carmelite friars in 1361, had fallen into ruins, monks of the order lingered in the town, and were to be found there at the close of the seventeenth century.

A young dressmaker in the town had often expressed to them her ardent desire to be a religious of Mount Carmel. Seeing her great virtue, the fathers themselves gave her the habit, and received her vows. There were always plenty of Irishwomen thirsting for religious life, and women of all ranks soon gathered round Sister Mary Teresa of St. Dominic, as she was called. One of the fathers collected alms for them in Spain, and in 1755 a house was built for them in the main street of Loughrea. It bore no external mark of being a convent; the lower part of it was arranged as a shop, and a milliner for many years rented it and carried on her business, while in the rooms above the nuns laboured, prayed, and suffered. The world knew nothing of them, they had no external mark of being religious, but they lived the lives of saints. Their poverty was extreme, and often they had nothing to eat, but they prayed fervently, and their wants were relieved in a remarkable way again and again. One day the prioress told the community to pray while she went out to beg, but she returned from her quest unsuccessful. Seeing her poor children faint with hunger, she bade them pray yet more fervently, and once again she ventured out on her weary errand. A stranger whom she had never seen came up to her, and silently put into her hand a piece of gold. The nuns, in their simple faith, always believed him to be St. Joseph. But persecution could not spare even this secluded and poverty-stricken community; information was given that they were ' *nuns*,' and officials were ordered to seize the supposed criminals, and search their house. The nuns were warned of the danger, fled during the night, and were housed by different friends. It suddenly flashed on the prioress's mind that she had left papers of some importance behind her, and she dared not risk losing them. So she dressed herself like a beggar woman, crept back to the convent and secured her property, and as she returned, met the officers on the stairs. But they never guessed she was anything else but a poor beggar, and let her pass without remark. The affair of the supposed convent was brought before the magistrates, and some charitable friend pleaded the cause of the religious, declaring they were only a few poor ladies who chose to live together and maintain themselves by their needlework. His remonstrance was listened to, and the nuns were allowed to return, but for many years the utmost caution and secrecy had to be observed. Their chapel was literally an 'upper chamber,' hidden at the top of the house, and they wore a plain, secular dress, but were always true nuns in heart and soul. A young lady once wished to join them, but having no money, was unwilling to become a charge to so poor a community. One day a person whom she had never seen in her life came to her door, and saying, ' You wish to be a nun, take this and accomplish your desire,' gave her the sum she required.

Times began to brighten. The nuns now sent out three foundations, the two first of which to Cork and Limerick did not succeed, but the third one sent to Dublin took root there and from it the other Carmelite convents in Ireland have taken their rise. At Loughrea the nuns now ventured to put on their habit, and in 1825 a house, standing on rising ground, completely out of the town, and with a good garden surrounding it, was built, and the nuns took possession of it. The community was still very poor, and received lady boarders in order to gain means for support. They also had a poor school, there being no other one for Catholic children in the place. Thus it became impossible for them to observe their rule strictly, and as it is always difficult in such a case to know where mitigation should begin and end, relaxation gradually crept in. But it is a remarkable fact that all through their career there were saints among them.

Mother Magdalene of St. John of the Cross used to spend hours on her knees adoring the Blessed Sacrament, and when her last hour came, she could only utter one sentence again and again, 'Oh! Love Divine! Oh! divine Love!' And light not of this earth shone around her, and sounds of celestial music came to welcome her to her home above.

Another nun had passed through a long life with the purity and innocence of a child. She died at last, worn out with extreme old age, and bearing the usual marks of advanced years, but after death the freshness and beauty of youth came back to the corpse. Some gentlemen who happened to see her in her coffin exclaimed, 'How vain these women are! they have actually painted a dead body;' but, say the convent annals very simply, 'she was not painted, but she was an angel.' In Mount Carmel at Loughrea lives such as these had passed away, prayers such as these had ascended up to heaven, and benedictions rested on the house. In 1850 the Sisters of Mercy opened a convent in the town, and the necessity for supporting a poor school at the Carmelite Convent ceased, and in God's good time the nuns were inspired to re-establish the rule of St. Teresa in its strict observance. In different ways and in many forms God's angels come pointing out the path that chosen souls must follow. To Mount Carmel at Loughrea such a message did not come in vain. It had been the birthplace of the Carmelite order in Ireland in times of persecution; it was to be also the birthplace of the reform, a *second Avila*. Entirely trusting in Providence for support, the nuns gave up their *pensionnaires*; a *grille* was erected, and strict enclosure restored; in short, every observance of the Carmelite rule, as reformed by St. Teresa, was adopted; so that when the General of the order visited the house, he observed he did not think that St. Teresa herself could find anything there to rectify.

Within these walls there is an inexpressible sense of rest and peace. We feel withdrawn for awhile from earth and its cares, and lifted up into a region above the weary world. Here saints have lived and died, and here their deeds are bearing fruit; here weak and feeble women are imitating the lives of angels, not for themselves only, but for us—for us who have to suffer, labour, and combat in the world outside. A visit to Loughrea wakes up many thoughts; the foremost certainly is this, When will the contemplative orders come back to Ireland? Out of her poverty, in the midst of her sufferings she has done much, will she not crown her work? In one respect only Ireland is behind not only foreign countries but even England herself. In all Catholic countries side by side with the *œuvre* of charity rises the house for prayer and contemplation. The white veils of the Sisters of Charity almost cover the land. The Frère des Écoles Chrétiennes passes us at every turn. The poor are

tended, cared for, honoured, and schemes for their
assistance and benefit succeed, multiply, and bear fruit,
because holy hands are lifted up unceasingly to God;
and while some are ministering to the Lord in the
person of His poor, others are sitting at His feet,
hearing His word. Who that has visited cities in
Catholic lands, but has felt the calm and hush that falls
on them, when, after making a round of the beautiful
works of charity which the town contains, the well
filled schools, the comfortable hospitals, the *asyles* for
every human woe, they enter within the gates of one
of those abodes of prayer and penance, from which
the busy world is shut out, where its maxims may
utterly be set at nought, where God is the sole Master,
and His praise the continual theme.   And even
England, poor England, so poor in faith, so full of
spiritual destitution, so scantily provided with religious houses, with orphans calling out for help, and
cries of misery on all sides; England has been wise
enough to bring back her praying orders to help on
the active.   And so, though the Minories, where once
the daughters of St. Clare lived and died, is now but a
crowded street in the heart of the metropolis, their
successors live and pray in its suburbs : there in the
dead of night, watching before the Tabernacle; there
in the early morning following in spirit along the way
of the cross.

Hard by their abode, the Carmelites, the true
daughters of St. Teresa, show us in very deed what
was the fashion of her life. A mile or two farther in
the great Babylon, and entering within a quiet chapel,
we find ourselves before Jesus exposed in His sacra-

ment, and too often, alas! alone, save for one faithful watcher kneeling at His feet. A little farther on, and in another convent, the scene is repeated.

In London alone there are more contemplative orders than in the whole of Ireland; for at present there are only three in the whole country, the Carmelites at Loughrea, the Franciscans at Drumshanbo, and the Redemptoristines, Dublin. It is quite certain that the need for active orders is great in modern days; but if the contemplative orders were wanted in the ages of faith, is it possible that they can be less necessary in an age of materialism and unbelief, when men are trying on all hands to destroy every token of the unseen world—in an age, too, of bustle and progress, and breathless speed, when the mighty power of prayer, and the lessons to be learnt in solitude, are too often forgotten? And if a life of penance was called for in the days when men lived simply and hardily, and cared little for animal comfort, is it not needed now when the luxury of the age has reached an appalling height, when comfort has become a god, and men shrink from enduring hardness? And experience shows that abundant blessings come in the train of religious orders. Active orders spring up and multiply by their side, their work is visibly blessed, and souls are won to God. These things we see, and what shall we say of those hidden from our eyes, woes averted, judgments delayed, blessings falling like the dew? For the sake of a few God would have spared the sinful cities of the plain; for the sake of a few He has patience still, proud and stubborn though the nations be.

The Sisters of Mercy at Loughrea have a very fine

convent, and their schools contain four hundred and
sixty-six children. They have also a House of Mercy
and orphanage, and visit the poor and sick. I was very
sorry I had not time to see their house, but I was
anxious to reach Gort before nightfall, as the twelve
Irish miles which lie between it and Loughrea had to
be traversed on an outside car. The road runs close
beside the lough, which is about two or three miles in
circumference. Its waters looked dark and gloomy, for
a storm was gathering overhead. Presently, down came
the rain in torrents, such as I do not think I ever saw
before ; but the car-driver was unmoved, and the horse
trotted quietly on. Along the road it was amusing to
see the way in which some of the peasant women met
the fury of the storm, by stooping till they were nearly
double, and thus letting the rain, which was driving
furiously, pass over them. Presently, the sky cleared,
and the sun came out and lighted up the landscape.
Part of the road to Gort is very pretty, passing through
some pretty woods, and close by several fine domains,
well planted and laid out. The rest of the way the
country is bare and rocky as before. As we neared Gort
the sun was beginning to set, and the stars came out in
the pale sky; peasants were coming home from the
market, some in the half carts, half cars, which are
used by the Irish poor, some walking ; but nearly all
barefoot, and in the pretty costume of the county. As
the sun disappeared it became extremely cold, and I
was very thankful when the car drew up at a large house
in the main street at Gort, which proved to be the
Convent of the Sisters of Mercy. There I had such a
welcome as one only meets with in Ireland, and cold

and fatigue were soon forgotten under the genial influence of affectionate hospitality.

Gort is a neat, clean, but wonderfully quiet little
town, and the visitor is involuntarily reminded of the
remark of the author of the ' Irish Sketch Book,' who
describes Gort as a town which ' seemed to bore itself
considerably, and had nothing to do.' There is a little
stir of life, however, twice a day, on the arrival of the
mail coach from Galway and Ennis, for at present this
old-fashioned mode of conveyance is the only available
one between the two towns. A railroad is in course
of construction, which is to join the Midland Great
Western line at Athenry, and which will be a great
boon to the traveller. Through the town of Gort
runs a broad clear river, on the banks of which
stands the convent. It is a large country house, which
has been transformed into a convent, while schools
have been built adjoining it. Behind the house are
good-sized grounds, planted with some of the finest
oak trees I ever saw, through which the river wends
its way. On a rising ground at the end of the
grounds is the little quiet cemetery of the nuns. The
schools here struck me as particularly good, the buildings well adapted for the purpose, and the children
thoroughly trained and well taught. There are infant
schools for boys and girls, another for elder girls, and
a small middle school. This latter is an absolute necessity in Gort, and the children of this class could
not otherwise obtain any education, there being no
other convent of any kind within miles. The chapel
is only a large room, fitted up for the purpose, but it
is very pretty, and has an air of devotion about it. It

was pleasing to see the Sisters, when the labours of the
day were over, assembling in their stalls to say their
matin office, forestalling thus by prayer and praise the
cares and troubles of the coming day.   There is an
old-fashioned, but clean and comfortable hotel at Gort,
almost facing a large plain building, which forms the
Catholic chapel.   A large stone cross stands in the
churchyard, and several people were kneeling round it
in prayer when on the Sunday after my arrival in Gort
I went to the chapel for nine o'clock mass. It was like
a little bit out of a foreign country suddenly set down
before my eyes; but on entering within the chapel the
scene as contemplated from the gallery was stranger
still.   The whole floor of the church is given up to the
poor, and there are no benches or chairs of any kind.
There they stood or knelt, grouped in various attitudes,
and in a variety of costumes.   The women, in their red
petticoats and blue cloaks, when standing together in
groups, formed a subject for an artist; here and there
were those not rich enough to possess the valued cloak,
some of whom had tied bright coloured handkerchiefs
over their heads, and others had arranged their poor
clothing as best they could. The occasional intrusion of
a straw bonnet, or, worse still, a *hat*, was a painful eye-
sore to the spectator.   There were quite as many men
as women, and of all ages, some greyheaded, fathers
with their little ones clinging round them, smart looking youths, and numerous boys.   When the consecration bell sounded the whole mass bent low, many
almost prostrate on the ground; it was like an Italian
picture, save and except that instead of sculptured
marbles or Gothic arches surrounding the multitude,

there rose the plain whitewashed walls of a poor Irish
chapel. These whitewashed chapels of Ireland, how
they jar upon the sight of those accustomed to see all
that is noble and beautiful adorning the sanctuary!
Yet what shrines they have been of faith and devotion!
what witnesses they are to the persevering, unconquerable faith of the Irish!

There were a great many communicants at this
mass, and when it was ended the priest took off his
chasuble, and advanced to the front of the altar.
There was a sudden rush. Up got everybody from
the floor, and the multitude packed themselves in a compact mass round the altar. The sermon was in Irish;
every eye was bent on the preacher, every ear strained
to listen, and it was evident, from the gestures of the
people, that their whole attention was given to the
discourse, and that every point went home. Certainly
Tennyson's satirical, but perfectly true, description of
the farmers who fill the fine old village churches of
England, with their Norman arches, their aisles, and
their transepts, could not be applied to the Irish
peasantry; for when speaking of the sermon, Tenny
son makes the auditor exclaim—

> An I niver know'd what a meän'd
> But I thowt a 'ad summut to saäy,
> An I thowt a said whot a owt to 'a said,
> An I comed awaäy.

The eloquent preachers in crowded city churches
would often rejoice to have an audience so hanging on
their words. I declared afterwards that I understood
the sermon very well; for it was the festival of the
Seven Dolours which formed the subject of the dis-

course; and the gestures of the priest, and the answering emotion of the people plainly told that they were bidden to endure patiently, and to suffer bravely after the example of her whose sorrows no mortal can ever equal. That Sunday was a cloudless summer's day, and after the last mass was over, the kind old parish priest took me to see the great lion of the neighbourhood, Kilmacduagh, some three miles distant. The diocese in which Gort stands rejoices in the poetical names of Kilmacduagh and Kilfenora. I suppose I need hardly remind my readers that *kil* is Irish for church, and hence the number of *kils* scattered widely over the country, which gave rise to the alarming answer given to a Saxon tourist by an Irishman. He had been to Kilsome, was going to Kilmany, and then on to Kilthemall!

The see of Kilmacduagh was founded by St. Colman in the seventh century. Here the cathedral was built, close beside a round tower, and surrounded by six other churches. We explored the ruins well, and I was fortunate in having a cicerone who had often visited them before, and took a vivid interest in them. It was irritating to see cattle and sheep grazing in the area, more especially as the place is held sacred by the people who bring their dead for burial in its precincts. The former owner of the place was proud of the ruins, and took pains to preserve them. It has now, unfortunately, passed into younger and more careless hands. It is supposed that one of these seven churches was a college chapel, another a monastery, and a third a convent—the other three being probably smaller churches or oratories dedicated to some favourite saints. The convent chapel is the most perfect, and the east window and several arches, with their corbels, show it to have been one of great beauty. The round tower is especially remarkable from its leaning seventeen feet out of the perpendicular, and it is certainly a most singular object. Tradition says it was built by Gobhan Saer, the architect of Glendalough and Antrim.

On leaving this interesting spot we drove through some pretty country, with distant views of the ' lonely hills of Clare,' all radiant with the sunshine, to Lough Cooter. It was pleasant to see all along the way how the people greeted the priest; they came out from their cabin doors, and children ran from their play to get a word from him. We met groups of peasants returning from the last mass at an outlying chapel, and between priest and people there was ever a kindly greeting. Lough Cooter is the largest lake in the south of county Galway, with many wooded islands lying in its bosom, and lovely views between them. The ' Castle,' belonging to the Gough family, is a modern erection, in the castellated style, standing on the west bank of the lake, and commanding a most exquisite view, while the lawn slopes down to the water's edge. Beautiful grounds, richly supplied with trees, surround the house, part of them planted and laid out, part left for the deer to wander about. A gateway and lodge stand at each end of the grounds; and after passing through the whole length, we returned by another route to Gort in time for the quiet Benediction in the little convent chapel.

Travellers from Galway and its neighbourhod proceed by coach *viâ* Gort to Ennis, and as there are many

emigrants, the coach is often full.   This was the case
on the morning on which I left Gort, and accordingly
two 'long cars' were furnished from the coach office,
which were rapidly filled with emigrants from Gort.
The whole *cortege* started from the office in the main
street, and it was a strange and sorrowful sight to see
the partings.   A crowd of people collected round the
passengers: mothers and brothers and sisters were saying good-bye, weeping, wailing, and sometimes howling;
kisses were given, last greetings exchanged; promises
to write soon, to send money over, and 'bring the others
out' were uttered, and, at last, away we went.   I noticed that the best were going—the young, strong, and
vigorous—the old, the feeble, and children were left
behind.   By my side sat two young girls, strong, healthy,
and active.   I was amused at their costume.   They
were going into the world, and had discarded the blue
cloak and stuck on their heads showy bonnets much too
small for them, profusely decorated with tulle and artificial flowers, and with broad strings of white ribbon.
Anything more incongruous for a journey to America
could not be conceived; but I was still further amused,
for when we were fairly out of the town passing through
the solitary monotonous country, and admiring friends
were left behind, out came the large shawls, in which
head, bonnet, and all were fully enveloped.   They became confidential, and told me they were going to
America to get places; and, on my suggesting that
they could find such at home, shook their heads and
said not with such wages as in America.   When they
were tired of talking they took out their books, and
began to read, and, peeping over the shoulder of the

one next me, I perceived the volume carried with her was a prayer book.

It is a long dreary drive of nineteen miles to Ennis, through an open limestone country, with low, craggy hills. In all this part of Ireland the eye wearies for the pretty villages and comfortable-looking farm-houses which give life and variety to the flat counties of England. The station at Ennis is a wretched one, the platform being of earth, and it was not improved by recent rain and the trampling of a crowd of emigrants. Although this is the terminus of the Ennis and Limerick line, the train was in no hurry to start. Everybody took their time, and just half an hour after the one named in the time bills the train set out. It progressed very slowly on its way, and I was not sorry, for it gave us the opportunity of an excellent view of Clare Abbey —close by which the line passes— one of the loveliest ruins I had ever seen, a graceful church, in the form of a cross, with east window almost perfect, and a lofty tower, and the ivy twining round about the broken arches, and covering the walls with a rich green mantle. On reaching Limerick, I implored a porter to get my luggage quickly, as I wanted to catch the next train for Charleville. 'But sure she's been gone this ten minutes. She was an hour after her time. But your train was so late, she could not wait any longer.' As I expressed my vexation, he said, in a tone of deep sympathy, 'There'll be a train *to-morrow*.' On making further enquiries at the station, it turned out that the trains do not profess to fit in with each other, and, as one of the officials expressed it, 'The great lines tries to eat up the little ones.'

CHAPTER XIII.

It must not be supposed that I have at all sufficiently enumerated the charitable institutions of Dublin; it would require more time than I had at my disposal to visit them all. Few, however, of those conducted by nuns escaped my notice, but there are colleges, schools, orphanages, and asylums of various kinds in a flourishing state.

The Christian Brothers have magnificent schools in Dublin attached to their principal house in North Richmond Street, and they have five branch schools in different parts of the city, and a flourishing establishment at Kingstown.

There were institutions also in Ireland that I much wished to see, but which I was not able to reach, more especially the Reformatory for girls at Monaghan, and that for boys at Glencree.

Another order, partly of Irish origin, has made great progress in Ireland—the Sisters of Loretto. I call it partly Irish, because, though it was founded by Mrs. Ball, an Irish lady, and its ranks filled by her country-women, the institute itself is a foreign one, and has various houses on the Continent. This is entirely an educational order, chiefly devoted to the instruction of the upper classes, although, as is universal in Ireland, free schools are attached to their convents. Several of the convents of this order are very fine buildings; the mother-house at Rathfarnham, near Dublin, is really magnificent, and is surrounded by fine grounds; when viewing the chapel, or walking round the cloisters of this convent one might fancy oneself in an 'abbey of the olden time,' when orders vied with each other in raising magnificent conventual piles, and cloister life flowed on in unbroken security and peace.

There are two convents of the order in Dublin, and another at Dalkey, built on rocky heights, and almost seeming to hang over the sea. The chapel is very pretty, and one hundred and eighty poor children are taught at the schools.

The residents in Dublin are certainly fortunate in their immediate vicinity to beautiful scenery, to which there is such easy access. Trains to Kingstown run every half hour, and convey the passenger along the coast of Dublin Bay with lovely views succeeding one another. From Kingstown the line proceeds to Dalkey, where the pretty island of Dalkey, about a thousand yards from the mainland can be visited, and where Killinny Hill rises in fine outline. Then we go onwards to Bray, in County Wicklow, so well known to the tourist; a charming and favourite watering-place for the summer months, and with hills rising on all sides. Bray Head towers boldly above the rest, and the scramble up it is richly rewarded when you have reached the summit, and behold distant mountains, Dublin Bay, Dalkey island, Kingstown, and the town of Bray itself lying in a rich valley; the blue sea washes the foot of the wild crag, the sunshine lights up the scene, and large white clouds are drifting over the sky, and the descent to the town is through wild tangled woodland paths.

There is a large, handsome Loretto convent at Bray, with fine grounds, formerly a gentleman's residence. We admired the ingenuity which had converted summer-house and dairy into an oratory, while an old ruin, supposed to be the fragment of some ancient religious house, now guarded the cemetery of the nuns.

There are large poor schools attached to this convent, receiving two hundred and sixty-seven children. The chapel is beautiful; indeed, in all the convents of this order no expense has been spared to make the building, and especially the chapel, beautiful and attractive.

On the Drumcondra road, long before we reach All Hallows Convent, there is a large and rather gloomy-looking house standing back from the road with a little garden before it; the entrance is at the side door, and about a quarter past two every day a little knot of people gather about the house. When the door opens they all go upstairs, and find themselves in a moderately sized room converted into a chapel; an image of St. Alphonsus Liguori is a conspicuous object, and a large alcove contains an altar handsomely vested and adorned. At one side of this alcove is a grating, and when at half past two a priest enters the chapel to give benediction, the voices of nuns are heard chanting behind the bars. The benediction over, the portress sternly banishes those who wish to linger, and the chapel is closed again. This convent is that of the Redemtoristines, or as the Dublin people call them the 'red nuns;' founded by St. Alphonsus at the

same time as his congregation of priests, and bound to
strict enclosure and contemplation. Having an introduction, I one day went into their parlour, where there
is a grating let into the wall, behind which soon
appeared a sweet-looking nun: her dress was very
remarkable; the habit is a bright red, the scapular
sky blue, a white coif shades the face covered by a
black veil, while a coloured miniature of Our Blessed
Lord hangs on the breast. This dress is worn as
symbolical of the office of the nuns, attendants round
the altar throne of One greater than any earthly
monarch. I asked the Sister what was the object of
her order; she said to be 'spiritual Sisters of Charity,'
continually praying for those who suffer and sin, and
for those whose vocation it is to aid them.

There are Carmelite Convents in Dublin, but they
are disappointing to those who know the convents of
this order in foreign lands, and who are familiar with
the life of St. Teresa. The Carmelite Sisters in Dublin
have not yet resumed their true place; they have not
yet recovered from the effects of the long persecution.
Before the active orders were founded, it was an
absolute duty for them to mitigate their rule, and lend
their aid to the work of education; but it would seem
now as if the time had come when they might resume
the strict observance of their holy and beautiful rule,
and become not teachers but apostles; ' Apostles
seeking souls, even as in the ocean bed is sought the
hidden pearl.' *

It is true there are difficulties in the way, but surely

---

* Père de Ravignan.

they are not greater than those which beset the path
of the Carmelites in France, when the storm of the
great Revolution had passed away. There, as in Ireland,
the wants of the poor were great ; for a time, the nuns
had to do the work of Sisters of Mercy, the education
of the young was important, and the restoration of
religion would have seemed to be best promoted by
active works of charity. Nevertheless, the Carmelites
never rested till they had regained their true vocation,
and restored the rule as their great reformer left it.
We went to one of the Carmelite Convents near
Dublin ; there was no enclosure, and the discordant
sound of a piano, on which a child was evidently learn
ing to play, jarred strangely on the ear, when we
thought of the stillness and repose which should
characterise the convents of St. Teresa ; of the
'hermitages' to which the Sisters were bidden to
retire ; of the solitude and silence which she so carefully enjoined.

They were not ' to work at curious and delicate
things which occupy the thoughts, and prevent their
resting in God.' ' They must not work all together,
for fear silence should be broken,' says their holy rule,
and we remembered the eloquent words of Père de
Ravignan, addressed to a novice of this order: 'Oh,
child of Carmel, follow the steps of your mother ; cross
the abyss, fly to the desert, encounter the night ; seek,
seek, and you will find, you will find God. Give yourself up, immolate yourself, and then you will bring
down on the souls of others and on our ministry the
benedictions and graces of which we stand so much in
need; cast away all that keeps you back ; another world

is waiting for you. To this world you are dead and crucified; forget it all, break through it all, destroy it all, and you will find a better life, because, then, you will live alone with God. You pass behind this *grille*, this door shuts upon you like that of the tomb. What does this cloister, this barrier denote? That from this moment you enter into the holy liberty of the children of God; you have found freedom. In the world there are chains, the yoke that must be borne; there we are slaves, slaves to our tastes, our habits, and our passions; slaves to the customs of the world, the usages of the world, its opinions and its requirements; in religious life is true freedom.'

After passing through a number of streets in the direction of Sandymount, it is quite a surprise when the visitor, after a sudden turn in the road, comes upon the open sea and fine range of sands, in which Sandymount rejoices, and for this reason it is a favourite resort of Dublin people. There is a beautiful church here, dedicated to the ' Star of the Sea;' a convent of Sisters of Charity, and the Carmelite Convent called that of ' Lakelands.'

The house is a good one with large grounds, and stands in an excellent situation. Attached to this convent is an orphanage, which the Sisters superintend.

It is managed by a matron with an assistant, and I liked it because it was more homely and simple than orphanages usually are. The matron, a good, earnest woman, with her heart in her work, apologised to me because the children had to dine in the kitchen, and there was no refectory to show me. I told her I was heartily glad to find it was so, and I thought the little discomforts and roughness they had to encounter would be an excellent preparation for their future life.

The charge of an orphanage is a great anxiety. And this anxiety does not end when a child has left the house. Those who have brought her up ought to keep an eye over her, correspond with her, become her resource in hours of trial, and look after her through life. Now that there are such numbers of active orders, there would seem to be no difficulty in transferring to their care the orphanages and schools, which at present weigh down the hearts of the poor Carmelites, and it is perfectly certain that the work would be far better done by the active Sisters, who are trained to the care of the poor, than by those to whom it is a *gêne* and a torment. Except in passing to the orphanage the nuns of this house keep strict enclosure, and observe all the other points of their holy rule which are compatible with their active duties. No doubt the time will speedily come when the observance of it will prevail in full vigour. I believe the same work of restoration of the rule is progressing at the Convent of Ranelagh, but the nuns are still burdened with a poor school in which they give the religious instruction only, and of course it would be far better to have the school under the charge of those who can take its whole management.

At Harold's Cross, almost opposite to the Sisters of Charity, is a Convent of Poor Clares; this community has grown up from the six Sisters who came in fear and secrecy from Galway in 1712, and who were dragged before the judges. It is a large community, and in 1830 sent out the foundation to Newry, which has been so successful. The convent is very large, and has extensive grounds. An orphanage is under the charge of these Sisters; it is quite separate from the convent, and the nuns have to cross the outer garden to reach it. It did not seem equally well managed with the other orphanages that I have seen, and the nuns evidently find it a great burden, and are fully conscious that they are unable to see after the children who leave, or to collect the funds for the support of the orphanage, as easily as religious of an active order would. We could not help longing to see the orphanage transferred to the Sisters of Charity close by, and then that the Poor Clares should adopt the rule of their order, as it was brought from Gravelines by their first Sisters, so that another 'Bethlehem' could be restored in Ireland, where, says the old chronicle, 'they prayed continually, for while they laboured with their hands, they used to be many times saying some kind of prayer in common, answering one another therein choirwise. They observed such silence that mid-day seemed to be night. They had mutual charity to help and comfort one another, rising continually at midnight to say matins, and never eating flesh; nor wore sock, shoe, nor stockings, but contented themselves with wooden soles or pattens under their feet, and observed all other things ordained by the first rule of St. Clare, with the straight statutes made by St. Collet upon said rule.'

Not far from the Poor Clares at Harold's Cross is the fine monastery of the Passionist Fathers, and a new church is in course of erection. The present one is small and without much ornament, but greatly frequented by the people.

Another interesting spot in Ireland, which I much wished to visit, is Benada Abbey in county Sligo. It was formerly an Augustinian Abbey, and after the dissolution fell into various hands, till at last it became the property of a Catholic, whose dying wish it was to give it back to the Church. He left sons and daughters behind him, and it did not seem likely that his wish would be fulfilled; but his children before many years were over had given to God not only all that they had, but the devotion of their whole lives. The sons are in the Society of Jesus, the daughters are Sisters of Mercy and Charity, and a convent of the latter order has been founded within the limits of Benada Abbey. By a singular coincidence, for it was not at all premeditated, the Blessed Sacrament was placed in the new chapel on the Feast of St. Austin. So after three long centuries one of the waste places of Ireland has once more blossomed like the rose. May it not be an augury for the future, and may it not come to pass that many of those ruined sanctuaries around which the people have so faithfully prayed will be once more devoted to the service of God?

CHAPTER XIV.

A JOURNEY through Ireland, and a stay of any length upon her shores, must necessarily leave many impressions on the mind of the traveller; and, in the present state of things, when the 'Irish difficulty' is a question of the day, the record of the impressions of even one individual may not be wholly useless. My last visit to Ireland was paid shortly before the Fenian outbreak, when the Habeas Corpus Act was suspended, the country 'proclaimed;' when timid ladies had lain awake at night, fancying they heard the tramp of the Irish Republic, and when a universal depression hung over the country. While in Ireland, I lived (with very rare and brief exceptions) entirely among the Irish, among those who had been long resident in the country, and rarely, if ever, quitted it.

Wherever I went I found Fenianism was disliked, feared, and disapproved of; looked on as politically unwise and morally wrong. Wherever I went I found people were loyal to the English Government; but, I must confess, it was the loyalty of the head, not that of the heart; and I believe the great cause of Ireland's miseries may be summed up in these few words: England is not loved, not trusted. The educated and the thoughtful Irish, who influence the classes below

them, believe that no good can result from the uproot-
ing of the English Government ; that attempts at
rebellion are certain to be unsuccessful, and can only
tend to disorganise and injure the country, and so they
discountenance them ; but there is none of that affectionate loyalty which forms a greater bulwark round a
country than armed men or ships of war.   There is a
universal discontent, arising from a vivid remembrance
of the oppression of the past, and a keen sense of
injustice in the present.

Englishmen say, What is the use of looking back
to the past ? In the first place it is natural to the Irish
character, and, secondly, the misgovernment of the
present tends to perpetuate it.   Remove the causes of
present discontent, and you will have done much to
obliterate the past from the minds of the people.   I
very much doubt whether those who so readily con-
demn the Irish for their habit of looking back, really
know what that past to which they revert consists of,
for the details of Irish history are unknown to a great
mass of Englishmen, and if it were not so, it is hardly
credible that, during the Fenian outbreak, a writer in
an English newspaper recommended the ' revival in
Ireland of the stern measures of Cromwell.'   How
few people know the real history, or the disastrous
consequence of those fatal measures.   Indeed, until a
very recent period, the documents and state papers,
which form the true foundation for authentic history,
were hidden away in a little cell in Dublin Castle,
covered with the dust of years.   A skilful hand dis-
lodged them from their hiding-place, and the ' records
of a nation's woe ' have at last seen the light of day,

and I only wish every Englishman and every English-woman were *compelled* to read these terrible revelations. The effect of the English government, only two centuries ago, was not only to ' suppress a religion,' but ' rather to extinguish a nation.' ' Let us conceive,' says Mr. Prendergast,* ' the dismay of a poor noble-man, with his wife and daughters, on the evening of the first market day after the 11th of October, 1652, when some neighbour came to announce the news proclaimed by beat of drum and sound of trumpet in the adjoining town. It was, in fact, the proscription of a nation. If he had been a colonel or a superior officer in the army, as almost all the highest were, it was a sentence of confiscation and banishment, and a separation from his now beggared wife and daughters, the partners of his miseries, unless he had the means of bringing them abroad with him. The Earl of Ormond, Primate Bramhall, and all the Catholic nobility, and many of the gentry, were declared incapable of pardon of life or estate, and were banished. The rest of the nation were to lose their lands, and take up their residence wherever the Parliament of England should order.

On 26th September, 1653, all the ancient estates and farms of the people of Ireland were declared to belong to the adventurers and the army of England; and it was announced that the Parliament had assigned Connaught (America was not then accessible) for the habitation of the Irish nation, whither they must transplant, with their wives and daughters and children, before the 1st of May following (1654), under penalty of death,

* *Cromwellian Settlement of Ireland.* By John Prendergast.

if found on this side of the Shannon after that day. It might, perhaps, be imagined that this fearful sentence was a penalty upon the supposed bloodthirstiness of the Irish.   But for blood, death and not banishment was the punishment, and the class most likely to be guilty of blood—the ploughmen, labourers, and others of the lower order of poor people—were excepted from transplantation.   The nobility and gentry of ancient descent, proprietors of landed estates, were incapable of murder or massacre;. but it was they who were particularly required to transplant—their properties were wanted for the new English planters. There is an anecdote told by an Englishman of the order of the Friars Minor, who must have dwelt, disguised probably (a not uncommon incident) as a soldier or servant, in the household of Colonel Ingoldsby, Governor of Limerick, that explains the reason why the common people were to be allowed to stay and the gentry required to transplant.   He heard the question asked of a great Protestant statesman ('magnus hæreticus consiliarius') who gave three reasons for it; first, he said, 'they are useful to the English as earth-tillers and herdsmen; secondly, deprived of their priests and gentry, and living among the English, it is hoped they will become Protestants; and, thirdly, the gentry without their aid must work for themselves and their families, or if they don't must die, and if they do, will in time turn into common peasants. . . . Connaught was at that time the most wasted province of the kingdom.   Sir Charles Coote the younger, disregarding the truce or cessation made by order of the king with the Irish in 1644, had

continued to ravage it, like another Attila, with fire
and sword. The order was for the flight of the Irish
nation thither in winter time, their nobles, their gentry,
and their commons, with their wives and little children,
their young maidens and old men, their cattle and
their household goods. . . . And now there went
forth petitions from every quarter of the kingdom,
praying that the petitioners' flight might not be in the
winter time, or alleging that their wives or children
were sick, their cattle unfit to drive. . . . The
petitioners were the noble and the wealthy, men of
ancient English blood, descendants of the invaders,
the Fitzgeralds, the Butlers, the Plunkets, the Barn-
walls, Dillons, Cheevers, Cusacks, who were now to
transplant as Irish. The native Irish were too poor
to pay scriveners and messengers to the council, and
their sorrows were not heard, though under their rough
coats beat hearts that felt pangs as great at being
driven from their native homes as the highest in the
land.'

The particulars of some of these petitions might
have moved a heart of stone: the aged, the palsied,
the imbecile, the dropsical, those in ' tedious and lan-
guishing sickness' cried out for mercy, and often could
get none. The work was accomplished, and ' Ireland,
in the language of Scripture, now lay void as a wilderness.' Five-sixths of her people had perished,
women and children were found daily perishing in
ditches, starved. The bodies of many wandering
orphans, whose fathers had embarked for Spain and
whose mothers had died of famine, were preyed upon
by wolves. In the years 1652 and 1653, the plague

and famine had swept away whole counties, so that a
man might travel twenty or thirty miles and not see a
living creature. Man, beast, and bird were all dead,
or had quitted these desolate places. The troops would
tell stories of the place where they saw a smoke, it
was so rare to see smoke by day, or fire or candle by
night. If two or three cabins were met with, there
were found there none but aged men, with women
and children, and they, in the words of the prophet,
' become like a bottle in the smoke, their skins black
like an oven because of the terrible famine.' In fact,
says Mr. Prendergast in his preface, ' in 1652, took
place a scene not witnessed in Europe, since the
conquest of Spain by the Vandals. Indeed, it is
injustice to the Vandals to equal them with the English
of 1652, for the Vandals came as strangers and con-
querors in an age of force and barbarism, nor did
they banish the people though they seized and divided
their lands by lot.' Cromwell's reign was brief, but
the effect of his cruelties remained in Ireland. The
imprisonment in Connaught ended, and by degrees
the country was repeopled; but the lands of the Irish
were confiscated, their property was gone, and if for a
short period there was some appearance that justice
would be done, all hope was lost again after the battle
of the Boyne, for that victory was followed by the
' Revolution Settlement.' By it the lands lately restored to the Royalist English and few native Irish
were again seized by the Parliament of England, and
distributed among the conquering nation.

At the court for the sale of estates forfeited on
account of the war of 1690, the lands could be pur-

chased only by Englishmen. No Irishman could purchase more than the site for a cabin; for to the condition of cottagers it was intended that the relics of the nation should be reduced. From that time to 1798 the penal laws remained in full force. ' Their main purpose was, on the one hand, to prevent the Irish from ever enlarging their landed interests, for which purpose they were forbid to purchase land; and, on the other hand, to contrive by all political ways, and particularly by denying them the power to make settlements of their property by deed or will, and by making their lands divisible equally among their sons at their death, to crumble and break in pieces the remnant that had escaped confiscation, and thereby to deprive them of all power and consideration in the state.' Such are a few records of the past on which Ireland looks back, and for which England owes her a long and heavy compensation. Not seventy years have passed since the repeal of the worst of the penal laws, and not forty have expired since Catholic Emancipation. How, in that brief space of time, can it be expected that a nation can recover from ravages like these? Even had the reign of full and free justice commenced in 1829, who could expect that the work of centuries (for the Cromwellian cruelties were only a continuation and aggravation of those heaped on Ireland since the Reformation) could be undone in less than half a century? But, alas! that reign of justice did not begin. Concessions to Ireland have been meted out at rare intervals, and with niggard hands, and many an element which ministers to discontent has been left to smoulder in the hearts of the people;

for how is it to be expected that Ireland will forget her past miseries while the badge of conquest is held ever before her eyes? The Irish Church Establishment is called a sentimental grievance; my impression is entirely the contrary, I believe it to be perpetually irritating and galling the people. They laugh at it, it is true, but they feel it nevertheless. Such a state of things could never exist for a day in England or Scotland, and yet both countries boast of possessing less sensitiveness, less imagination than the Irish. To the Irish the Establishment is perpetually witnessing to the fact: 'You are a conquered people, you are not an independent part of a great empire; we have tried through long ages to force our new religion upon you, and though you have resisted us, you shall still have the result of our fruitless efforts before your eyes: we will not let you forget the past. Your fathers built cathedrals and parish churches; we took them from you, and for fear you should forget the fact, we will keep them still. True, they are no use to us; our clergy have no flocks, our bishops nothing to do, but you shall keep your barn-like chapels, or impoverish yourselves in raising your churches, because you shall not have your own, for you are a conquered people.'

In days gone by the proprietor of a large tract of land in County Clare refused to give a site for a Catholic church; 'the people worshipped in the open air, carrying stones in their hands as they journeyed to the place of meeting, that they might not kneel in the mud. A sort of wooden canopy placed on wheels was constructed to protect the movable altar, and is still preserved as a memorial.* Stories such as these linger in the minds of the Irish, and the supremacy of the Establishment remains to keep the memories of them alive.

Stories which illustrate the absurdity of the system fly about Ireland in all directions, and are related with bursts of merriment round the fireside. A Protestant clergyman was once reproved by his bishop for holding his Sunday service at an unusually late hour. He replied that he could not help it, for he had to wait for his clerk till he came back from mass!

' In the parish where I live,' said an Irish gentleman to me, ' the clergyman has 300*l*. per annum, and there is not one single Protestant in the place. The church is occupied simply by his own family and household.'

Closely connected with the Established Church is the terrible practice of 'souperism,' to which I have already alluded in these pages. I shall at once be told that it is foreign to the question, because souperism has nothing to do with law, and can neither be enforced nor repealed by Act of Parliament. But it can be repealed by public opinion; and were its real working and results known, I believe public opinion would not be appealed to in vain, and in saying this, I am thinking less of the fairness and justice of Englishmen, than of their wish to heal the discontent in Ireland.

The evil done by souperism in estranging the two nations is incalculable. It is perpetually putting English people in an irritating light before the eyes of the Irish. They come as foes, not as friends. Amidst all

* *The Church Settlement of Ireland.* By Aubrey de Vere.

their sufferings and persecutions, the Irish have kept
their religion intact. From Henry VIII. to Queen
Victoria they have clung to their faith, and ' soupers'
are like robbers come to pillage their homes; and they
còme with English hands and English voices; from the
lady who boasts in Connemara that she has converted
an ' aconite ' (i.e. acolyte) to the Bishop of Oxford,
who highly approved and commended the 'conversion
movement,' which, be it well remembered, *originated
in the time of the famine.* 'If,' says the Protestant
Chancellor of Cork, one of the few Protestant clergymen who abhor and expose the ' souper ' system, ' his
lordship has been totally misinformed, I am very sorry
for it; but I am fully persuaded he would see cause
to change his mind if he were acquainted with the facts
which I and so many other clergy would have furnished.'

Dr. Forbes visited Connemara some ten or twelve
years ago, and with his usual rigid impartiality endeavoured to test the ' reports' of the souper societies.
If the subject were not such a sad one, the shrewd
remarks of the worthy Protestant doctor would be
very amusing. The Irish Church Missions had declared they had between 5,000 and 6,000 converts in
West Galway, and that their labours had thus rendered ' a district extending fifty miles in breadth
characteristically Protestant, which but a few years
ago was characteristically Romish.' This, says Dr.
Forbes, ' must be regarded rather as an expression
of an amiable and sanguine enthusiasm, commingling
the hopes of the future with the over apprecia-
tion of the present, than the sober definition of a

reality;' for he goes on to remark that county Galway is only eighty miles long, and its population by the last census before this statement appeared, 298,564. He went to visit Clifden workhouse, where he finds 840 inmates, ten of whom are Protestants. But then of course it is but fair to admit that 'converts' would not be found in the union, as their temporal wants are well attended to. The same report, to which Dr. Forbes's attention was drawn, stated that in addition to these 5,000 or 6,000 converts, who are supposed to take up fifty miles of the county, and leave the remaining thirty for the happy 298,064, 'nearly 5,000 children of *converts* or *Romanists* daily attend the scriptural schools of the Society.' But when the Doctor came to investigate the matter, he thought 'it would be interesting to know what was the relative proportion of the two classes of children,' and believes that ' the great majority of these children are not only the children of Catholic parents, but are in no other way Protestants, except as attending such schools, and a certain portion of them going to the Protestant Church;' and adds that the Catholic parents themselves told him ' they permitted their children to join these schools chiefly for the sake of the food and clothing supplied to them.' Dr. Forbes was evidently convinced at the end of his researches, that the great wealth of the souper societies had been almost thrown away, as far as gaining converts was concerned, and only tended to keep up a spirit of irritation and dislike in the minds of the people. ' There is only one disadvantage,' says he, ' attendant on the use of the " stirabout" weapons employed by the missionaries, in the

handle it gives the enemy to maintain, even if conquered, that they are defeated by carnal, not by spiritual weapons;' and he continues, ' the triumph of the
Protestants, if they are to triumph, would be purer,
grander, and more decisive, if they could boast that
their victory was the exclusive result of the goodness
of their cause, and their own personal friends.   At
present they certainly give nearly as good grounds to
their enemies for bestowing on Protestantism the nickname of the ' Stirabout Creed,' as the honest Laird of
Rum in olden times gave to his Catholic subjects for
bestowing on it the nickname of the ' Religion of the
Yellow Stick.' I give the history of this transaction
in Dr. Johnson's own words : ' The rent of Rum is
not great ; Mr. Maclean declared he should be rich if
he could let his land at two pence halfpenny an acre.
The inhabitants are fifty-eight families, who continued
Papists for some time after the laird became a Protestant.   Their adherence to their old religion was
strengthened by the countenance of the laird's sister,
a zealous Romanist, till one Sunday, as they were
going to mass, under the conduct of their patroness,
Maclean met them on the way, gave one of them a
blow on the head with a *yellow stick*, I suppose a cane,
for which the Erse has no name, and drove them to
the kirk, from which they have never since departed.
Since the use of this method of correction, the inhabitants of Egg and Canna, who continued Papists, call
the Protestantism of Rum *the religion of the Yellow
Stick.*' Dr. Forbes winds up his remarks on souperism
by saying that to the minds of many ' it will appear unjustifiable to seek to attain Protestantism in

Ireland at the risk of the comfort or peace of a nation
which is profoundly devoted to Catholicism, proud of
its peculiar doctrines, and happy in the practices they
enjoin.'

It is the fashion to say that were the Establishment
swept away, souperism would become more rampant—
that all the Protestant clergy then would become a sort
of spiritual Bashi Bazouks, instead of being, as the
majority now are, quiet country gentlemen with nothing
to do. But facts prove the contrary, as it has been
truly said, 'The ascendency would be too obviously
absurd if it acknowledged the Catholicism of the nation
as the permanent order of things; that Catholicism it
therefore is forced to regard as but an accident, destined to vanish before the zeal of a church planted for
the purpose of compelling the nation to come in.'* And
Protestant bishops are continually asserting that the
Irish Church is a 'missionary' one, and the heathen to
be brought into its pale are the Roman Catholics. An
English clergyman, a man of cultivation and intelligence, and of the 'High-church' school runs over for
a few weeks to Ireland, and when summing up his
'impressions' on the state of religion in Ireland,
quotes the opinion of a friend which he evidently
approves of and indorses. 'Where is that Church of
the future to be found? I think I see a *nucleus* near
home, and where you would least expect to find it in a
Church despised and rejected of men, a Church that has
'laid her body as the ground and as the streets to them
that walk over. I could not but think of the Church of

* *The Church Settlement of Ireland.* By Aubrey de Vere.

Ireland—*not* the Irish branch of the English Church, but the Church of the *people* (not the *priests*) of Ireland —as the fifty-first of Isaiah was read yesterday. I know the Irish people well, and their faith, love, and poverty, and through all their poverty, " the riches of their liberality," and I cannot think that God ever did desert or ever will desert them. They have long lain under an *incubus* of Romanism on the one hand and of English persecution on the other. In our days the English element of oppression has been removed; there is nothing now to complain of, but *Rome* has latterly been making her yoke heavier and heavier. The present Archbishop Cullen has been striving to introduce *Ultramontanism* and all its darkest doctrines, and *at present* he has filled the land with his priests. But I do not think he has sensibly affected the faith of the people, and I rather hope that a time of reaction may be at hand, how to be brought about I know not; but yet I think the dawn is even now brightening the sky. I do not think the Irish people will come *as a body* into the English *Established* Church, nor do I *wish* them to do so, but I *do* think a time is coming when the Church, casting off its slavery to Rome, will return to the faith of St. Patrick and St. Columba, and then to it will flock the better part of the State Church, and we shall have (whether I live to see it or not) a *free* Catholic Church in Ireland, a church *free* from Rome, and *free* from England's *oath of supremacy*, but of the ancient Catholic faith and apostolic succession, and ready to communicate with every church holding like faith. What a support would such a church be to the poor *government-ridden* Church of England! How nobly the Irish people would then be avenged of her who laid a yoke on them in Henry the Second's time, which has ever since pressed into their flesh.'*

If such a farrago of nonsense can be put forth by a clergyman of this stamp, what can not be expected from those of the Exeter Hall type?

In the course of my travels, I came across a priest, well advanced in years, who had spent his whole life labouring hard for the good of his people. He was a very superior man, warm-hearted, genial, and considerate towards all. He would never have spoken a harsh word to any who differed from him, and kindly deeds for others seemed to be spontaneous to his nature. Yet such a man is obliged to say publicly, 'The elaborate machinery for the subversion of the Christian faith of the destitute poor, and for bringing up and rearing their children in Protestantism, is a thing unknown in any other part of the civilised world, nor would it be tolerated in any.' And he asks: 'How are we to encounter this enormous and infamous traffic, which is carried on around us, and sustained by English gold?'

Favourite instruments in the hands of the soupers are placards of the kind most likely to insult and outrage the feelings of the sensitive people amongst whom they live, and the walls of quiet towns and villages, filled with Catholics, are stuck over with, 'Is not the Pope Antichrist?' and 'Rome, the mother of Harlots;' and in the parish of the very priest I have been speaking of, the rector of the Established Church placards the walls

* *A Holiday in Ireland in* 1861.

with a sentence which he plumes himself on having invented: ' The Papacy came hot from hell, and its presence makes a hell upon earth.' If the placards of the Fenians are torn down, and those who posted them are liable to punishment, because they tend directly to rebellion, surely the perpetrators of such outrages, which most assuredly tend *indirectly* to the same end, should be restrained. If insults such as these to the faith of a nation are allowed to pass unpunished—if men in England, who load Ireland with good advice, who profess to be perpetually studying her interests, do not raise their voices against it—it is no wonder that Fenianism breaks out, and that not an Irish Catholic's heart really clings to and trusts in the good intentions and good faith of what is called, in refined irony, ' the sister country.' The intense nationality of the Irish has often been spoken of. I do not think anyone but those who have lived in the country can form an idea of its strength. An Englishman is said to love his country; but for the most part—owing, no doubt, to the state of quiet prosperity under which we have lived so long—it shows itself in a calm content, and a lofty contempt for the inhabitants of less favoured lands. With the Irish it is a passion, a motive power for their daily conduct, the theme of their conversation, the object of their thoughts. Not a nun in a quiet convent but whose heart beats quick when Ireland is spoken of; the poor and the ignorant take a vivid interest in the hopes and fears concerning the future of the country. Can this spirit of nationality be turned in the direction of an attachment to the United Empire? The Irish, who are

bid to love England, find themselves under a sovereign
who, in her long reign of thirty years, has but twice,
for a few days, set her foot on Irish shores. They see
the heir apparent make the tour of half the world, but
knowing nothing of the scenery, habits, and character
of the people of one of the fairest parts of his future
empire; they see their chief ruler come and go with
every change of ministry, no sooner having learnt something of the people than he is ordered away; they see
him, on coming into office, take an oath containing
words which they believe to be blasphemous before
God and grossly insulting to them; they see a charter
persistently refused to their Catholic University—a
system of education introduced 'which ignores the nationality and excludes the religion of the country, in
which the schoolmaster is afraid to read one of Moore's
ballads, for fear he should be thought to be teaching
sedition, and the crucifix kept hid in a box in a corner
of the room.'* And is it to be wondered at, then,
that their affections turn to the past, 'and their pride
attaches itself less to the greatness of an empire in
which they have an unequal part than to recollec-
tions sad and dear in which none claim a part with
them'? †

Of course no one can live in Ireland without perceiving that some of the evils that exist might be re-
medied by the people themselves, and that a certain
amount of the fault may be laid at their own door.
They brood too much over the past, they are too easily
depressed by difficulties, and they allow minor dissen-

* *Dublin Review,* April 1867.
† *The Church Settlement of Ireland.* By Aubrey de Vere.

tions to split up their interests and prevent the action
of a united people.   The demands of a united Ireland
no English government could resist, but when there
is little hope there is little union.   ' It is often asked
why Ireland has not sent more petitions to Parliament
on the subject of the Church.   It had little hope of
success.   A nation that has ceased to hope has become formidable.' *   These things are well known to
the thoughtful among them, and it is their task—not
our's—to point them out.   As for us, I know not with
what face we can preach to the Irish, and thrust our
superior commercial superiority in their faces—we who
are descendants of those who have done them such
bitter wrong.

> Unstanch'd is the wound
> While the insult remains.
>   Distrust the repentance that clings to its booty ;
> Give the people their Church, and the priesthood its right ;
>   Till then to remember the past is a duty ;
> For the past is our cause,
> And our cause is our might.†

The ' Irish Homes ' that I have tried, however im-
perfectly, to describe, are a witness to what the Irish
can do and have done ; out of their poverty, and their
suffering, and their difficulties they have raised one
after another of these noble institutions, which in all
material things may vie with the grand establishments
in England, on which English wealth has been so
lavishly expended ; while from the spirit in which they
are carried on, they far excel the results of our splendid
efforts.   In these Irish Homes I have tried to show the

---

* *Church Settlement, &c.*   † Aubrey de Vere.

'Irish hearts' which animate them. These witness to us of what Irishmen and women can do and have done. They have not dreamed away their lives, given up enterprises in despair, talked about 'poor despised Ireland,' and then run away from her to follow in the train of English fashion; they have remained in their country, worked for her, lived for her, suffered for her, and the land where hearts such as these can be counted by thousands, where homes such as these can be found at every turn, I cannot believe is destined to perish.

Success and prosperity are not God's best blessings for individuals; they may not be for nations.

> Endurance it was that won,
> Suffering than action thrice greater.*

Ireland in her suffering and her poverty may be more blessed than her prosperous neighbours; what looks like failure may be in reality a success, and when the deeds of nations shall be reviewed, poor and despised as she is now, Ireland may be found to have played no ignoble part in the world's history; but surely it is not impossible that the time should come when England will at last generously and entirely repeal the wrongs of Ireland, when the past will be forgotten in the peace and content of the present, when America will find no longer any rebellious spirit to fan, and when the kingdoms will be so united that it can no longer be said with truth—

> The emerald gem of the western world
> Was set in the brow of a stranger.

* Aubrey de Vere.

INDEX.